JOURNEYS

Through

PARADISE

Pioneering Naturalists in the Southeast

GAIL FISHMAN

UNIVERSITY PRESS OF FLORIDA

Gainesville · Tallahassee · Tampa · Boca Raton · Pensacola
Orlando · Miami · Jacksonville · Ft. Myers

05   04   03   02   01   00   6   5   4   3   2   1

Library of Congress Cataloging-in-Publication Data

Fishman, Gail.
Journeys through paradise: pioneering naturalists in the southeast /
Gail Fishman.
p. cm.
Includes bibliographical references (p.) and index.
ISBN 0-8130-1874-9 (acid-free paper)
1. Naturalists—Southern States. 2. Natural history—Southern States.
3. Fishman, Gail—Journeys—Southern States.
4. Southern States—Description and travel. I. Title.
QH26 .F47 2001
508.75--dc21   00-051030

The University Press of Florida is the scholarly publishing agency for
the State University System of Florida, comprising Florida A&M
University, Florida Atlantic University, Florida Gulf Coast University,
Florida International University, Florida State University, University of
Central Florida, University of Florida, University of North Florida,
University of South Florida, and University of West Florida.

University Press of Florida
15 Northwest 15th Street
Gainesville, FL 32611–2079
http://www.upf.com

Florida A&M University, Tallahassee

Florida Atlantic University, Boca Raton

Florida Gulf Coast University, Ft. Myers

Florida International University, Miami

Florida State University, Tallahassee

University of Central Florida, Orlando

University of Florida, Gainesville

University of North Florida, Jacksonville

University of South Florida, Tampa

University of West Florida, Pensacola

Illustrations

Contents

Contents

For the men and women who have devoted their lives
to identifying and protecting the earth's flora, fauna,
and natural resources,
and
For my mother and to the memory of my father.
I would not have done it but for you.

Preface

THIS BOOK PROFILES thirteen curious men who ventured into North America's southeastern wilderness between early 1700 and early 1900. Their interest ran deeper than merely cataloging different plants and animals; they would know the natural world's whys and hows. Over time and under primitive conditions, their toilsome studies defined differences in species. They lived and worked at their profession as this country grew from a prize coveted by distant countries to a remote colony of the fledgling British Empire to an emerging world power. Their stories will appeal to those interested in the human and natural history of this country and to anyone who has a dream, for each of these men's dreams come true. We owe thanks to those who began assembling facts and folklore long ago.

No book can be written without help and encouragement from others. Angus Gholson whetted my appetite by sharing stories about pioneering naturalists and how the land had appeared a short time ago in his boyhood when he began rummaging the woods for plants. Gil Nelson planted the seed for this book and provided advice and photographs. Thanks Angus and Gil. Special thanks to Fred and Pat Harden and Sue and Martin Plotkin for endless support and enthusiasm, to my friends and family, and, most of all, to my mother, Marie Tener, for always being there. The following people provided water, sunshine, and nutrients to help it grow: Wilson Baker, Smith Banks, Keith Bradley, George Chapel, Eleanor Dietrich, George Ganz, Bill Hilton, Milton Hopkins, Estelle McElveen, Dr. Delma Presley, Janisse Ray, Dr. Vivian Rogers-Price, Dr. Mark Schwartz, Greg Seamon, Dr. Susan Stephenson, Sharyn and Larry Thompson, David Sims for the map, the reference staff of the Leon County Public Library, the staff of the State Library of Florida and Florida Archives and Records Management, the staff of the Georgia Historical Society, Dr. Tom Scott of the Florida Geological Survey, Roger Hammer of Miami-Dade County Parks, Alíce Warren-Bradley and Ernie Lent of the Charles Deering Estate at Cutler, Louise Kirn of Apalachicola

National Forest, David Danley of Pisgah National Forest, J. Drayton Hastie of Magnolia Gardens, The Nature Conservancy, Tracy Hayes and Cathy Jenkins of Drayton Hall, Robin Will and Joe Reinman of St. Marks National Wildlife Refuge, James Burkhart of Okefenokee National Wildlife Refuge, Joan Stibitz of Andersonville National Historic Site, Sandy Madsen of the Florida Park Service, and the Association for Institutional Research for being understanding about my sudden, extended absences from work.

Chris Hofgren and the University Press of Florida believed these stories were worth sharing. Steve Gatewood and Dr. William Rogers read the entire manuscript and Rita Lassiter, Greg Seamon, Chris Trowel, Charlie Williams, and Kenneth Wurdack read selected chapters and offered suggestions for improvement and pointed out errors and inconsistencies. Thank you.

As the author, I am only the conduit for others' words and chose to follow the most accepted version. If I have learned anything from this adventure, it is that history lives best when it is disputed and facts are separated from fiction. Any mistakes are entirely unintentional and wholly my responsibility.

Introduction

THE GENTLE MOUNTAINS, regal forests, and shadowy swamps of North America's southern lands held a special lure for early naturalists and their successors. To them, the expansive wildlands were an unread book awaiting translation. Naturalists dedicated to their task were blessed with passion, insatiable curiosity, and a desire to learn. They endured deprivation, hardship, and possible death in a strange country.

They observed and wrote of the customs and learned dialects of numerous native nations. Armed only with knowledge of European species, the first bold students of natural history listened to native people and absorbed their sense of animal habits and plants used for medicines, food, dyes—and which plants to avoid. Knowing plants meant the difference between eating and starving, between recovery and illness. Plants formed the first information highway of our lives. Traveling by horseback, boat, and foot, pioneering naturalists tramped with eyes scanning from ground to treetops for any unfamiliar vine, bird, or insect. Always they searched for the unaccustomed and obscure. Their studies supplied the underpinnings for those who continue studying the natural world.

Plant presses, paper, pencils, books, a blanket, simple medicines, a pot or two, knife, firearm and ammunition, salt, and rice made up the bulk of their pack. They stepped away from society and families into a land where death might come from an untended cut, a twisted ankle, the pierce of a malaria-bearing mosquito, or the wrath of Indians angered by continued invasions of their homelands. Heat, damp, cold, and explosive thundershowers accompanied them. Their hearts must have quickened as they entered each unknown area. Even into the early 1900s, scientists faced a land with few improved roads and spotty communication systems. Possibilities of discovering new specimens for science and the quest for adventure led them onward.

They gathered seeds, pressed leaves, dug bulbs and roots, took cuttings and seedlings, trapped, snared, and shot animals, caught butterflies, birds, beetles, snakes, frogs, turtles, and spiders. After drawing a creature, they might set it free or dissect the carcass, observe striated musculature padding the skeleton and delicate bindings of sinew and bone, taste the flesh, and preserve the skin. They worked in harsh weather with little equipment and wrote their notes by moonlight and stuttering firelight, serenaded by wolves and wildcats hunting the night. They dealt with uncooperative pack animals, learned to caulk a leaky boat, and were often the first Europeans to scale a mountain or drink from the headwaters of a mighty river. The country was a polyglot of Spanish, English, French, and other European tongues, not to mention the staggering variety of dialects peculiar to specific native tribes. We remember Daniel Boone and David Crockett as brave explorers while forgetting the first explorers who meant to describe this country. They traveled with the intent to learn, not conquer, with little armament beyond what was necessary to provide food and obtain specimens.

Returning from a trip did not mean their work had ended. They procured boxes and jars, completed the preserving process, copied notes and descriptions to send with carefully packed specimens, and saw their harvest safely stowed aboard ship. Bundles, boxes, and barrels of preserved plants, skins, seeds, rocks, human artifacts, and living plants and animals were sent over the sea. Sailors jettisoned such nonessential cargo in rough weather. Thirsty crew members opened specimen jars and drank preserving rum, tossing other contents overboard. Hundreds of ships foundered in stormy seas or fell prey to pirates. Nonetheless, an astonishing amount of material reached Europe.

Those naturalists were a hardy breed, conversant in natural science and proficient in specific fields. The men featured in this book are only a handful of all who studied America. Each was chosen for his commitment to science and the legacy he left behind. Their evocative descriptions unlocked nature's secrets. Most became famous in their day, but a few received little recognition beyond natural history's circle. Reading their adventures and looking at the Southeast today it is almost impossible to imagine that such a world existed. But it did.

From the late 1600s into the 1800s, scientific knowledge increased at a dizzying pace. Despite what we have learned, we have not come close to answering all questions posed by the world around us. Scientists continue searching, facing harsh weather and hostile environments with improved equipment and communication. Opportunities to study natural history remain boundless and while it may not be financially rewarding, such work is infinitely exciting.

There is almost no place in the contiguous United States that has not directly or indirectly felt the influence of human engineered intervention: timbering; dams; chemical applications; stream alteration; wholesale displacement of plants, animals, and terrain. Currently safeguarded areas have not been exempt from modification in the past, but continued protection will preserve many places visited by the men included in this book.

To understand who they were, what compelled them to pursue their work, and what America was like during their lifetimes compared to the late twentieth century, I drove a small van, fitted for camping with a bed, propane stove, cooler, and many maps. The land I traveled has been plowed, paved, cut over, rearranged, and explored for centuries. My intent was not to find patches of untrammeled wilderness, but to visit places easily reached by anyone. I hope readers will explore some of the areas mentioned herein, realize the dramatic changes that have occurred, and value the remaining pockets of natural lands all the more.

The naturalists in this book crossed each other's paths and forged new trails of their own, traded information, discussed theories, argued conclusions, and studied customs, sought knowledge, and passed their wisdom on. Although they made no great speeches, fought no military battles, and seemingly left no spectacular history, they led extraordinary lives. We are, indeed, fortunate that they possessed an astounding desire to study and to describe this paradise.

New Map of Georgia, with Par[t]

Drawn from Original Draughts, assisted

Collected by Eman: [B]

THE RIVER MISSISSIPPI

The Remainder of the Natches

Kappa

Chikasaws English

The Akansas

CHAUC[TAWS]

Aneeperees

Tacheoule Manik

G E O R [GIA]

C H A U C T A W S

in Amity with the French

L O U I S I A N A

P A R T   O F

U P P E R   C R E E K S

Coussa

Great Talasee

Wokokoi

Ockoi

Island Eschinalatche

Oitumpkee

Ocha

Taskeechi Puckney

Albamous River

P A R T   O F

F L O R I [DA]

Namiaba

Mobilians

Isle aux Statues

Tanfaw

Tabouscha

Apalachean

Fort St. Louis

Chetimachas

Mobile Bay

Mouth of the Mobile

I.S. Ross

Bay St. Amb[rose]

Bayogoula

Thatchagoula

Tilipani

Mississippi River

New Orleans

Isles de la Chandeleur

Lau Breton

Sitimachas

Tchouché

Mouth of the MISSISSIPI

ASCENSION BAY

West Longitude from London

G U L F   O F   M [EXICO]

English & French Leagues 20 to a Degree

MAP I. This 1749 map of Southeastern America demonstrates
a limited knowledge of interior regions.
Courtesy of Georgia Historical Society.

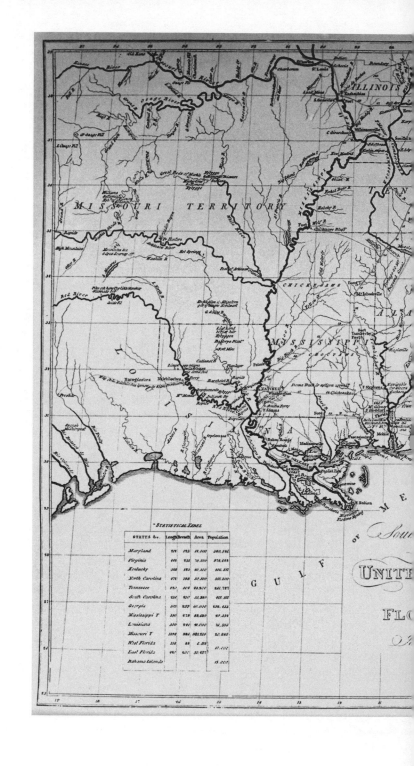

First Contact

And indeed, most of the Plantations in *Carolina* naturally enjoy a noble Prospect of large and spacious Rivers,
pleasant Savanna's, and fine Meadows, with their green
Liveries, interwoven with beautiful Flowers, of most glorious Colours, which the several Seasons afford; hedg'd in
with pleasant Groves of the ever-famous Tulip-tree, the
stately Laurel, and Bays, equalizing the Oak in Bigness and
Growth; Myrtles, Jessamines, Wood-bines, Honeysuckles,
and several other fragrant Vines and Ever-greens, whose
aspiring Branches shadow and interweave themselves with
the loftiest Timbers, yielding a pleasant Prospect, Shade
and Smell, proper Habitations for the Sweet-singing Birds,
that melodiously entertain such as travel thro' the Woods
of *Carolina*.

—John Lawson, *A New Voyage to Carolina*, 1709

Twenty-one years after Columbus bumped into the New World, Juan Ponce de León ground his longboats against the sandy beaches of a recumbent land. Other Spanish ships had preceded him, but Ponce de León claimed the territory, which extended past present-day Georgia to the low country now called South Carolina, for Spain in 1513. He called it Florida. Spain then began supplanting native cultures of the new land with its own.

Estimates vary, but at least two million indigenous people, comprising approximately six hundred tribes speaking about five hundred distinct languages, populated North America at the time of European contact. They had established their own religions, governments, and codes of conduct. Southeastern tribes gathered plants from surrounding forests for food, medicine, and dyes. In some cultures each family maintained its own farm plot and in others communal fields were planted. Their villages were connected by tracks winding around mountains and through vast forests, such as the Occaneechi Path, the Natchez Trace, and the Great Warrior Path, used for social visits, trade, and warfare.

A few million people spread across the continent had a minimal impact on the land. Rivers and streams provided a gracious plenty of sweet, clean water for crops, drinking, and transportation, and a variety of game animals roamed the Southeast. *Our Country and Its Resources,* published by Scientific American in 1917, estimated that America's original forests contained more than five trillion board feet of lumber spread over eight hundred million acres.

Florida's peninsula had been above sea level for about twenty thousand years when Native Americans first moved in; pollen records of that period indicate that north-central Florida's pine, sandhill, and broadleaf forests were much like they are today. Sand pine scrub clutched the loose sands of the central ridge and nosed into South Florida. About five thousand years ago, sea levels rose a bit and pushed the water table higher. Florida's southernmost scrub gave way to cypress swamps and sawgrass marshes, and the Everglades began forming. When the first Europeans touched shore, Florida's interior had become a mixture of xeric (dry) or mesic (sometimes wet) pinelands and wetlands. *Spartina* marshes guarded the northern coasts, mangrove swamps protected the subtropical southern half of the state, and, in between, sandy beaches offered open access to the seas.

The Appalachian Mountains bristled with tall, green pines, and

MAP 2. By 1816, familiarity with the Southeast's coastline and inland reaches had improved considerably. Note the statistical table in the lower left corner.
Courtesy of Georgia Historical Society.

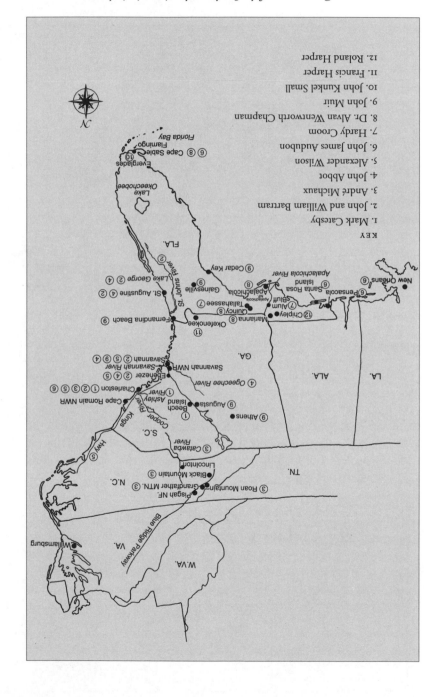

MAP 3. Current map of the Southeast showing principal areas associated with naturalists in this book.

Map by David Sims.

KEY

1. Mark Catesby
2. John and William Bartram
3. André Michaux
4. John Abbot
5. Alexander Wilson
6. John James Audubon
7. Hardy Croom
8. Dr. Alvan Wentworth Chapman
9. John Muir
10. John Kunkel Small
11. Francis Harper
12. Roland Harper

mixed forests marched over the rolling Piedmont Plateau and faded into the flat Atlantic Coastal Plain sparkling with lakes, Carolina bays, and cypress swamps. Rivers twined through wide salt marshes rippling with *Spartina* and black needlerush grasses to empty tons of fresh water into the briny ocean. Broad beaches, backed by humped sand dunes, shifted with tides and currents. Breezes cooled by the water's surface blew toward the coastal plain and punched against warmer air overlying the land, resulting in thunderstorms rent by jagged threads of lightning that kindled dry grasses. Flames crackled over the land until stalled by wetlands or burned over areas. Animals fled before the blazes and returned in a few weeks to feast on tender green shoots growing in luxuriant response to nutritious energy released by the conflagration.

It was a magnificent land and those who came from plundered European countrysides saw that America possessed an abundance of natural wealth: tall, straight pines for ship's masts, fine-grained live oaks for spars and ribs, minerals, bounteous rivers, game animals, and room. The sheer size of the thinly settled land and abundant numbers and varieties of flora and fauna suggested limitless resources.

With certainty that a fantastic land lay over the sea, other countries launched independent voyages. Explorers sailed across virtually uncharted waters guided by maps based on conjecture and imagination. If they sailed far enough, it was almost impossible to miss the Americas and each nation vied to claim as much of the New World as possible. That the lands were already inhabited was a minor inconvenience.

Ships returned to Portugal, Spain, France, Holland, and England with stories that gained embellishments in each narration. Costly gems, sumptuous spices, and glittering gold lay beyond the horizon, bringing the claimant personal glory and pecuniary rewards. Finding shorter trade routes or new lands assured recognition for the sponsor. Politics and religion played underlying roles in world expansion as European powers established settlements.

England's ships had skirted the New World's shores in the middle 1500s, yet it waited decades before attempting a permanent settlement, annoying expansionists eager to Christianize heathen Indians before Spain converted them to Catholicism. Englishman John Sparke wrote in 1589 that Florida would be a perfect place to raise cattle; hides were a valuable commodity.[1] If England were to become a dominant nation, it would have to expand beyond its island's borders and end its dependence

3

upon other countries for goods it could not produce. In addition, the new land was a place to dispose of the unwanted residue of its over-crowded cities.

Spain sent ship after ship to the New World. Spanish law required that each sailor plant orange seeds at every stop, sowing a one-drug pharmacy across the ocean. They were seeds of bitter orange, intended to prevent scurvy, once the scourge of all seamen. Ponce de León probably planted the first oranges in Florida. Hernando de Soto's men likely planted young orange trees across Florida in 1539.

After landing near Tampa Bay and pitching camp, de Soto sent out eight horsemen to explore the country. Before their horses, weakened by the voyage, became mired in bogs, the Spaniards discovered six Indians and killed two, demonstrating that they meant business. The next day, Sunday, soldiers set out to capture the Indian town, but the people es-caped through marshy woods. De Soto was an ambitious man, intent upon gathering riches for himself, his men, and his country and convert-ing Indians to Catholicism by force if necessary.

If his actions against the native people of North America seem cruel, remember that battles of that era were loud and brutal, up close and per-sonal. From all accounts, however, de Soto often sent his men to kill unarmed villagers, leaving bloody wounded as a warning; a tactic that worked well. As well trained and expert shots as the native armies were, they were no match for mounted, armored men with advanced weapons.

Tormented by humidity, rapacious insects, hot summers and cold winters, and hunger, his army marched across the present-day states of Florida, Georgia, South Carolina, western North Carolina, Tennessee, Alabama, and Arkansas. De Soto was dead by the time the remnants es-caped through Texas and Mexico. The men worked their way over moun-tains and rivers, through forests, swamps, deep sands, and slick clay searching for treasure. He didn't find any, but his troops were probably the first Europeans to see the Mississippi River.

De Soto's men traveled in a period that archaeologists have named "Mississippian." This culture began around A.D. 800, and a growing de-pendence on corn as a major food staple by the early 1500s resulted in a region populated by tightly knit communities governed by chiefs said to be descended from the sun. Similar among the people were their beliefs about how the world was created and why things happened as they did. In order to protect their land, each chiefdom contained a warrior group.

Although many of the nations spoke a derivative of a particular language group, each spoke a different dialect. For instance, Cherokee and Tuscarora stemmed from the Iroquois language, but neither could understand the other.

As de Soto's army snaked through the land, the soldiers captured people from different chiefdoms. Most important were those who could speak and understand another language. Many a conversation passed down a line of people speaking a variety of languages before an answer was obtained. Long marches through uncharted country took a toll on the troops. They feared hunting alone and went out in large hunting parties, which provided safety from angry Indians but scared away game. The soldiers stole food from the Indians, assuring that some would starve during the lean winter months. Nonetheless, de Soto's army also shriveled; by the time they reached Arkansas, it was in a sorry state.

The soldiers followed the Arkansas River to the Mississippi through a valley pocked with swamps and Mississippian towns. As the men approached, villagers ran away, carrying their corn if they could. A few miles below where the Arkansas joins the Mississippi, de Soto reached a small town called Guachoya, located near present-day Arkansas City. The chief was willing to share his large store of corn and beans, but just across the river a more powerful chief ruling a large town named Quigualtum sent his war canoes to inquire about the Spanish.

De Soto was not a fool and knew that his force was vastly weakened, not only in strength and numbers but in spirit. He had to reach the Gulf of Mexico and believed it was a short distance away, but the chief of Guachoya claimed to know nothing of the great water. De Soto sent one of his men to scout ahead, but he also reported no sign of the Gulf.

Despondent over failing to find enormous wealth, his men, horses, and food supplies dwindling, de Soto despaired of reaching the sea across densely forested swamps. The rigors of travel and leadership coupled with a poor diet weakened him and he fell ill. We cannot know what ran through his mind at this time. Perhaps he knew he was going to die, leaving his men without a leader, far from safety and surrounded by hostile Indians. De Soto lashed out in a final display of desperate anger and ordered a vicious attack on a nearby sleeping village called Nilco, proving that the Spanish were still a superior force.

It was mid-May of 1542. The army had been searching for treasure for three long years and now their forty-two-year-old leader lay dying.

De Soto named Luys de Moscoso to take his place and died on May 21. Not wanting the chiefs to know that de Soto was dead, de Moscoso secretly buried de Soto and explained that the Spanish leader had ascended to heaven because he was an invincible god. The Indians, skeptical about the Spaniard's divinity, noticed the disturbed earth and suspected that de Soto was dead; an anxious de Moscoso exhumed the body and committed it to the big river that night.[2]

Trying to gain a foothold in Florida, a French expedition landed at the mouth of the St. Johns River in the early 1560s. Jacques le Moyne sketched and painted Timucuan Indians dressed in animal skins, bird feathers, and clothing fashioned from long grey moss and other plant materials. Hoping for a peaceful place to live, a band of French Huguenots returned in 1564, established Fort Caroline on the St. Johns, and lived in peace with their Timucuan neighbors. In 1565, colonist Nicolas le Challeux described the surrounding land as thickly forested hills full of wild game. The colony was nearly wiped out in September of 1565, however, by Spanish soldiers who considered the land theirs and felt fully justified in attacking heathen Huguenots and Indians.

A party of Spaniards, left behind to guard the reclaimed land, treated the Indians poorly: ruining their crops, pillaging, and enslaving captives. Frenchman Dominique de Gourgues mounted a secret raid in early 1568. The sailors were not even told their destination or their mission until the ship was well away from France. Quietly landing on Cumberland Island, de Gourgues met the Timucuan Chief, Saturiba, who had befriended the first French settlement. The Frenchmen and the Timucuans allied forces, attacked the Spanish soldiers, and recaptured Fort Caroline.

De Gourgues had made his point and returned to France where he received a hero's welcome. The king played down the whole affair lest it spark a war with Spain. Spain decided to ignore the matter, but it established a mission at the mouth of the St. Johns River. More than two centuries would pass before France would raise its flag over northwest Florida again.

England's Sir Richard Grenville led an expedition of seven ships stocked with nearly six hundred men to America in 1585. Sir Walter Raleigh, Grenville's cousin, underwrote the voyage, which first detoured to Puerto Rico and Hispaniola where Grenville traded for supplies, seized a few Spanish vessels, and stole other items before tacking along America's eastern coast. Privateering assured a tidy profit and relieved tedium. Artist John White and scientist Thomas Hariot were among the crew; White drew animals while Hariot wrote of the new land, publishing *A briefe and true report of the new found land of Virginia* in London in 1588. A new edition with White's illustrations was issued in 1590. Though well known at the time, White's drawings slipped from favor in light of new information but were rediscovered in 1709 by Sir Hans Sloane, who later showed them to Mark Catesby. Catesby copied seven drawings and used them in his own work without giving credit to White.

It was no accident that many chronicles, written by explorers paid from royal coffers, gushed praises of the new land's climate, ease of living, friendly natives, and, always, the lure of gold. Reality proved the opposite. The climate, hot or cold, was often harsh, one had to work continuously to grow crops, natives were beginning to wish they had been less welcoming, and gold was as elusive as Ponce de León's fabled Fountain of Youth. But those who looked to the future knew that hard work would bring success.

John White was named governor of England's first colony on Roanoke Island and brought 150 settlers over in 1587. Supplies ran low and some colonists became disillusioned. White shepherded the disappointed people back to England, planning to replenish supplies and return as soon as possible.

The fleet of supply ships was prevented from sailing because the Spanish Armada was on the prowl. White did attempt to cross with only two ships, but they were attacked by French vessels and forced to return to England. Almost three years passed before John White and a fleet of supply ships arrived in August of 1590. The remaining colonists had vanished, leaving only the name of an adjacent island, "Croatoan," carved in a tree. White's granddaughter, Virginia Dare, the first child of English parents born in the New World, was among those lost.

Storms prevented White and his men from searching Croatoan; reluctantly they returned to England, reaching there in October. Besides a letter written in Ireland to Richard Lakluyt in 1593, nothing else is known about John White. He may have died while on another of Raleigh's voyages in 1606, when Bridgit White was appointed administratrix of her brother's estate. John White's fame survives in the early glimpses of the New World he drew in 1585.

The London Company founded Jamestown in May 1607. Starvation and disease nearly decimated the colony in the early months, and John

Smith left to barter or beg food from the Indians. Chief Powhatan captured Smith and legend contends that his daughter, Pocahontas, gained Smith's rescue. The lucky survivor returned to Jamestown only to be thrown into prison by starving settlers. Luckily, a supply ship arrived in time to save Smith again. Many new settlers had been rousted from crowded city streets so it is no wonder they knew next to nothing about farming or hunting and relied almost completely upon provisions from England until Indians taught them to plant corn. Years passed before the colony became self-sufficient.

John Rolfe touted tobacco as a viable income source for Virginia and the colony banked on a single, labor-intensive crop demanded by Europe. Tobacco was thought to cure or ease head pains, kidney stones, blisters, toothache, bad breath, and ward off plague. Eton students were whipped if they did not regularly smoke. Though it brought wealth to many, tobacco eventually robbed nutrients from the soil and Virginia planters were a land-hungry lot by necessity, constantly acquiring virgin land to grow the plant. Though hundreds came to work the fields, more labor was constantly needed for the demanding crop.

The year 1629 was a pivotal one for Jamestown. Twenty Africans disembarked from a Dutch trading ship and were sold as indentured servants, essentially beginning American slavery. In the same year, the Virginia House of Burgesses held their first session there and for the next few years Jamestown was the colony's center of activity. Moving the capital to Middle Plantation in 1698 sounded Jamestown's death knell.

Self-sufficient or not, the swelling Virginia Colony wanted a college. With Governor Francis Nicholson's backing, James Blair, the Church of England's colonial agent, appealed to London. A college, he said, would train ministers and educate youths, thereby helping save colonists' souls. To that argument, Sir Edward Seymour, one of the Lords of the Treasury, thundered, "Souls! Damn your souls! Make tobacco!"[3]

Blair persisted and England eventually granted land and funds for the College of William and Mary. Middle Plantation became the site of the colonies' second seat of higher learning when the cornerstone was laid on August 8, 1695. America's first college, Harvard, had been chartered in 1636. The third oldest, Yale, was formed in 1701 to offset Harvard's growing liberalism.

Middle Plantation, renamed Williamsburg in 1699, was situated on a peninsula between the James and York Rivers and bustled with political activity until Richmond became the capital in 1779. Had the College of William and Mary not been well established there, Williamsburg might have gone the way of Jamestown.

Plucky young clergyman John Banister caught the eye of the Temple Coffee House Botany Club and the Bishop of London, Henry Compton. One of Compton's duties was to fill positions in the colonies and when a post opened in Virginia, the Bishop seized the opportunity to send Banister who would also be an unofficial botanist.

Banister arrived in 1678 and was astounded by the strange new world. He soon buckled down and during fourteen years in Virginia sent 340 species of plants as well as drawings of plants, insects, and mollusks, and scores of reports on natural history, Indians, and daily life to England. His interests were all-encompassing and little escaped his notice. Banister's lively narratives were a splendid addition to science and other English scientists, John Ray among them, used his drawings and portions of his reports to augment their own publications. While on an exploring trip with William Byrd in May 1692, Banister was mistaken for a deer and shot by Jacob Colson, one of Byrd's woodsmen. Colson was later acquitted of the death *per misadventure*.[4]

In 1700, John Lawson sailed from England for Charleston because he had a yen to travel and had met a man who said Carolina was the best place. James Petiver, London apothecary and botanical collector, may have hired or urged Lawson to go to America. At least Lawson was acquainted with Petiver's solicitations for botanical specimens if not the man. In a letter dated April 12, 1701, he promised to send Petiver "Animals vegitables etc. I shall be very industrious in that Imply I hope to yr. satisfaction & my own."[5]

Virtually nothing is known of Lawson before he arrived in Charleston, but he must have been a man of substance for the Lords Proprietors quickly tapped him to explore and survey Carolina's interior. Lawson boasted of covering one thousand miles in fifty-nine days though the actual journey was closer to half that distance. Given the time's travel conditions, he can be forgiven for overestimating the mileage. Lawson was assisted by Indian guides and kept copious notes on the land's natural history and native people, and he began a vocabulary of Indian words. On the way back from this excursion, the party stopped at Richard Smith's home on the Pamlico River. It was probably there that Lawson met Hannah Smith, who became his "beloved Hannah." She bore him at least one daughter, Isabella, though the couple never married.

During his eight years in America, Lawson co-founded the towns of Bath and New Bern in North Carolina, worked on an account of his travels, and surveyed new settlements. He returned to London in 1709 to oversee publication of his book, *A New Voyage to Carolina*. The Lords Proprietors called upon him to return to America to aid Swiss adventurer Baron Christopher Von Graffenreid in settling a colony on the Neuse River. Lawson sailed from Gravesend with 650 Palatine emigrants in January 1710. The voyage took more than three months over pitching seas.

Lawson and Von Graffenreid, helped by two slaves and two Indians, began a trip up the Neuse in 1711. Tuscarora Indians, angry at increasing numbers of arrogant settlers, found a target for their ire in Lawson's small party. Von Graffenreid declared himself under the Great White Queen's protection and was freed. Lawson was executed, probably by having pitch pine splinters stuck into his body and lighted, a gruesome method he had described in his book.

The Tuscaroras may have recognized Lawson as the man responsible for the newest settlement, New Bern, or they may have been ready to punish any European. Von Graffenreid finagled his own release and by his own admission did not say much in Lawson's defense. Soon after Lawson's death, Von Graffenreid left America.

Ironically, death came from people Lawson considered better than whites. "They are really better to us, than we are to them; they always give us Victuals at their Quarters, and take care we are arm'd against Hunger and Thirst: We do not so by them (generally speaking) but let them walk by our Doors Hungry, and do not often relieve them. We look upon them with Scorn and Disdain, and think them little better than Beasts in Humane Shape, though if well examined, we shall find that, for all our Religion and Education, we possess more Moral Deformities, and Evils than these Savages do, or are acquainted withal."[6]

A New Voyage to Carolina was the first major attempt to describe the New World's natural history. The bird lists exceeded anything written by prior inquirers. Lawson's light shone brightest during his sojourn in Carolina for he tumbled rapidly into oblivion after his death though his book remained in print for several years in German and English editions.

To Hannah and Isabella he bequeathed two homes, large land holdings, and a trunk, which has since become lost, containing several writings. His will had been written on August 1, 1708, when Hannah was pregnant and their unborn child was also named an heir.

The Neuse River must have been beautiful when John Lawson began his last short journey almost three hundred years ago. In 1997, the waterway achieved a dubious honor by being named one of the Twenty Most Threatened Rivers on a list generated by American Rivers, a conservation organization dedicated to preserving the nation's rivers. At the end of the twentieth century, close to one million people had settled in the Neuse River basin. Seepage from aging sewage treatment facilities and surface water runoff contribute to degrading the once clean river.

But back in the 1700s, the huge new land seemed almost too large to tame. More settlers were needed to strengthen England's hold. Concerned about the growing number of London's poor, James Oglethorpe and twenty other gentlemen hatched a plan in 1732 to export the city's less fortunate inhabitants to a new American colony named after King George II. The former city dwellers were expected to purchase seed and tools with a start-up allowance and work their own plots of land. England would buy materials produced by the colonists—hemp, flax, wine, and raw silk. After a two-and-one-half-month voyage, the party landed about fifteen miles up the Savannah River on February 1, 1733. Oglethorpe directed that trees be cleared to accommodate the town of Savannah. To keep colonists working, he banned hard liquor and slavery. The first years were hard. Not only were settlers unfamiliar with working the land, but farming was impractical in the sandy soil and the heat was, at times, unbearable. There was not a hint of cooling shade with all the trees gone. Supplies always ran low and Spain shook its sabers at Georgia until the 1740s. Not surprisingly, colonists soon ignored Oglethorpe's injunction against drinking and demanded that slavery be adopted. André Michaux, passing through Savannah in 1786, described it as a village of fifty houses built on sand dunes overlooking the river.

Thanks to contributions of men like White, Banister, and Lawson, scientific knowledge about North America increased dramatically in the late seventeenth and early eighteenth centuries. The startling influx of newly discovered species from around the globe almost overwhelmed scientists trying to devise workable classification systems; animals were designated as wild or domestic, plants were trees or shrubs. Before Linnaeus came along, scientists had used Latin phrases to describe plants and animals, but they were not standardized. Therefore, if a specimen of, say, an oak seemed just slightly different from one looked at yesterday, a new descriptive phrase was written or a few words added or deleted to the previous phrase. Descriptions were unwieldy, cumbersome, and difficult to remember, and before long they were like snowflakes in that they all seemed different.

John Ray, a forward thinking English naturalist, was the first to use anatomy to codify groups of plants and animals. Carolus Linnaeus, Sweden's famous taxonomic botanist, devised the binomial nomenclature system giving each plant or animal species a unique two-word Latin name. He presented his methods in *Systema naturae* in 1735 and *Genera plantarum* in 1737.

Linnaeus dominated botany throughout the 1700s. Using sexual attributes, he divided plants into classes and orders based upon the number, arrangement, and structure of their flower parts. There were those who called his method artificial and found flaws in it. There were those who found it offensive because it was based on sex. Botanists continue refining the system to this day.

The reasoning behind why and how plants and animals grow and live where they do, geographical distribution, was not clearly understood until almost 1900. Climate, soils, rainfall, topography, all determine the geographic range of a species. Some species evolve to survive with certain conditions, such as sea turtles and land dwelling tortoises and birds that have lost the ability to fly. No wonder many early naturalists had difficulty making sense of America's animals. It seemed plausible that the New World's creatures should correspond to European species, and some were similar but many were not in the least related.

As the eighteenth century progressed and growing cities were established on the coast, the country seemed crowded and settlements began pushing into the unknown interior. Interest in natural history and science continued rising, but studies written by the first naturalists had only scratched the surface. Time was ripe for a boom of scientific discovery in the New World.

CHAPTER 2

Illuminating Natural History

Mark Catesby
(April 3, 1683–December 23, 1749)

All the lower (which are the inhabited) parts of Carolina, are a flat sandy country; the land rising imperceptibly to the distance of about an hundred miles from the sea, where loose stones begin to appear, and at length rocks, which at the nearer approach to the mountains, increase in quantity and magnitude, forming gradual hills, which also increase in height, exhibiting extensive and most delightful prospects. Many spacious tracts of meadowland are confined by these rugged hills, burdened with grass six feet high.

—Mark Catesby, *The Natural History of Carolina, Florida and the Bahama Islands,* vol. 1, 1730

MARK CATESBY arrived in Williamsburg on April 23, 1712, from England. Having celebrated his birthday on the high seas, he was twenty days into his twenty-ninth year when he landed. In the preface to his benchmark work, *The Natural History of Carolina, Florida and the Bahama Islands,* Catesby shared a rare glimpse of his early life: "I soon imbibed a passionate desire of viewing as well the animal as vegetable productions in their native countries . . . Virginia was the place, as I had relations there, which suited most with my convenience to go."[1] Then capital of Colonial Virginia, Williamsburg was filled with the cacophony of commerce and politics. Catesby came to explore the colonies with a small budget. Fortunately, his sister Elizabeth had immigrated to America with her husband, William Cocke, shortly after 1700. Using their home as a base and armed with introductions to prominent families prepared by Dr. Cocke, Catesby stayed in relative comfort during his travels.

Mark was born April 3, 1683, likely at Castle Hedingham, home of his maternal grandparents. His antecedents were men of means, employed in the profession of law with side interests in botany and antiquities. The extended Catesby family owned several homes scattered around England. Uncle Nicholas Jekyll kept a flourishing botanical garden and had more than a passing acquaintance with naturalist John Ray.

Since Mark came from a well-to-do background, he must have received a decent education but showed little interest in pursuing a legal career. Increasing popular interest in natural science and visits to his Uncle Nicholas's garden, where the boy could have met Ray, might have been catalysts for studying nature. No known likeness of Catesby survives, only a description written by a friend: "tall, meagre, hard favored, . . . a sullen look . . . extremely grave or sedate and of a silent disposition; but when he contracted a friendship was communicative and affable."[2] Peter Kalm, a student of Linnaeus, thought the naturalist nearsighted, which could explain his somber countenance.

Catesby spent seven years in America, principally in Virginia, during his first visit. A lively young gentleman, he passed time hunting, socializing, and studying natural history. He may not have thought much about a book as he casually observed flora and fauna and collected samples and seeds. Governor Spottswood sent one of Catesby's seed packets to Henry Compton, the botanical bishop, but Compton died before acknowledging the gift. Samuel Dale, skilled apothecary and botanist, and William Sherard, a well-connected Oxford botanist, also received specimens.

Catesby did not amass large quantities of samples on the first visit, but he learned where to look and how to prepare specimens, and he made contacts in the colonies and in England.

After returning to England in 1719, Mark found he had acquired a reputation among natural historians. Catesby met Sherard, who had filled the gap left by James Petiver's death in 1718, and Sir Hans Sloane, court physician and president of the Royal Society. He was also introduced to Colonel Francis Nicholson just before Nicholson sailed to begin his appointment as Royal Governor of South Carolina. Nicholson agreed to sponsor Catesby with an annual pension of £20 upon the latter's return to America to search for new species. This must have been a relief to the young man. His prospects had been hazy in 1712, when he first disembarked in America, and after seven years away from his homeland Mark Catesby might have wondered just what he would do with his life. A path soon became clear.

Members of the Royal Society, established in 1660 to promote scientific discussion, needed someone in America to further and improve the works of Banister and Lawson. Catesby was a likely candidate. He showed aptitude as a scientist and artist; in addition, he was relatively young, with no family to support, and no vocation. His seven years of experience in the new land proved he was up to the task. He was chosen for the job in late 1721.

After several delays Catesby left England in February 1722, bound not for Virginia, but for Carolina. At what he reckoned the halfway point across the Atlantic he noted an owl, swallows, and a hawk with a white head, breast, and belly. The ship had almost reached Charles Town when a contrary wind blew it back into the Gulf Stream. Two weeks passed before port was reached on May 3, 1722. Mark described the voyage as pleasant, but not short, and Charles Town must have been a welcome sight.

Charles Town was first settled on the west bank of the Ashley River in 1670. Settlers faced constant danger from the Spanish, and friendly Indians helped defend the village more than once. Ten years of worry convinced townsfolk to move to a thumb of land between the Ashley and Cooper Rivers, and there Charles Town has remained. By the early 1700s, Charleston, the spelling officially adopted in 1783, was a hub of commerce, travel, and southern hospitality.

England wanted Carolina to produce silk, olive oil, and wine, but the climate was not suited to those goods. What Carolina did have was a plentitude of timber, deer, and wetlands ideal for growing rice. Between December 1706 and December 1707, more than one hundred and twenty thousand deer hides were shipped from Carolina to London. In return, England sent many supplies and foodstuffs.

Most of Carolina's towns eventually became self-sufficient and were able to ship substantial products abroad. By the 1730s, rice was a leading export crop for South Carolina. Prosperity did not come without worries for plantation owners. Whites numbered fourteen thousand and blacks numbered around thirty-two thousand in 1724. Fears of a slave rebellion scratched at every planter's mind, but large-scale farms demanded a huge workforce.

Spring would have been in full bloom in May, when Mark arrived. With backing from the Royal Society and Governor Nicholson, Carolina's most influential doors were opened for the English botanist. If he proceeded at a languid pace during the first visit, his second stay was frenetic. Soon he was collecting specimens, taking notes, drawing sketches. At least seven months elapsed between his departure from England and the arrival of his first shipment there. His English patrons, with their indefatigable appetites, waited impatiently, but they had no notion of the hard going their collector faced in America's wilderness. Catesby could not collect and send fast enough to satisfy.

Mark meant to gather botanical examples in every season, though that was not always possible. A swelling in his cheek, treated by crude surgery in September, kept him confined into December. While he was recuperating, a storm stripped trees of leaves, cones, and seeds. He would have to wait a year to collect those samples.

Settlements were expanding over Carolina, stretching the edge of America's frontier. Along the coasts, great swaths of pine forests broken by secretive swamps spanned the distance between towns and plantations of the Carolinas and the land then called Florida. Catesby joined others or hired Indian guides to accompany him, especially when traveling through unknown lands. Travel was slow; often trails had to be cut. Nothing moved faster than a horse, a boat, or one's own feet. Rumors of Indian attacks peppered any conversation.

Like Lawson, Catesby wrote favorably of Native American customs and traditions. Out of respect, neither man wrote of ceremonies concerning religion, marriage, or death. Indians were "averse to reveal their secret mysteries to Europeans," wrote Mark. Though Catesby recognized several different nations, he lumped them together under such categories as: Their Habits; Of their Arms [few used bows and arrows since the English had supplied them with guns]; Their Persons; Of Their Sagacity; Their Drunkenness [a vice to which they became addicted only after Christians came amongst them]. In describing a cradleboard that could be slung over the shoulder or hung on a tree when the mother was busy, Catesby mused it seemed a handy invention, "and I can't tell why they may not as well to us, if they were introduced here."[3] For the most part, Indians were peaceable and the women were patient, kind, and indulgent to their children. He made special remarks of their hospitality and assistance in the preface to his *Natural History,* for they carried his boxes, hunted and prepared his food, and built bark huts to protect him and his collections from rain. Neither Lawson nor Catesby considered indigenous people an impediment to settling the continent, but neither knew the enormity of the land nor the numbers of people to come.

I WANTED TO VISIT CHARLESTON, for it was a city through which almost all of the men mentioned in this work passed. When friends Pat and Fred Harden rented a cabin at James Island County Park near the city and invited me to join them in March 1999, I didn't hesitate to accept. Leaving late in the day, I scooted up the ramp to Interstate 10, set the cruise control, and switched on some traveling music. Pastures, pine plantations, truck stops, and fields lined the roadside until it passed through a portion of the Osceola National Forest, and there, floating against the sharp blue sky, was an exquisite swallow-tailed kite, white with black points, long pointed wings, scissored tail. The bird made the trip worthwhile and reminded me to slow down and enjoy the journey. Once past Savannah, weather deteriorated and I found my way to the snug cabin through leonine winds, blustery and cold. Pat and Fred would not arrive until Monday night.

Unfortunately, morning's weather was still unsettled. Irritated winds kneaded grey clouds and stirred up gusts that rattled cabbage palms and thrashed wax myrtles. An egret lost its elegance as it tried to land in the marsh. Buffeting gusts blew it up and down like a carousel horse. It was stinging cold. Watching the storm from the warm cabin, I remembered that Catesby had set out for the Cherokee lands in March of 1723. The tribe had been at war with another nation and less likely to bother white travelers. Memories of Lawson's death must have lingered in his mind. I hoped he'd had better traveling weather.

The Ashley River region and Kiawah, Sullivans, Johns and James Islands, south of Charleston, were Mark's favorite collecting spots. They were close to the city and he could make the most of his time there. In the forested river swamps Catesby found wood storks, ivory-billed woodpeckers, Carolina paroquets—America's only native parrot—many species of waterfowl, and bobolinks, called rice-birds because they commonly fed in rice fields. Hundreds of rice-birds were shot each year; they were deemed a choice delicacy and a pest as they could devastate a rice field in an afternoon. Unlike passenger pigeons and paroquets, the bobolink survived. Huge cypresses must have graced those swamps, but they are gone. Still found here are pitcher plants, sundews, and butterworts—all wetland species.

Winds abated by late afternoon so I bundled into a warm jacket and headed for the marsh trail. Nasty weather kept others indoors while crimson cardinals, formal mockingbirds, and chatting myrtle warblers happily escorted me along the paved path. The trail passed through a bamboo thicket, or canebrake. A few steps off the trail and I would have been lost from sight. William Bartram had described an expansive canebrake on Pensacola's outskirts in 1775: "The Canes are ten or twelve feet in height, and as thick as an ordinary walking staff; they grow so close together, there is no penetrating them without previously cutting a road."[4]

The Stono River slices between James and Johns Islands and creeks draining into the larger stream lace the marshland. Catesby had walked near here, for in a few words he blithely related a momentous discovery. Slaves building a levee on the Stono near Charleston, "dug out of the earth three or four teeth of a large animal, which, by the concurring opinion of the Negroes, native Africans . . . were the grinders of an elephant; . . . they could be no other; I having seen some of the like that are brought from Africa."[5]

I stood near a tidal creek that joins the Stono and watched faint glimmers of the setting sun eke through thinning clouds. I shivered, not from cold, but from thoughts that I was near places where the Englishman, burdened with sacks of wilting plants and a heavy game bag, had once

walked. He would have been hurrying to his base, an island plantation or a Charleston home, to begin drying leaves before they became bent and broken, to gut the birds and sprinkle tobacco powder over the skins, to write his observations while they were still fresh in his mind.

Quiet now that the storm had spent its energy, the marsh seemed unchanged. Looking over silent grasses, ignoring the glint of a buoy light, I imagined this was how Catesby saw it. But the land behind was dissimilar. Now, James Island County Park has 125 developed campsites, a water park, and bicycle and boat rentals. Outside the park, homes and businesses line the roadways. Sounds of airplanes and cars and lights from street lamps and neon signs distort the night.

Songbirds had called it a day, and turning toward the cabin in the gloaming, movement in a small pond near the trail caught my eye. A pair of mallards displayed their ingrained courtship ritual as hen and drake stretched alternately out of the water. I watched for a short time and felt like a voyeur.

Pat and Fred arrived about 10:00 P.M. Monday. We headed into Charleston the next day in much improved weather to meet their friends Bob and Bobbie Lee and tour the city. Three centuries of history oozed from every crack in the city's uneven sidewalks. Tourists were encouraged to park and take one of the frequent trolleys or walk the narrow streets. Overshadowing historical aspects, a throng of restaurants catered to every taste and price range, tempting visitors to sample their fare. We gave in to temptation often and walked off calorics in Charleston's open-air market. Aisles were packed with a variety of goods and echoed with conversations and commerce.

At every intersection of the several blocks–long market, clusters of quiet black women sat weaving sweetgrass baskets, wearing ragged cardigans or old flannel shirts to guard against afternoon's chill. While their nimble fingers worked, their inscrutable eyes watched for a likely buyer or an unsavory person who might choose to take their wares without paying.

We noticed small groups of young men and women in crisp blue uniforms, and discovered they were from a French destroyer, *Jean le Viene*. The ship was in port for a few days and open to the public. It was a short walk to the dock and we decided to take a tour. Many of the crew did not speak English, and we couldn't speak a phrase of French among us. Fortunately, the ship was hung with signs reading "visite" underscored with directional arrows so we knew which way to go. Crew members left on board as well as those ashore were busy looking all around. Though they probably wouldn't get farther from their ship than a few square blocks, they drank in atmosphere through their eyes.

Had Catesby's ship docked near this wharf in 1722? The harbor would then have been filled with tall masted schooners nodding to each other as they rode at anchor. Concrete and asphalt constrained the industrial seafront now; the harbor had been altered to accommodate larger, deeper draft vessels. Then as now, the waterfront rang with accents from many lands.

The sun was ducking behind the broad Atlantic as we returned to our vehicles. Fred, Bob, and Bobbie Lee headed off in one car as Pat and I drove along the Battery and Charleston's quiet residential streets. Waterfront homes severely damaged by hurricane Hugo had been bravely restored by their owners. Charlestonians have a history of digging in their heels and standing their ground in the face of whatever is flung at them. The homes echoed that attitude, flaunting their vulnerability to the ocean's fury a road's width from the seawall.

This had been a day for soaking up the city. Tomorrow we would visit Ashley River plantations. Around 1670, a number of plantation owners from crowded Barbados had been drawn by Carolina's inexpensive land. Those families formed Charleston's nucleus. Within a few years, commodious homes hosted by gracious owners bordered the Ashley's marshy banks, land well suited to growing rice. Catesby had access to forests, cypress swamps, brackish marshes, and lodging at those comfortable dwellings, but pyromaniacal Union troops burned many homes in February 1865; time has taken others. Middleton Place, Magnolia Gardens, and Drayton Hall are the only plantations preserved and open to the public at this time.

March 17, 1999, dawned a stunning spring day as we set out for the river plantations. In Catesby's time, the trip could take an entire day; the road was rough, often flooded. Traveling between Charleston and the river plantations by boat was easier and took about four hours. We followed Highway 61 from Charleston, which nearly follows the original river trace and is easily traversed in a few minutes.

Our first stop was Drayton Hall. John Drayton, a descendant of one of Charleston's founding families, purchased the site in 1738, several years after Catesby had returned to England. The ad that Drayton read stated that the property contained a good house and an orchard with several varieties of fruit trees. A house may have been there in Catesby's time, but whether he visited the property cannot be said.

Visitors feel instantly welcome at Drayton Hall. A wide, double staircase leads to the porticoed entrance of a Georgian-Palladian–style house sturdily built of red brick manufactured locally along the river in the Charleston area. The key to this architecture is balance, and inside and out this house speaks symmetry. Drayton Hall, now owned by the National Trust for Historic Preservation, is maintained as it was when the Drayton family moved out and the Trust took over. Parts of the house have been replaced, but nothing has been restored, for that would mean that later trends incorporated into the interior would have to be ripped out. One descendant, for example, installed a Federal-style mantle. There is no electricity or plumbing. Paint on the walls is estimated to be one hundred years old. Knowledgeable guides can answer almost any question and they will often remind visitors not to touch the historic paint. Dozens of inquiring fingers a day would quickly rub the paint away.

Drayton Hall is the only plantation house that escaped burning during the Union troops' sortie through the state. A persistent story credits the owner with eating strawberries to which he was allergic and scaring the soldiers with his swollen, splotched complexion, but that is false. Wisely, the owner placed warning flags indicating yellow fever around the house. Yellow fever was not a disease to trifle with, so the Yankees skedaddled and Drayton Hall survived.

Our guide suggested we close our eyes and imagine sounds from the 1700s. Going back in time after listening to the guide's description was easy. I stood in the middle of the open yard and conjured pools sprouting supple rice plants. Pots clattered from the kitchen, harnesses jingled and shouts wavered from the stable, laughter resounded from the building used for weaving and carpentry, and low, resonant singing drifted from beyond the trees.

Our next stop was Middleton Place, owned by a private foundation. Middleton dates from the late 1730s, so it's unlikely that Catesby was hosted there either. It was lunch time and we'd worked up an appetite while touring Drayton Hall. Middleton has a good restaurant, but figuring the confusing entrance fees took a little time and being hungry did not help our collective disposition. We were finally admitted, parked the car, and walked through formal gardens to the restaurant.

FIG. I. Drayton Hall on South Carolina's Ashley River.
Courtesy of Drayton Hall, National Historic Site.

We'd noticed two contented Jersey cows grazing on the extensive front lawn as we drove in. Just before we reached a reflecting pool, a commotion sounded behind us and then a man's shout, "Look out! Clear the way." One cow had slipped out and she was no longer contented. We dove out of the way, but the family ahead of us, oblivious to the noise, was nearly run down. The bewildered cow stampeded down the paths with her caretaker in pursuit while her partner bawled from the lawn. Finally, the escapee was persuaded through a gate, the pair was reunited, and we safely strolled the garden's precise paths.

Middleton's grounds are spacious and many outbuildings remain. Henry Middleton had begun laying out formal gardens around 1741. "It took one hundred slaves ten years to build the gardens," our tour director later explained. The home must have been glorious at that time. A few trampling horses and flashing sabers laid waste those flowered beds on a February afternoon in 1865. Soldiers burned the main house and its flankers. The troops must have gleefully torched those buildings because their owner, Williams Middleton, had signed South Carolina's Ordinance of Secession. (An ancestor had signed the Declaration of Independence.) Williams fled and sent his wife to Columbia with valuables for safety. Union troops spared Charleston and burned Columbia, so the Middletons lost nearly everything. Their library housed some ten thousand books, most gone up in flames. When the Middletons returned, only a few brick walls were standing. The once beautiful gardens were in ruins. Paintings taken by a Union medical officer were finally reinstated after ten years of written pleas from Williams.

Williams Middleton borrowed money from his sister and rebuilt one of the flanker buildings. Here the Middletons lived, every day gazing on the crumbling walls of their former home, constant reminder of a splendor forever gone. The walls fell in the 1886 earthquake, but the Middletons had gone to live with a daughter by then.

When Middleton Place came under the auspices of a private operating foundation in the 1970s, appeals went out to family members to donate items that might have been found in the home before it was destroyed. Gardens and reflecting lakes were fully relandscaped with precise formal paths and terraces leading to the river. Upstairs walls of the flanker rebuilt by the Middletons were hung with Audubon prints and a copy of Catesby's *Natural History* rested in a glass case. Of all the memorabilia, Catesby's book held the most allure for me.

The afternoon waned and we were tired, but since we passed by Magnolia Gardens on our way to the cabin, we decided to stop. If we had stopped there first, we might never have seen the other plantations. Magnolia, one of the first Ashley River plantations, is owned and operated by the Drayton family.

Thomas Drayton, Jr., and Stephen Fox were among Charleston's early Barbadian colonizers. Fox acquired land about ten miles up the Ashley. Drayton married Fox's daughter, Ann, and inherited land that came to be called Magnolia. Thomas and Ann built their home during the 1680s. No image of their home exists; it burned in the early 1800s, but memoirs state that it was modeled after the Drayton family estate in Northamptonshire. An essential complement was a formal English garden, and by the time Thomas died in 1717 the garden encompassed more than ten acres.

Catesby must have passed by here in 1723. Thomas Drayton III would surely have invited the Englishman to stay and explore the grounds. The naturalist might have rambled down this very path to the river. Nearly six decades later, British troops camped on Magnolia's grounds as they prepared to capture Charleston during the Revolution.

John Drayton, builder of Drayton Hall, was Thomas's younger brother and would not inherit the family land. He was able to purchase nearby acreage and would eventually purchase the Magnolia property. An entire book could be devoted to explaining not only the family's lineage, but their contributions to settling the Southeast.

Thomas Glen Drayton had no son and in 1825 willed Magnolia and other lands to his grandsons, Thomas and John Grimké, provided the boys took Drayton as their legal last name. They did so. John began studying for the ministry and Thomas ran the plantations. Unfortunately, Thomas was accidentally killed during a deer hunt and the holdings passed to John. He continued his ministerial studies and, while attending a seminary in New York, fell in love and married Julia Ewing from Philadelphia. Julia was apprehensive about moving south because of the large slave population. John wanted to create a paradise that Julia would never want to leave and he poured energy into the gardens. At the same time, he competently ran several plantations and served as Rector of St. Andrew's Episcopal Church a short distance from Magnolia Plantation.

Reverend Drayton's aunts, Angelina and Sarah Grimké, were among the first women to vocalize antipathy to the oppression of women and to slavery—so much so that they were banished from South Carolina. They moved north and continued their crusade. After they spoke in Philadelphia's new Pennsylvania Hall, a riot broke out and a mob burned the building. The Grimké sisters became unpopular there too.

Though he owned several hundred blacks, John must have harbored some of his aunts' views. Going against state law, John built a school at Magnolia and taught slave children to read, write, and do sums under the guise of teaching religion. The schoolroom serves as an office today.

The second plantation house was burned during the Civil War. After the war, John moved a summer home from the mountains and raised it on the burned-out foundations. Drayton sold several properties and opened the gardens to the public to make ends meet. Then phosphate was discovered underneath Magnolia's fields. It sold at the fantastic price of $60 per ton, and John quickly started mining operations. When he realized that strip mining was ruining the land he halted the operation and forever forbade it in his will. Damage was done, but fortunately not on the entire plantation.

Though not as grand as Drayton Hall and Middleton Place had once been, the existing plantation house is comfortable and reflects the personalities of owners past and present. Fine porcelain bird statues stand on priceless antique furniture. A treasure trove of natural history books are protected under glass cases in an upstairs room: Audubon's elephant portfolio, two copies of Catesby's work, Wilson's *Ornithology,* François Michaux's *American Sylva,* and wildlife prints lining the walls—oh my, how my hands itched to turn the pages of those magnificent books. But they are old, so old, and must be protected from dust and bruising fingers.

We had had a full day of sightseeing and gratefully headed back to the cabin. Near the highway, advertisements for new developments crept in between older, less expensive dwellings. Their wood siding could not remember paint and was adorned with ghost herds of deer hides and antlers. Tilting couches shedding clots of stuffing beckoned neighbors to sit a spell and gossip as the world rolled by. As the Charleston area expands, these small, rural enclaves fall before progress, converted into choice livable land for exclusive developments and golf courses. It's another chapter in a long story of one culture overtaking another and of wildlife habitat forever lost.

In the past three days, I'd glimpsed a shadow of the area Catesby combed. In his rambles around the countryside and interviews with dwellers, Mark adopted some stories and rejected others. He had passed on, in almost the same words, Lawson's tale of the devil-fish, or manta ray, a huge animal with a semi-kleptomaniac personality, which had purposely entangled its horns in a ship's anchor ropes and absconded with the vessel for a sprightly run, later returning the craft to its original anchorage.

I initially thought it a tall tale, but revised that opinion on February 10, 1999, after hearing a news report about a manta ray that had become snarled in a small fishing boat's anchor line and, panicked, began swimming. On February 22, I phoned the New Smyrna Beach Coast Guard Station and spoke with Mr. Heitkamper, a Coast Guard Auxiliary volunteer, who confirmed the story. A forty-one-foot rescue boat had been dispatched to the scene about one and a half miles offshore after receiving a distress call concerning a sixteen-foot fishing boat being pulled in circles by an unknown creature. Crew transferred the anchor line from the smaller craft to the cutter and attempted to haul in the rope. Sensing a shift in the rope's tension, the ray surfaced. It had been towing the small boat for about two hours and must have been tired. Witnesses estimated the animal to be about eighteen feet wide and to weigh nine hundred pounds. When the rope slackened the big ray slipped free and swam away. Mr. Heitkamper said he knew of no other reports of boat-stealing rays.

Animal encounters aside, and weather and health permitting, Catesby had worked with dogged determination. Exasperated by repeated insinuations that sponsors were not getting their money's worth, Catesby wrote to Sherard: "I wish I would know what you required and by whome. I hope it can't be expected I should send Collections to every of my Subscribers, which is impracticable for me to doe . . . I protest before God I never can be more industrious in collecting whatever I could possibly meet with either those few days that I was at Savannah Garrison or Since."[6]

In truth, Sherard and Sloane each anticipated complete collections. Catesby had neither time nor means to collect for everyone, but he did his best. Sloane had an insatiable appetite for all nature's curiosities. No example was too big or too small and, in addition to Catesby, Sloane had linked himself to collectors around the globe. His medley of minerals, plants, animals, shells, and human artifacts became the foundation of the British Museum's natural history collection.

On a trip in May 1999, I drove south across South Carolina on U.S. Alternate 17 from Jamestown to Walterboro toward another collecting site, far from Charleston's comforts, favored by Catesby. He often traveled with troops heading for Fort Moore on Beech Island on the Savannah River. Catesby had described the region as one of the "Sweetest Countrys" he had ever seen; small hills and numerous creeks reminded him of Kent. He hunted buffalo there and late in the summer of 1723, witnessed a magnificent sturgeon run up the Savannah River's rapids above the fort.

Once past Moncks Corner, manufactured housing businesses, convenience stores, and fast food heaven line the highway. A hop and a skip across Routes 63, 363, and U.S. 278 took me to Allendale and Highway

125, which carries traffic out of the coastal plain and onto the rolling Piedmont through the Savannah River Site that now squats on Catesby's sweet country, about fifteen miles south of Augusta, Georgia, on South Carolina's side of the river. A series of dams gags the river above Augusta. The rapids have been tamed but sturgeon still spawn.

A line of empty guardhouses and a large sign ordering drivers not to stop or stand on the roadside mark the entrance to the Savannah River Site, built in response to the Cold War. At one time, personnel stationed at the gates would have checked credentials before letting cars enter. Five reactors began producing materials used in nuclear weapons in the early 1950s, primarily tritium and plutonium-239. This was a secure area with an array of support facilities, staff housing, two chemical separations plants, a heavy water extraction plant, a nuclear fuel and target fabrication facility, a tritium extraction facility, and waste management facilities. Today the installation processes and stores nuclear material and develops new technologies to treat nuclear and hazardous wastes left from the Cold War.

The Department of Energy owns the 198,344-acre site. Security is not as stringent now; the guardhouses wait. Westinghouse Savannah River Company has been responsible for many operations since October 1, 1996. Approximately 13,000 people work here, making this one of South Carolina's largest employers. A call before my trip to make sure the road was open to through traffic brought assurance that it was.

The complex is dedicated to protecting the surrounding natural resources. The U.S. Forest Service manages a timber and forestry research center and the University of Georgia maintains the Savannah River Ecology Laboratory for the Department of Energy. A variety of wildlife live in or use the area: alligators, deer, turkeys, bald eagles and endangered red-cockaded woodpeckers, peregrine falcons, shortnose sturgeons, and wood storks. Indeed, the highway passes through stands of healthy longleaf pines.

Flagging on the pines used as nesting trees indicated a monitored red-cockaded woodpecker community and new growth showed that managers used prescribed fire, but those warning signs were annoying and distracting. I thought about pulling off the road and taking a few photos to see what would happen, but why risk the hassle?

There is, however, one spot where passersby are permitted to stop for a few minutes and read a historical marker that tersely explains the death of a town. Established in 1873, the Ellenton post office was situated near the marker. The town was chartered in 1880 and residents went about their business with the usual ebb and flow of human activity until the early 1950s when the federal government bought the town and surrounding area to build the nuclear plant.

The sign does not relate what happened to the post office or other town buildings. It is one thing to have your childhood home blown down by wind or burned up by fire, but here is an entire town gone—schools, churches, graveyards: all gone. If former residents desired to return and visit the place where they grew up, said their wedding vows, buried a family member, they could not. Stopping there was eerie and I felt sure a hidden camera surveilled the spot.

New Ellenton is on Route 19, a few miles northwest of the Savannah River Site. I did not go there, but I did log onto the town's Website. Photographs of the original town are posted; the most poignant was taken on the highway approach to Ellenton of the standard black and white sign announcing the town. In the photo, the sign has hand-lettered boards nailed around it with a message that no one could have read completely without stopping. "It is hard to understand why our town must be destroyed to make a bomb that will destroy someone else's town that they love as much as we love ours. But we feel that they picked not just the best spot in [unreadable] but in the world. We love these dear hearts and gentle people who live in our home town."

Old Ellenton has passed into history and so has Fort Moore. Beech Island is indicated by a sign a few miles south of Augusta, but at that point I was swept along with traffic flow heading for the city. Once past Augusta's crush I pondered Catesby's work.

In an age that sought to bring rigid order to chaotic nature, he faced an insurmountable task. With few previous studies to guide him, Catesby meant to describe plants, animals, people, and landscape of the Carolina region. He answered the challenge with an energy that might leave us, in our convenient modern age, breathless. In describing the land, Catesby lumped the Carolina soil into three categories, hedging his bets on a distant fourth: rice land (swamps); oak and hickory land; pine barren land; and most sterile of all, shrubby oak land. Based on evidence of inland shells, he correctly assessed that the low southern country had once been underwater.

Large longleaf pines, also known as pitch pine and yellow pine, grew on high sandhills between rivers and marshes. Frequent fires kept under-brush low, allowing grasses to dominate. Settlers referred to such pine-lands as barren because they seemed devoid of anything other than grasses and trees. Longleafs were slow growing but their durable lumber was used more than any other for headings, staves, shingles, doors, floors, and staircases. The butter-colored wood assumed the patina of molten honey with age.

Catesby wrote that a pleasant Carolina, "happily situated in a climate parallel to the best parts of the Old World, enjoys in some measure the like blessings."[7] Summer months he rated as sultry, but where land was cleared of trees, sea breezes were free to refresh the air. Serene, moderate tempera-tures from September to June more than compensated for summer's blaze. After tropical diseases, such as malaria and yellow fever, began picking off the populace, those who could afford it relocated to more healthy climes during sweltering summers.

Short-lived frosts came in December and January, Catesby extolled; compared to England, Carolina's winter was short and mild. The first blossoms appeared in February and April's showers brought spring to a peak of beauty. Occasional and violent thunderstorms struck May through July and long rainy periods fell in August and September. About every seven years, hurricanes blew against the coasts, though they were "much mitigated in their force by the time they reach Carolina." Other than big storms, the sea seldom made great changes in the landscape, but the coast was in a constant state of change, Mark surmised succinctly, as it "gets and loses alternately and gradually."[8]

About the only detraction Catesby would admit was that farmers and Indians burned the woods from February through March to clear under-brush and promote fresh growth. Wood smoke and added smoke from tar-kilns tainted the otherwise sweet air. The Atlantic tempered winter along the coast, but Catesby found that on the whole northern colonies were colder than European countries lying on the same latitude.

With funds running low, Catesby ended his work and boarded a ship bound for the Bahamas. While lying on the sloop's deck, he pondered birds flying overhead and postulated that rice-birds followed ripening fields from south to north. Migration was hardly understood at that time and many believed birds lay torpid in caverns, hollow trees, and even underwater during winter. Catesby rejected such tales as absurd.

Most of his observations were based on common sense. People clung to the notion that plants falling under the common name of snakeroot could cure a venomous snake's bite. He had supplied numerous samples of plants accompanied with his caution that a bite could not be cured by any concoction made from snakeroot.

He gathered samples and painted and returned to England in 1726 with publication on his mind. As he wrote in the preface to his *Natural History*, "The illuminating natural history is so particularly essential to the perfect understanding of it."[9] Catesby knew a lavishly illustrated book would sell to those who could afford it. His first hopes were dashed because of engraving costs, but Joseph Goupy, French watercolorist and etcher, saved the day by teaching Catesby how to etch the plates himself.

His was an ambitious project, describing all of America's creatures and plants. Mark labored under the misconception that everything to be found resided in fair Carolina, and he returned to England certain that he had described most of what there was to find in America, except for insects. The ranges of many species overlapped the area he covered, from present-day southeastern Virginia to a bit of eastern Georgia. Those areas were rich in diversity, but only a small representation of America's natural wealth. There was much more to be described, but Catesby's book remained the standard for nearly a century. Despite the title of his book, Catesby never did visit Florida as we know it. Back then, Florida reached up to Carolina's border and Georgia was not on the map yet.

Catesby drew from others for his own work. He relied upon Lawson's book for corroboration and for explanations of things he had not been able to study himself. Evidently Mark copied some of John White's drawings; although he credited Lawson's influence in his discourse on Native Americans, Catesby claimed all drawings as his own. Catesby's catfish is almost a mirror image of White's. His motives are unknown. Perhaps Catesby never saw a catfish or his own drawings had become damaged or lost.

In order to stretch his modest finances, Catesby released his work in a series. The first volume was released in 1729 and the second in 1743. The Appendix, the final installment, was released in 1747. Still, Mark ran short of funds. Peter Collinson, a new face in the naturalist circle, loaned Catesby money without interest. Collinson, a wealthy merchant and devotee of nature, sponsored many others, most notably John Bartram.

Once the project was underway, problems arose in determining correct colors and shapes. Around 1741, Catesby contacted John Bartram to send specimens of whippoorwills and whip will's widows, birds he had neglected to describe. In addition to working on the *Natural History,* Catesby directed hired colorists, refined his notes, dashed to meetings, delivered lectures, pottered in his London garden, and advised others about ornamental cultivation.

Space, or rather, lack of it, dictated that plants and animals be placed together and plants were often pictured in bud, flower, and fruit at the same time. Mark Catesby was probably the first natural history artist who tried to pair birds with the plants that provided their food or shelter. Descriptive discourses supplemented each drawing.

Catesby's *Natural History* signaled the dawn of wildlife art. Modern field guides are descended from those early, laboriously produced books, and hold an accumulation of research, a collective natural history that has been building since before great trees were cut, sweet waters sullied, and clear air obscured.

As seen today, Catesby's subjects appear flat and lack the meticulous detail of Alexander Wilson or the vitality of John James Audubon. Catesby was a self-taught painter and apologized for it, "As I was not bred a painter I hope some faults in perspective . . . may be more readily excused."[10] Few creatures are not readily recognizable anyway, even by a casual observer. In this context, his work stands on its own merits; it set the way for those who followed. Here was a work for others not to imitate but to better.

At age sixty-four, Mark Catesby married Elizabeth Rowland, a widow with a grown daughter, in a quiet ceremony on October 8, 1747. His health began declining in the summer of 1749, and he died on December 23, 1749, leaving Elizabeth and two children, Mark, aged eight, and Ann. They might have been his children from an earlier marriage, though no record can be found. In any case, Mark and Ann were born before Catesby married Elizabeth. He left little money to his family, but he did leave the plates and a few copies of his *Natural History.* Elizabeth lived on proceeds of the books, but had to reduce their price. She died in 1753 and Mark's children inherited their father's art.

Two hundred and fifty years later, Mark Catesby has slipped into near oblivion. His art and studies, especially of birds, were overshadowed by Alexander Wilson's *American Ornithology,* published about eighty years after *Natural History;* Wilson would later be obscured by John James Audubon. Catesby's reputation lasted longer in England, though his book was published before Linnaeus redesigned the classifying regime, making many of the names in Catesby's book obsolete. Mark Catesby's name dwindled from American consciousness, except among the coterie of scientists. Such is the vagary of fame.

Catesby was working on the *Hortus Britanno-Americanus* when he died. In this work devoted to America's trees, Catesby had a chance to correct some erroneous information given in the *Natural History* and to include some trees and shrubs not mentioned in the earlier work. But the smaller *Hortus,* published a few years after his death, lacked the broad appeal of his first work and wanted his fine touches.

Catesby had painted 263 large watercolors while in America, separate from those that appeared in the *Natural History.* King George III purchased the paintings in 1768 for £120. For years they rested in Buckingham Palace and were moved to the Royal Library at Windsor in 1833, where they were little used and ignored. They were rediscovered and presented in England and America once again in 1997.

If Mark Catesby was publicly forgotten, he was remembered by the scientific community. Listen for the bullfrog's *basso profundo* voice issuing from a river or lake and remember that its scientific name is *Rana catesbeiana.* Thomas Walters named the pine lily *Lilium catesbaei* in 1788, long after Mark's death. Its eye-catching apricot-colored flowers peer above tawny grasses of pine savannahs from southeast Virginia to Florida.

As Catesby had depended upon Lawson's study, so others depended upon Catesby's, notably Peter Kalm, John Bartram, and Alexander Wilson. The book drew John Abbot to Virginia. John James Audubon must surely have referred to it. Though Catesby had more than a casual interest in nature, he did not begin earnest studies until his thirties. Had John Banister and John Lawson not been killed, Mark Catesby might not have achieved the measure of fame that he did. Their deaths opened the way for Catesby to create a landmark study of America's natural curiosities.

CHAPTER 3

The Bartram Legacy

John Bartram
(May 23, 1699–September 1777)

William Bartram
(April 9, 1739–July 22, 1823)

I am daily waiting for further orders & recommendations from Court, but our Friend Peter ordered me to take my son or A servant with me & as thee wrote to me last winter & seemed so very desirous to go there: now thee hath A fair opertunity so pray let me know as soon as possible our vesail is to sail in about two or three weeks.

—John Bartram's letter of June 7, 1765, informing William Bartram of his appointment as Royal Botanist and the impending trip to Florida

The shores of this great river St. Juan are very level and shoal,

extending, in some places, a mile or two into the river,

betwixt the high land and the clear waters of the river, which

is so level, as to be covered not above a foot or two deep with

water, and at a little distance appears as a green meadow,

having water-grass and other amphibious vegetables grow-

ing in the oozy bottom, and floating on the water.

—William Bartram, *Travels,* 1791

ON DECEMBER 20, 1765, John Bartram and his son William, Mr. Yates, Mr. Davis, and a slave launched a dugout canoe onto the St. Johns River at Cowford near present-day Jacksonville. Their mission was to trace the river to its source. Mr. Davis acted as hunter and guide for the party and his slave rowed and cooked, wrote John. It must have been a cold day, and crowded in the vessel with five people and supplies.

King George appointed the elder Bartram to the post of Royal Botanist for the recently acquired property in 1765. Since Ponce de León's landfall, Florida had bounced among Spain, England, and France. During the Seven Years' War, 1756–63, Great Britain captured Cuba, and demanded Florida from Spain in exchange for the island. Spain acquiesced and abandoned her mainland forts and settlements. Anxious to learn what the southern lands promised, his Majesty wanted detailed reports and drawings. Probably no white colonist had followed the St. Johns' sinuous length until the Bartrams made their journey.

John and Elizabeth Bartram emigrated from England in 1683 to escape religious persecution and help settle William Penn's Quaker colony built on the site of former Swedish settlements near Philadelphia. Their grandson, John Bartram, was born on May 23, 1699, and along with his younger brother, James, grew up on the family's farm. The boys' mother died soon after James's birth in 1701.

Their father, William, remarried in 1707 and fathered two children with his second wife before moving his new family to North Carolina in

1711, leaving John and James behind. William Bartram was killed during a Tuscarora Indian raid in September of that year, possibly part of the same warfare that led to John Lawson's demise. Mrs. Bartram and the children were captured but returned to Pennsylvania in 1712.

John revealed little about his youth in his writings. Accounts mention a delicate child not always in the best of health. Some place John's interest in plants in his middle years, but in a letter written May 1, 1764, to Peter Collinson, an English merchant, Quaker, and natural history enthusiast, Bartram revealed an attraction to plants since age ten, though he neither knew their names nor had books to teach him. His mother dead, left behind by his father and then his father slain, raised by his grandparents, perhaps the young boy found cheer in woodlands surrounding the farm, which laid a foundation for a lifelong appreciation of nature.

All his life John felt the sting of his scanty education though he had attended solid Quaker schools. In an earlier letter to Collinson, dated November 3, 1754, John took umbrage at derisive comments about his faulty English, protesting that the truth was more important than correct grammar and spelling. Bartram hungered for knowledge, reading everything he could find about paleontology, botany, zoology, medicine, and geology. Worries about his own health led him to study medicine and he practiced on his neighbors. The son of a farmer, John became a farmer and employed innovative procedures, such as letting fields lie fallow and rotating crops. He designed and built five stone houses, cutting some of the blocks himself.

A keen observer with an intelligent, inquisitive mind, John knew what he wanted and aimed for his goal. His personal letters, journals, and other writings show a man spare and concise in his language. He was a thoughtful man who considered everything and, once presented with a question, tenaciously pursued it until a satisfactory answer was obtained. Acquaintances and family members portrayed him as a learned man who sought the society of educated men.

Above all, his abiding passion was botany. John turned over the wood-lots near his farm at Kingsessing, Pennsylvania, for seeds and plants. Each new discovery spurred his desire to find another. Conceiving of a garden representing all the plants he could find in America, as well as samples sent from abroad, John planted the country's first known botanical garden.

Showing off gardens and hothouses filled with New World curiosities was the rage across Europe. Through his American contacts, Peter Collinson had provided many specimens found in those gardens and cabinets. Bartram began supplying plants and seeds to Collinson in 1733. By 1734, eagerly responding to the merchant's requests, Bartram's passionate hobby had become a demanding activity and the two formed a strong trading relationship. A typical list sent to John in 1738 requested multiple specimens of berries, fruits, cones, and acorns from several species and included strict instructions on preparing and packing young plants. Collinson and Bartram did not always see eye to eye, yet the bond across the Atlantic was strong. The merchant and the farmer never met but their friendship lasted until Collinson died in 1768.

John's family increased significantly when twins, William and Elizabeth, arrived on April 9, 1739. Toddling through fields, following his father around the growing garden, William displayed a propensity for botany. Quick of mind and as observant as his father, the son grew to view things differently. Where John saw a succinct scientific description, William beheld colors in an artist's variant hues, shapes, and purposes in a poet's imaginative, romantic language. While John examined plants and wrung every exact shape and color from them, William caressed leaves and turned a small bird over and over until it became as familiar as his own skin, and when he wrote of them and sketched their likeness, they sprang to life again.

Largely through his connection with Peter Collinson, John's botanical expertise became increasingly known across the colonies and abroad. Bartram joined Benjamin Franklin and others in forming the American Philosophical Society in 1743. Naturalists found their way to John's home, as they would continue to do throughout William's life. Peter Kalm, a Swedish botanist and former student of Carolus Linnaeus, visited the Bartram household in 1748. During his American investigation, Kalm expressed wonder at the variety and enormous girth of some trees, only to be told by old settlers that the largest trees had already been cut. The land was nothing like it had appeared sixty years before, they said. It was a refrain to be chanted as the years advanced; you should have seen it fifty years ago, forty, twenty.

In addition to time spent gathering plants, there was endless paperwork. Bartram kept journals of his trips and nurtured a vigorous correspondence with Collinson, Carolus Linnaeus, and Benjamin Franklin, among others. Writing at night by candlelight, he penned two copies of letters and notes, sending one and keeping the other for referral when an answer was received several months later. Letters sent abroad were usually wrapped in dry tobacco leaves to keep hungry insects at bay.

Since farming commanded John's time during most of the year, he scheduled his collecting trips to follow the fall harvest. As his hobby became more businesslike, he frequently traveled farther from home for longer periods. Currency was rarely the payment for the specimens; Collinson often sent bolts of cloth, household items, and clothing. Most of those items were readily available in America and what John repeatedly requested were books to help in his work. Instead, when Bartram sent specimens he could not name, Collinson had them classified and returned to John. The merchant was sure they would be of better use than the constantly requested books.

John's forays provided opportunities to observe the land. In letters and conversations he expressed concerns about the country's disappearing forests, noting especially the extensive erosion caused by removing sheltering forests from river banks. John advocated reforestation and advised at least partially replacing what was destroyed by agriculture and construction.

In William's fourteenth year, 1753, John took the boy on a collecting trip to the Catskills. Billy, as John called him, gathered plants, watched, sketched, collected birds, and prepared the skins himself. Bartram felt the boy showed promise, yet he worried about Billy's future. Writing to Collinson in 1755, soon after Billy's sixteenth birthday, John voiced his concern. Proud of his son's talent, the father fretted that drawing and botany would not provide a living. John wanted Billy to support himself, but had to admit that hard labor disagreed with the boy.

William sent some bird skins to English ornithologist George Edwards in 1756. Edwards later sent the skins to Linnaeus who used them to classify new American species. The next year John sent some of his son's drawings to Collinson.

It must have been frustrating to be John Bartram's son and share his love of nature. William seemed always to stand in the shadow of the spotlight cast upon his father, even after John's death. After all, Linnaeus had called John Bartram the world's greatest natural botanist. That was high praise for a self-taught man and a hard act to follow.

There is no doubt that John, vexed by his son's dreamy nature, tried time and again to turn Billy into a businessman. And there is no doubt that while Billy wanted to please his father, the young man's heart lay in the wilderness. William turned down an offer to be Dr. Alexander Garden's assistant and apprenticed himself to a Philadelphia merchant. After the tutelage period ended, and with financial backing from his father, William set up a trading business on the Cape Fear River in North Carolina in 1761. John's half-brother, also named William, lived nearby and Billy lived at Ashwood, his uncle's home.

When England received Florida as spoils after the Seven Years' War in 1763, Peter Collinson urged King George to name John Bartram as his royal botanist. Not only would the appointment bring John deserved prestige, it would assure a yearly income of £50 to ease some of Bartram's financial woes. John wrote William with news of his royal commission and requested that his son close his business and join the expedition. William wasted no time settling his affairs.

John arrived at Ashwood in July. Father and son left in August 1765, bound for Charleston. The town was almost a century old and no longer the frontier settlement found by Mark Catesby. While there they visited Dr. Garden, who shared their passion for plants. The spicy white gardenia is a living tribute to Dr. Garden.

Having tramped many enjoyable hours through the low country, crossing some of Catesby's long vanished footprints, John and William departed Charleston in late September. They passed through Augusta and observed sturgeon running the rapids, as Mark Catesby had seen in 1724. While following the Altamaha River toward Fort Barrington, Georgia, they became lost. John, aged sixty-six, tired easily but was revived by the discovery of a slender, smooth-barked tree. They camped nearby and regained their proper direction the next day.

Although John did not make specific mention of the tree in his journals, William returned and collected seeds during his search ten years later. The Bartrams named the tree *Franklinia alatamaha* in honor of Benjamin Franklin. The tree has not been found in the wild since John Lyon saw it in 1803, though it thrives in cultivation. More than likely, any *Franklinia* tree growing in a modern garden is descended from seeds collected almost two centuries ago.

William fell in love with the verdant Southeast and when the king's expedition was over, he decided to stay behind and try his hand at running a rice and indigo plantation near the St. Johns River. John was against the idea, but purchased slaves in Charleston and shipped them to

Billy in Florida in 1766. William soon faltered in his venture and the next few years were a low point. He found himself ill-suited to any vocation save one, and his father did not approve of it. Dispirited, Billy returned to Philadelphia in the fall of 1767, found work as a farmhand, and tried the mercantile trade again. Clearly, William was unsuited to business and he was unhappy.

Collinson wrote with good news in July 1768. Margaret Cavendish Bentinck, Duchess of Portland, had engaged Billy to draw all land, river, and sea shells for £21. Scarcely a month later Collinson died. Dr. John Fothergill, another of John's long-time correspondents, wrote to Billy in autumn of that year with a commission to draw mollusks and turtles for another £21.

William could not forget the lush, steamy South and returned to Cape Fear to fulfill his commissions. But he wrote from St. Augustine in 1772, an almost desperate letter, telling his parents that he would stay in the southland and immerse himself in that which he had been born to do, the only thing he was good for. William was happiest in the woods, discovering, drawing, observing. Predictably, John strongly disapproved of the plan. Father and son were again at odds.

Luck turned William's way in 1773 after he contacted Dr. Fothergill with a proposal to collect plants in Florida. Fothergill agreed to pay William £50 per year plus expenses. William returned to Philadelphia to prepare for his journey.

The unsettled young man was nearly thirty-four years old when he arrived in Charleston in March 1773, trailing a string of debts and business failures. Unable to adapt to a life of which his father approved, William embarked on a journey following his own hopes and dreams. He roamed through southern Atlantic coast marshes and swamps and across the interior to the Appalachian Mountains for nearly a year, accompanied by John M'Intosh.

Spring 1774 found him in Florida, retracing part of the St. Johns River. He returned to Georgia for the winter. Setting out from Charleston the following spring, he tramped through northwestern South Carolina and western North Carolina, across Georgia and Alabama, turning south to visit Pensacola. A boat carried him to Mobile, and then to the Mississippi River.

William returned to Georgia in January 1776 to ramble over red clay hills and brooding, never-still rivers. The Cherokees had not yet been forced from their home, and Bartram referred to the southern Appalachians as the Cherokee Mountains. William found the Cherokee intelligent, freedom-loving, honest, and just, willing to die for their land and rights.

Trekking a vague path around Georgia, at last there was nothing to do but turn north for home. An overland journey delivered William to his father's house in January 1777. His family had not heard from him in almost two years; his father thought him dead. John was an old man by the time Billy returned, and his health had not been good for some time. John Bartram, the most famous American naturalist of his time, died that September.

After his father's death, William stayed home, assisting his brother in managing the garden, filling orders for seeds and cuttings, and lending his erudition to a flood of naturalists exploring America. The garden needed to be reclaimed, as it had lain untended during the British occupation, 1777–78. William, no longer called Billy, finished his report to Dr. Fothergill and began a book about his journey. Visitors kept coming, for even though John was gone, the son was in residence.

André Michaux, botanist to the king of France, first visited the garden in 1786. Later that year, William fell nearly twenty feet from a cypress tree, suffering a compound fracture to his right leg. The leg did not heal correctly and bothered him for the rest of his life. After all the miles he had traveled, his most serious accident occurred at home.

The garden was in full glory by 1787 when a Constitutional Convention delegation led by George Washington visited. Michaux came again in 1789 and drew William away for a day's botanizing south of Philadelphia. William returned home the next day while Michaux continued on. Alexander Wilson dropped by in 1802 and William encouraged the Scots schoolteacher to study birds. The young man learned quickly under William's direction and taught himself to draw and paint. Wilson published the first volume of his *American Ornithology* in 1808.

Thomas Jefferson invited Bartram to serve as the natural history advisor on an expedition up the Red River in Texas in 1805. William, then sixty-six, declined because of his age and stiff leg. Four years later Wilson requested William's company on an exploratory trip to St. Louis and, again, William cited his age and aching leg as good enough reasons to stay home.

William had published *Travels Through North and South Carolina,*

Georgia, East and West Florida, the Cherokee Country, the Extensive Territories of the Muscogulges or Creek Confederacy, and the Country of the Chactaws in 1791. Europe was enthralled with the romantic view of the wild New World embodied in his animated descriptions and detailed drawings. Americans embroiled in wresting the land from native people and nature, however, were put off by his flowery prose. The book was subsequently published in Ireland, Germany, and France. His drawings and writings appeared around the world. William became famous in his own right.

Each morning William recorded the weather and noted the birds he saw. On July 22, 1823, after describing a plant, he stepped outside to stroll among the world's flowers and trees. At age eighty-four, an artery burst in his lung. He crumpled to the ground and died in his beloved garden. He was buried the next day. No one knows exactly where.

Viewed primarily as a great naturalist, William Bartram was also a historian and an artist. A life-long note taker and record keeper, he compiled a calendar record of 215 avian species, noted their habits, and discussed their migration patterns. He did not see board feet of lumber or the site of a new town in a forest. He saw beauty and a haven for spiritual revival. Living and traveling through the land at the time of the nation's birth, he, like his father, recorded first-hand observations of people and places we will never again know.

Each Bartram left a legacy of scientific contributions. Together, father and son were a commendable team, responsible for sending 320 new plant species to England. Their prodigious talents earned for both the respect of the most influential and famous men of their day.

OF ALL THE PEOPLE IN THIS BOOK, William Bartram left the easiest path to find and follow—Florida's St. Johns River. It took three trips to cart our gear down the wooden dock to *Gator,* a sleek twenty-two foot Hunter sailboat, tall-masted, bearing a small outboard bolted to its stern. The boat belonged to Fred Harden, jaunty entomologist (mosquitoes his specialty) and William Bartram aficionado. I had cheerfully accepted an invitation to join Fred in following a portion of Bartram's trip on the St. Johns. *Gator* would be our home for the next seven days.

We sailed north from Sanford, Florida, to the upper end of Lake

George, actually downstream, on the St. Johns, one of the northern hemisphere's few rivers that flow north. So, upstream, against the current, is south and downstream, flowing with the current, is north, making directions a bit confusing.

Our trip lasted from May 14 to 21, 1997, squeezed between other commitments and appointments. Time bound us, but we answered to no other authority for this escapade. We could end any time and be home in a day or two. Attempting to mimic Bartram's trip, we hoped to encounter similar situations, though we traveled in vastly improved conditions 223 years later.

Our equipment included three small coolers, way too much food, a shelf of Bartram books and field guides, binoculars, an assortment of cameras and lenses, clothes, sunscreens, hats, rain suits, a portable toilet, and an array of possible necessities—bungee cords, bits of rope, tarps, tools, several rolls of duct and electrical tape, spare gas cans, oil, and so on.

On his four-year passage, William traveled on foot, horseback, or in a small boat powered by a crude sail or by his skill as an oarsman. A fur-lined hide served as his bed and the sail doubled as a tent. He carried a burlap sack of rice as his staple food and a supply of precious paper, pens, and plant presses. He fished and hunted and accepted invitations from settlers along the way. When William began his journey, the colonies were on the brink of breaking from England. Florida remained under British rule during the Revolution and Billy tramped through Georgia and the Carolinas while the country was at war.

At last everything was loaded onto *Gator*. Sunlight bounced from the white hulls congested around us, intensifying the shallow, tepid basin's heat. *Gator's* small motor cranked on the first pull and rumbled evenly, burping smelly exhaust. Water lapped at the bow as we cast off. Fred backed the boat slowly from its berth while I nudged a newly painted, bright blue dinghy tied to the stern out of the way. The dinghy was our ticket to getting ashore.

We motored slowly out of the marina, passing long rows of houseboats and yachts that reduced *Gator* to the size of a dinghy. Underway at 1:50 P.M. on a simmering Thursday in May, *Gator's* slow speed pushed a welcome breeze in our faces. Ahead, a power plant's tall, striped stacks would be welcome landmarks when we returned. We entered the big river and I looked starboard to see cars flying over the stream on the concrete arcs of Interstate 4. Beyond them, upstream, the river widened into

Lake Monroe. Fred turned *Gator* to port, downstream, between columns of profusely green trees and shrubs scribing the St. Johns' turbid waters. From that perspective, we might just as well have been on the river with Billy.

William had begun his St. Johns' journey near the river's mouth in mid-April 1774, and headed southward. Soon after embarking, he encountered a storm. He collected a supply of dry wood and spread his sail from the trunk of a large oak tree to the ground for shelter. It was not the first storm William waited out, nor would it be the last. For the rest of his life, he rarely slept a whole night, especially when thunderstorms were crashing about. John Bartram suffered a lifelong fear of thunder and William likely inherited a similar aversion.

But there were more fearsome trials than weather during his pilgrimage. The lands he traveled were beautiful, spacious and unspoiled from our vantage point, but they were not benign. Occasionally William had to pause in his travel because of Indian troubles. Cougars, bears, and wolves still owned the forests. Miles spread between settlements. Had William been injured or become ill, he might have died.

In the published account of his journey, William rarely mentioned companions. But his report to Fothergill indicated he sought the company of traders, Indians, and other travelers, frequently adjusting his schedule to fit theirs. No matter where he traveled, William passed through Indian towns; some were thriving and others long abandoned. The naturalist always got on well with Native Americans, unlike his father, who mistrusted them and thought they must be kept in line by brute force.

The Seminoles called William Puc Puggy, the Flower Gatherer. William later published his observations of various Indian tribes. He concluded the essay with drawings of public buildings, layouts of Indian towns, and hopes that the dwellings could be searched and the findings recorded before time and greed and disregard obliterated the ancient remnants.

When the Spanish had arrived near the St. Johns' mouth in the early 1500s, they found Timucuans in residence, engaged in fishing, farming, and trading with other tribes. Comprising at least fifteen separate tribes, the Timucuan Nation shared a common language. By the mid-1700s, murder, slavery, and diseases had decimated the powerful nation. When John and William explored the St. Johns for King George, the once prosperous Timucuans were gone, but the two observed the remains of Timucuan shell mounds melding into the forest. Burial mounds and kitchen middens, composed of cast-off shells, broken pottery, bones, and other trash, lined the St. Johns. Bitter oranges grew wild between the villages of tribes who had taken over the abandoned Timucuan fields, as well as scattered plantations and trading posts built by white settlers. Later, William chose abandoned mounds for his camps when he could. Invariably, they rose above the river and were more open than the surrounding area.

I wondered what traces we would find in 1997. Most of Florida's mounds had been scavenged by pot and relic looters and by state and county road departments. Crushed shells make excellent roadbeds. My mind drifted backward, trying to grasp the fragile concept of time and changes levied on the river since the Bartrams had made their way upstream.

Trees lining the river were much the same as William listed, oaks, pines, magnolias, palms, and cypress, but thicker today. William described open vistas and meadows of succulent grasses, especially on the eastern side. Growth had been a bit more heavy on the western side, but only at the edge; behind lay pine savannas and marshes. On both sides he could see in the distance twinkling water in ponds and marshes. At night he looked up at a brilliant, starry sky, which would be difficult through today's leafy canopy. People living on the river then would have required wood for cooking, homes, tools, and canoes, and they would have cleared rich bottomlands for crops. Frequent wildfires probably burned through higher areas, too, which would account for the uncluttered spaciousness Bartram had seen.

In the nearly ten years between William's first St. Johns' voyage with his father and his own exploration, the scenery had changed. Plantation owners had laid axe and saw to the land, believing that forests and groves bred mosquitoes and should be destroyed. Fields—indigo, cotton, and corn—and buildings had replaced the consoling forest, leaving few shade trees. William found solace under a shady canopy and like his father deplored wanton destruction. Practices his father had observed decades earlier had not abated as new settlers cut acre after acre, mistakenly believing their actions would bequeath no ill effects.

Fred hugged the eastern bank, mindful of entangling the mast in overhanging trees. *Gator's* steady engine tarnished slightly one thing we had hoped to find in following John and William's wake—the river's voice. The water slipping past the bow was almost as old as the earth and had traveled far before becoming this river. Pulled from oceans and streams by the sun's irresistible heat and cast back as snow, sleet, and rain, water moves around the world, witness to all since time began. The liquid surrounding the hull could have come from an ocean far away, a lake in Africa, or held underground for ten thousand years until it burst forth from a spring an hour ago. There are stories to hear in water.

Some geologists believe the St. Johns began as a lagoon in the late Pleistocene, but more recent thoughts place its beginnings on a beach-ridge plain. Swales between relict Pleistocene beach ridges helped determine the directional flow. At three hundred miles in length, the St. Johns is the longest river wholly within Florida. Its drainage basin encompasses 8,840 square miles. The headwater marshes once covered close to seven hundred square miles, but the land has been drained for mosquito control and the marshes now total about two hundred and fifty square miles, less than half of their original area. We still have plenty of mosquitoes and flooding is more frequent in the reduced marshlands. The St. Johns Water Management District has been buying back acreage to restore marshes at a cost in excess of $100 million.[1] The river does not readily flush pollutants, even with a storm surge. In low-water periods, tides may cause a reverse flow as far south as Lake Monroe, 161 miles upstream. From the grassy headwaters twenty-five miles north of Lake Okeechobee to the mouth at Mayport, the grade drops less than thirty feet, about an inch a mile. It is not so much a descending grade that drives the waters northward as a series of tributaries and springs that encourage the river to seemingly flow uphill.

Geologists divide the St. Johns into three segments. The southern segment includes the headwaters to about Sanford. The middle or offset segment continues to Palatka, and the final segment runs from Palatka to the St. Johns entrance into the Atlantic. We were floating on the middle one, considered the oldest, the one that feels the southernmost influence of salty tides. Along the way, salt water captured when the region shifted from a marine habitat to a primarily freshwater system escapes into the St. Johns and flows to reunite with the ocean. If we were to dive underwater at those salty vents we would find relict sea creatures stuck in a memory of a larger ocean.

This is a blackwater river, its waters tinted with tannins from surrounding vegetation and stained even darker from sewage and other pollutants; though naturally the color of strong tea, its clarity was greater in Bartram's time. Today, the St. Johns waters run inky and visibility extends only a few inches. Impossible to see the bottom.

Gator drew a little more than two feet, and the river's depth averaged about nine feet though frequently it dipped to more than twenty feet. The depth finder, set at five feet, beeped intermittently. We might have passed over a submerged log, a school of fish, a prehistoric looking garfish, or one of the many alligators living in the river. Manatees call the St. Johns home for part of the year, but we thought they had left for the season.

The air was palpably hot and the humidity hovered at a barely tolerable level. Even the water looked hot. There was no way to escape the heat, a situation we had in common with William.

"There's the Wekiva River," Fred called, indicating a stream feeding into the St. Johns. Fred and his wife, Pat, live on the Wekiva, a broad, clear river, too shallow for a sailboat. It's a river designed for the mellifluous travel of canoes and kayaks; motorboats should use it cautiously.

Fred turned over the tiller and went below to find a large envelope stuffed with charts and maps. Johnboats puttered by, sparkly bass boats roared on, and bulky houseboats chugged past. Few slowed as they surged around us; larger boats seemed less inclined to slacken their forward momentum. *Gator*'s motor cavitated in the troughs of their departing wakes. Gear rattled and fell from shelves. We probably cursed their disturbance as much as they cursed our snail-like pace, but we waved to each other just the same.

Hauling up from below, envelope in hand, Fred spread a smorgasbord of maps and charts before me. "We are here," he pointed. Looking at detailed blue bends and curves on the paper I recognized where we were. Fred's finger moved ahead. "Here, I think, is about where Beresford Plantation is and here's where Bartram met the alligators at Idlewilde Point. We'll make Hontoon Island State Park tonight and tie up there."

Maps imposed an order on our journey. I traced curves with my finger and watched for the next bend. Here the river turned east and then headed north again. Its grimy waters flowed between green banks as surely as the blue streak was captured within the black outline. The charts plainly showed where the river's sharp turns had been cut, making a route easier for barges and leaving muddy crescent lakes behind small swampy islands.

"How far north can we go on this trip?" I asked.

"Oh, as far as Lake George for sure, and maybe up to Palatka."

On a car trip last winter, Fred had scouted ahead for marinas. We would need lots of gas and lots of ice before the trip was over and we would have to spend at least one night anchored out, not safely tied to a dock. It seemed a long way to Lake George at our slow speed, but time was not important. For now, we were content to glide along, drinking in the land's lushness. Lost in our reverie, we were startled by a fast motor's snarl and a man's shout coming from behind.

"Hey!" he yelled, "your dinghy's loose!" He drew alongside smoothly and his wife tossed us the wayward craft's painter. We called our thanks; without the little boat, going ashore meant swimming with gators. A less honest person might have kept it; we were fortunate that it had been returned. Lashing a firm line to a stern cleat, we scolded the bobbing blue boat as if it had escaped like a wandering child to make its own river exploration. For the rest of the trip, our eyes repeatedly scooted to the stern to make sure the dinghy was still with us.

Attuned to the water's tempo once more, we discussed the river's edge. Its gentle flow did not contribute much to wearing away the banks, but looking closely, we saw subtle erosion caused by the scrubbing waves tossed by speeding boats. Trees sometimes succumbed. The spiny, weathered trunk of a long-fallen sabal palm resembled the enormous backbone of the great fish in Hemingway's *The Old Man and the Sea*. In low floodplains, erosion appeared a trifling concern. Trees and shrubs grew to water's edge; their roots helped anchor the soil. Shallows along shore sprouted grasses that absorbed some of the waves' power and gave tiny aquatic creatures shelter from predators. Flowing water follows the path of least resistance and this river has changed course on its own. Invisible to us on the water, but in perfect sight of anyone flying over the river, are noticeable dark green commas of vegetation escorting the river's main stream, sure signs of where the water used to go.

Cottages, marinas, and permanent homes crowded together where high banks rose. Weathered docks and boathouses stoically bore action on the river. Older docks tilted and sagged, victims of continual water wear. A few new structures were elaborate affairs of steps leading up and down to decks on various levels, perfect for sunbathing and parties. Here and there, sea walls had been replaced when slapping waves wore them out.

Fred kept a casual bird list. We saw snowy egrets, great blue herons, green herons, tri-colored herons, great egrets, and little blue herons, as William had noted two hundred years ago. Pileated woodpeckers torpedoed overhead, but the dramatic ivory-billed woodpeckers were gone. We saw no sandhill cranes though William described eating soup prepared from them and allowed that he would rather listen to their voice than dine on one.

William wrote of enormous cypress trees bordering the river and bustling with Carolina paroquets fluttering about the tops hunting for seedballs, their favorite food. Cypresses still spread their fringed limbs streaming graceful falls of Spanish moss over the floodplain, but even the largest is puny compared to the giants of early Florida. The last of the massive trees fell prey to loggers in the 1930s, when mile-long rafts of logs as much as nine feet in diameter floated to the mills at Palatka. The colorful paroquets are no more.

We can read words of people who lived in past times and observed abundant wildlife, clear waters, magnificent forests, and extraordinary encounters with different cultures. But we can only read of these things; we cannot fully experience such a world. We float over unclouded waters of a spring-fed river, yet we are afraid to drink directly from it. We easily find deer in the southern woods but we will never be startled by a shadowy form that might be a passing wolf or have our hearts set thudding by a panther's scream in the pitch of night.

What remains on the river, thankfully, is an abundance of ospreys. Their bulky nests balance high in trees and on man-made navigational towers. Almost ready to fledge, the well-feathered young were still on the nest. Now and then one stood and beat its wings in muscle building flaps; soon they would fly. Watchful adults scolded from their sentry posts, never growing accustomed to the activity as every passing vessel received a tongue lashing. Did they chastise us for the transgressions of those who once shot these birds for sport?

During the heyday of steamboats, beginning in the early 1800s, gaudy paddle-wheelers brought tourists and supplies. By 1860, steamers from Charleston and Savannah made weekly rounds and advertised target practice at birds and alligators as a pastime. Ospreys are now protected by federal law. It would be difficult to shoot one and get away with it on this river; someone is always around the bend.

Ospreys cruised above the water, paused, beat their great wings in a stall, and plummeted to the surface. Sometimes they captured a small fish, and sometimes one so large they struggled to lift it. A successful bird, circling and swooping with a forward-facing fish clutched in its talons, showed off the catch while its mate called from the nest. Landing with food, the parent tore off pieces of meat with its ferocious beak and delicately offered tidbits to clamoring young.

One big bird angled toward the water like a landing seaplane, disappeared in a large splash, then rose, shuddering droplets like a wet dog. A biologist friend later suggested they were washing off bits of fish gore and blood clinging to their legs and feathers. It made sense, but it was rather comical watching a graceful osprey perform a deliberate, slow, clumsy dunking, lacking all the deadly skill and excitement of a swift plunge.

A big alligator broke the surface ahead then slowly sank as we approached. Supreme in their watery realm, reptiles reclined on grassy banks. William Bartram had written of thrilling alligator encounters on the St. Johns. We were glad that dinghy still tagged behind.

The river widened into a shallow lake. The channel turned to port and took us to Hontoon Island State Park, accessible only by water. Florida's Park Service operates a small barge that ferries mainland visitors across the narrow waterway. An uncovered, floating dock allows those who arrive in their own boats to tie up. It is a short walk to the offices and restrooms. While we signed in, a bearded young man came into the office and questioned us about *Gator.* He was an Americorps volunteer for the park and had been girdling overabundant trees and helping with prescribed burns. When his job was over, he wanted to take his own small sailboat around Florida. We believed he would. The desire to see the "out there" never dies in some people.

Back on the boat, it was dinner time. Fred set up a one burner butane stove under the bimini and I faced the first challenge of preparing a meal in the cramped space down below. Shifting and lifting in close quarters was a bit frustrating, but surmountable. I chopped ingredients, handing them up to Fred with cooking instructions. Meals requiring little cleanup were a must, for dishwashing was difficult. I silently thanked a friend who, while on a southwestern camping trip, had taught me how to clean up after a meal using a half cup of water. Maybe it wasn't 100 percent sanitary, but it was efficient.

When Billy needed dinner, he used a "bob" tied to a short, stout line attached to the end of a long rod. From his description—three large hooks securely tied back to back, covered with hair from a deer's tail, shreds of a red garter, and multicolored feathers—I could not imagine how any fish, once hooked, could escape from such a contraption. William competed with alligators, but he did not worry about mercury levels in his catch.

After landing his fish, William cleaned it, gathered wood for his cooking fire, and used salt and sour oranges for flavoring. Afterwards, he organized notes by flickering firelight. He prepared multiple copies of every specimen, cached bundles at homes, and shipped packages to Dr. Fothergill from trading posts along the river.

One evening, William's companions caught a large mud turtle for supper. At first Bartram was apprehensive about eating it, not because of its appearance, but because they would not be able to eat the entire creature. His companions seemed not to mind the waste as they sat in the midst of plenty. Herds of deer and flocks of turkeys filled the woods and rainbows of fish shimmered in the clear water. A committee of vultures waited in a nearby tree for their own feast of the hapless turtle's remains.

After dinner we sat under the bimini as alligators began prowling the still water. I asked Fred if he could imitate the distress call of a baby gator. He obliged. A six-foot long alligator swung around and swam a few feet toward us, casting a baleful eye, if an alligator can do such a thing. Involuntarily, my heart sped up. We were safe in a boat at least three feet above the water line, but my subconscious saw a predator coming. The reptile decided we were bluffing and returned to hunting. I tried to imagine the dread that Billy would have felt in the same situation. His boat was only inches above the water and he would have encountered gators much larger than the ones we saw.

The Florida Fish and Wildlife Conservation Commission (FWC) has kept records of alligator attacks on people since 1948. In fifty years, there have been 236 attacks on humans. Florida now averages eighteen reported attacks per year, counting bites from twelve-inch babies that were picked up. Since 1948, there have been nine fatalities and six additional cases where the victim may have died of other causes before the alligator's attack. Given Florida's burgeoning population, those statistics reflect fewer encounters than expected.

As more people live and play along Florida's waterways, the alligator's habitat shrinks. Unfortunately, humans find it amusing to throw marshmallows and chicken legs to alligators. Gators may appear dull-witted, but they will return to the spot expecting food. Anyone who lets the family pooch near water where the reptiles dwell may find the howling pet clenched between a gator's powerful jaws in a froth of churning water— not a pretty sight. Any gator hanging around places where humans gather is classified a nuisance animal; a call to the FWC will bring a licensed trapper who captures it. The animal will not be released in a different area, but is killed, its hide and meat sold.

Alligators are strong animals, dangerous if provoked. In their natural state, they avoid people. It is unlikely they would attack a boat. It *is* likely that they will try to remove fish or other food from an unattended boat or camping site. They are not animals people find cuddly, but females are protective of their nests and a grunting baby will bring an adult on the double. If a gator manages to survive babyhood and avoid a confrontation with a human, or another gator, it should live about sixty-five years. E. L. McIlhenny, who made a lifelong study of alligators, estimated that mature males average twelve to sixteen feet long. The biggest one he ever measured was nineteen feet two inches long. These days gators greater than fourteen feet are rarely found. Hunted almost to extinction by the 1960s, they have made an astonishing recovery under protective laws that were first put into place in 1973. About one million alligators live in Florida's lakes and rivers today, and though they are no longer on the federal endangered species list, they are protected by Florida law. The knobby reptiles represent the wild essence of Florida's rivers, lakes, and swamps.

Hunting alligators disappeared from sight as rising darkness enveloped Hontoon Island and the river. A weak breeze stirred, but not enough to blow away hungry mosquitoes. They had little taste for Fred, who has spent nearly his whole life studying their behavior and how to kill them.

"These are mostly blind mosquitoes," Fred commented. When Bartram was here, great hatches of mayflies filled the air. Billy wrote of clouds of innumerable millions in the evening. Scores of them, shimmering, released from their aquatic prison, floated, bobbed, and rose in the sun-shot air to mate and mate and mate before falling back to the water again. But mayflies are gone from this part of the river, replaced with blind mosquitoes, which are actually non-biting but very annoying midges. Mayflies require clean water to survive. Blind mosquitoes prefer dirty water. There were, however, plenty of blood-thirsty mosquitoes on the hunt soon after sundown, despite Fred's claim.

That is not to say the St. Johns was free of mosquitoes in Bartram's time. A little north of Hontoon Island, William sought a suitable camp-site, but the land was low and swampy. He found a higher spot, but there was a troubling gator trail worn broad and deep, leading from the river. Having little choice, he collected firewood, drew his bark from the water, and prepared his bed under a spreading oak. The day's strength-sapping heat, biting mosquitoes, and the certainty that he would not have a peaceful night shrunk his appetite. He kindled a fire and the languid air barely shifted. The smoke, he vainly hoped, would deter alligators and mosquitoes. No sooner had he fallen asleep than he was awakened by screaming barred owls. As they are wont to do, when one begins calling, all join in.

Dazed for the moment, he then noticed a large alligator attempting to take fish from his boat. He chased it away and fell into another fitful sleep only to be reawakened by the owls. The alligator was closer. William roused up the fire to keep himself awake, grousing that mosquitoes alone were enough to hold sleep at bay. He had little rest that night and hoped to evade the whining pests in the morning—only to find they had bed-ded down in his canoe and were only too happy to greet him. He cut leafy branches to beat them from the boat.

With great foresight, Fred had mosquito netting drapes made for the forward and main hatchways. A few skeeters slipped inside as we ar-ranged drapes over the openings. Later, I ignored them and watched the night sky from my short, narrow bunk, grateful for a small breeze. The first night passed peacefully and I thought this might not be so bad.

In the morning, Fred rowed the dinghy a short distance to the main-land marina while I rearranged food and utensils. When he returned with ice, I repacked coolers as we motored to open water. Our goal today, Friday, was to cross the shallow lake to a spot where Fred believed the remains of Beresford Plantation lay.

A mighty storm had waylaid William before he could reach Beresford. He rode out the tempest anchored in a marsh. Limbs and leaves flew through the air as trees bent and broke around him. Upon reaching the plantation after the storm he saw that almost every house had been blown away and the crops nearly destroyed. He spent three days there, drying his books and specimens and surveying damages with the owner.

We eased carefully across the lake; the bottom was close. Even though we had raised the keel, the depth finder beeped a constant warning. We watched for pilings and snags, remains of steamboat docks, beneath the surface. One could damage or disable *Gator* if struck. Grasses and a broad mat of lily pads guarded the shallow, boggy shore and we could not get close. Fred rowed the dinghy as close as possible and waded to shore to explore while I stayed onboard, making notes and studying Billy's journal. He returned in about an hour and reported that he had found brick rubble that must have been the plantation house site.

We threaded our way back to the river's main channel. It was Friday, the beginning of the weekend, and rushing boat traffic had picked up. *Gator* labored over the swells like a huffing elephant. We counted the number of other sailboats on one hand. By afternoon, long, sleek, powerful cigarette boats were out. Fred said they were headed for Silver Glen Springs on Lake George. Using a handheld radio, Fred called ahead to the Astor bridge, requesting them to raise it for us. We might be slower than other boats, but we stopped traffic and raised bridges. The bridge tenders were unfailingly nice. Sailboats mean job security.

"St. Francis Dead River should be just around the next bend," Fred remarked. "Billy made camp here one night where the river doubled."

The St. Francis is not a true river but a short water arm that tapers off into the floodplain. Coming around the bend we saw that the bank was a little higher and from a distance appeared sandy. We anchored the sailboat up in the St. Francis and loaded cameras into the dinghy. As Fred rowed, I scanned the jade green lily pads and spotted our first limpkin, a bird that Bartram had also found but could not name as it had no European counterpart. The Indians called it *Ephouskyca,* crying bird. Limpkins often call at night; the sound is quite unnerving to the uninitiated.

When we reached shore, we found that it was not sand at all but bleached snail shells. In the shallows, the opaque water achieved clarity over ancient shells. Stirring the waters raised shattered fragments; reflected sunlight threw prismatic lavenders and pinks glinting against the surface. Poking around the shallows, we found pottery shards and some shell bits naturally cemented together. A botanical search turned up sour oranges and an indigo plant. Cultivated indigo came from India by way of Africa. Slaves had processed the leaves and stems in a tedious, smelly procedure for beautiful blue dye. America's Revolution had put an end to its profitability as an export crop, and after the arrival of synthetic dyes and slavery's demise indigo growers either turned to other crops or failed. Indigo plants can still be found growing wild near water and floodplains.

This was all that remained of the mound where Billy camped. Native people had hunted, celebrated, married, raised their children, argued, buried their dead here. Evidence of their existence was now undoubtedly encased in the foundation of an asphalt highway. A sand road led away from the river. Discarded cans, bits of clothing, and campfire ashes, trash from a modern era, littered the site. Water steadily ground the shells and pottery pieces, returning them to the earth.

Friday night we made Lake Dexter. Bartram had commented that the water "was shoal and very clear"[2] near there, but such is not the case today. Boat traffic had definitely increased and we decided to head directly for Lake George on Saturday and take our time exploring on the way back. Silver Glen Springs emptied into Lake George, but would be too crowded to maneuver *Gator* on a busy weekend. This was our second night on the boat and the first night anchored out. Fred ran an anchor light up the mast. We turned in when mosquitoes turned out. Barred owls *who-ahhhed* from shore, frogs kept up a steady din, and every now and then a fish plopped. Alligators primarily hunt at night, and if we had

FIG. 2. William Bartram's rendering of alligators on the St. Johns River.
Fig. 1 is a bellowing alligator; Fig. 2 represents a feeding alligator.
Courtesy of Florida Archives.

shone a light across the water we would have seen their eyes reflecting ruby in the light. Maybe we didn't want to bother them. Maybe we didn't want to know how many were out there. Drifting toward sleep, mulling over Billy's adventure near here, at Idlewilde Point, I was glad we were safe aboard *Gator.*

Billy had pitched his camp under a sheltering live oak on a point of high open plain. Alligators had begun to roar and appear in uncommon numbers along the shores and in the river in the calm, cool evening. At best he could hope for snatches of sleep between bouts of talkative owls and foraging alligators. He collected firewood for cooking and a night fire. Supplies being low, he had to fish for supper. He readied his "bob," but his attention was drawn to a horrific alligator battle.

> Behold him rushing forth from the flags and reeds. His enormous body swells. His plaited tail, brandished high, floats upon the lake. The waters like a cataract descend from his opening jaws. Clouds of smoke issue from his dilated nostrils. The earth trembles with his thunder . . . from the opposite coast of the lagoon emerges . . . his rival champion. They suddenly dart upon each other . . . They now sink to the bottom folded together in horrid wreaths. The water becomes thick and discouloured. Again they rise, their jaws clap together . . . when the contest ends at the muddy bottom of the lake, and the vanquished makes a hazardous escape . . . The proud victor exulting returns to the place of action. The shores and forests resound his dreadful roar.

After the animals had settled down, William hurriedly paddled to a small lagoon behind the point. Afraid he might lose his gun overboard, he left it behind, and armed himself with a club. Before reaching his destination, alligators attacked from all sides and the canoe nearly upset. "[T]wo very large ones attacked me . . . their heads and part of their bodies above water, roaring terribly and belching floods of water over me. They struck their jaws together so close to my ears as almost to stun me, and I expected every moment to be dragged out of the boat and instantly devoured."[3] Using his club, he beat the creatures off and by changing course, Bartram finally made it into the lagoon and quickly caught more fish than he needed.

Alligators harassed him after he returned to camp, especially one about twelve feet long that dared come too close. William ran to fetch his fusee, a small flintlock musket. The animal withdrew but challenged again, at which time William shot the bold alligator. Unbothered for the moment, William continued cleaning his fish, but soon another reptile rose from the river and Bartram had to quickly withdraw or find himself as the gator's meal.

Sensing that he would not spend a peaceful night at this site, William pulled his little boat nearly free of the river and removed most of his gear to camp. Clearing the area of any impediment in case of attack, he charged his gun, set the fish and rice on to boil, and planned a retreat if necessary. Because a cypress swamp lay behind his campsite, he would have no choice but to push off in the boat or climb a tree. Looking over the river he viewed a surprising sight. The water was roiling with fish passing through a narrow spot heading for the lake. Feeding alligators were so thick he could have walked across the river on their heads.

The feeding behavior William observed has been witnessed since. Alligators and other crocodilians form a line to feed on fish streaming through a narrow opening or channel. When one animal moves out of line, another takes its place. This cooperative feeding is different from opportunistic feeding that takes place when fish become trapped in a drying pond. There is little fighting during cooperative feeding, but opportunistic feeding can be competitive. Scant attention is paid to human observers during either type of group feeding as the animals concentrate on the matter at hand—eating.

Leaving the alligators to their feast, William returned to his dinner. While going over some notes, another disturbance broke out behind him and he saw two black bears coming his way. Firing his gun into the air sent the bears tearing away through the swamp. Despite the afternoon's commotion, the night settled down and Bartram did get a few hours of rest.

Henry Wansey, an English Quaker who visited Bartram's garden in 1794, made a joking reference to William's alligator tales. The naturalist, offended by the jest, withdrew from conversation. Alligators fascinated Bartram. Like it or not, they were his almost constant companions on the river and he experienced many close calls. He drew several sketches of them, and it appears his pencil took off on a flight of fancy. Bartram's alligator resembles a mythical fire-breathing dragon more than the actual creature.

Between clashing thunderstorms, whooping owls, and marauding gators, it is doubtful that William had ever found a good night's sleep on the river. But sleep came easily to me. It must have been about 2:00 A.M. when loud engines and lights sweeping through the portholes popped me from my bunk. Fred bolted from the forward berth. It took a moment for our sleep-addled brains to recognize the noise. Two airboats with big spotlights streaked across the night. Frog giggers. We stumbled back to our bunks as the boats rumbled away, cut their engines, and then roared again as they worked the shoreline. We were jolted awake once more as they raced past the sailboat with engines roaring and bright lights snouting through the darkness. I fell back to sleep quickly and the rest of the night passed uninterrupted.

Boat traffic intensified on Saturday as we neared the twin wooden structures that guide boats into and out of Lake George. Several ospreys nested on the railings and their young turned a curious golden eye as we passed. Forster's terns, laughing gulls, and ring-billed gulls lined the top rail. For the first time we saw cormorants. Slowing the motor, Fred handed over the tiller so he could ease to the bow and began raising the sails, determined to sail across this open water. I watched the compass, for the shoreline appeared the same in all directions. We stayed out of the main channel, but bass boats zinged like fireworks everywhere as anglers searched for the right fishing hole.

Weak winds brushed the canvas, periods of silence until the next boat whizzed by. We barely moved under sail. The air was still under a broad hazy sky sketched with thin, high clouds. The day turned close and oppressive. Heat blanched color from the surroundings, turning the sky barely blue, the water pale grey, and the distant trees a whisper of shadow along the shore. Giving in to drowsiness, I went below for a nap.

Tormented by continual heat, hungry mosquitoes, and brazen alligators, Billy gave in to sleep one warm afternoon, too. He awoke refreshed and it was probably the best sleep he had on the whole trip.

After a short nap, it was no cooler and the shoreline looked unchanged. "Have we moved?" I chided. Indignant for a moment, Fred gave in, lowered the sails, and cranked the motor. We headed for Camp Henry, a small fish camp on the mainland across from Drayton Island, where Lake George narrows and becomes a river again.

Camp Henry's covered docks showed their age and a few pilings did not even reach to the dock proper. It was nigh impossible to tie the sailboat to the covered dock because of *Gator*'s mast. Marge, an easygoing woman who ran the place with her husband, said we could anchor off-shore, dinghy in for ice and showers. Besides showers, Camp Henry, which also features boat-motor sales and repairs, offers sturdy concrete block cabins, RV spaces, and a small store with a modest stock of food and a larger selection of boat-related equipment.

Safely anchored, we rowed in for ice and phone calls home. I claimed a shower. In Florida's hot summer, it does not take long for sweat and grime to accumulate. Fred stocked up on ice and chatted to Marge about the river and William Bartram. "Oh, I just read his book," she said. Bartram fans were everywhere.

She told us to contact a woman named Mona who lived on Drayton Island. "She'll know the history of the place," Marge said, and gave Mona's phone number to Fred. He called but no one answered, so we decided to try again on Sunday. "She'll show you that oak tree Billy Bartram slept under," Marge called out as we left.

By the middle of May, Billy had neared Lake George and thrown in with a group of traders heading upriver. He followed their heavily laden boat, enjoying the company and safety they provided. The morning was fair, but as they approached the entrance conditions changed and the waters grew rough, "behold the little ocean of Lake George, the distant circular coast gradually rising . . . I cannot entirely suppress my apprehension of danger. My vessel at once diminished to a nut-shell on the swelling seas."[4]

Winds whipped the lake and before they had gone very far across the angry water, the men headed their boats for the shelter of Drayton Island. Billy could not pass up a chance to explore, even with a storm blowing. From the number of mounds and pottery remains still evident, he surmised that the island had once been heavily settled by Indians, though it was then uninhabited except for deer, turkeys, bears, wolves, bobcats, squirrels, raccoons, and opossums. Bears savored bitter oranges, William wrote. He found a particularly beautiful species of multicolored lantana and a new species of morning glory.

With daylight and the storm waning, Billy contemplated the scene, "as I reclined . . . at the foot of a live oak."[5] A storm-free night then passed and William and the traders made an uneventful voyage across calm waters the next day.

At twelve miles long and five miles wide, Lake George is large enough to become really rough. It was calm for our crossing, though the weather sweltered, and predictions hinted at storms on Saturday. Billy had faced a blustery lake about this same time of year and we might have a similar experience.

We savored red wine after dinner. Venus glowed in the gathering twilight, and lights onshore twinkled through the trees. A few anglers, late leaving the river, idled by. One bucketed for home, oblivious to gathering darkness, and our sailboat tugged at its anchor in the big wake he threw. The air cooled and we were reluctant to go below, but mosquitoes began their nightly serenade and quest for blood. Just as we were draping the netting over the hatches a large boat grumbled past—a big tug, several stories high, strung with lights all around, heading upstream across Lake George. We watched until it disappeared. An eerie sight it was, all those lights dangling across the lake and into a night as black as a bottle of Bartleby's ink.

Above a leaden sky, dawn broke somewhere Sunday morning, but from our anchorage we could see only mounded clouds. At Camp Henry, Marge alerted us to approaching storms. We tried Mona again. Still no answer. Marge assured us that Mona was around, try again. It looked like a bad weather day, so we discussed our options.

We could walk to Mount Royal, several miles from Camp Henry. When both Bartrams traveled the St. Johns in 1765, they stopped there. At that time there were no settlements; all appeared wild and savage. A large orange grove, palms, and live oaks surrounded the mound and an Indian highway ran from the mound to an artificial lake. By the time Billy returned in 1774, trees had been cleared and the land planted with indigo, corn, and cotton. Luckily, the mound had not been destroyed, probably because its height afforded a view. We could walk there, or we could explore this northern end of Lake George around Drayton and Hog Islands by boat. We opted for the latter.

Drayton is an island of approximately ten thousand acres. Most of it is low and swampy. Hog Island, a good bit smaller, lies behind Drayton. We aimed *Gator* through the ragged water to a point where Billy first viewed the lake while his boat had shrunk to the size of a nut-shell. Fred rowed through rough water and we explored the shore, but could not penetrate the thick shrubbery. Pulverized shells extended a few feet into the water. I stirred them with my foot, but without sunshine they were solemn in their aspect. Broken pottery bits lay exposed on the bottom. We returned to the boat; the weather was getting rougher.

FIG. 3. A high, open shell mound at Salt Lake near St. Johns River
similar to those William Bartram sought as campsites.
Courtesy of Florida Archives.

Behind protecting islands, waters were calm along the shore, and determined people hunched over fishing poles watching as we heaved past.
We continued our circuit, around Hog Island's back side and the southern end of Drayton Island. Not many other boats were on the lake, for
obvious reasons. A squall could skitter across before you knew it.

Gator pitched and rolled in two-foot seas. Powered by the small engine in unsettled water, the boat lost its grace and stumbled along. Cat
paw waves spilling small lips of white foam over their crests chased bobbing crab floats across the lake. Those little white caps indicated winds of
ten to twelve knots. Fred checked lines and every now and then looked to
make sure our course headed for Camp Henry. The dinghy yanked petu-
lantly at its towline, resentful of being dragged along. We were, like Billy

and the traders, anxious to be off the big lake. Fred said the water around Camp Henry would be calm and it was.

Going ashore for more ice, Fred made another call to Mona. She was home and said she would be delighted to pick us up the next morning for an island tour.

After a windy day, the night was calm, but in the morning pale grey clouds haunted the horizon and insinuated a stormy afternoon. Still air and humidity crouched over the lake as a well-used, open skiff plowed toward us, wielded by a dark-haired, attractive young woman accompanied by a sprite of a child named Lake. Mona's parents had purchased one of the island's older homes in the sixties. She had spent her teenaged summers on the water and later moved around the country before returning to the island some years ago.

Drayton Island was named after chief justice William Drayton of the South Carolina Draytons. William Drayton, who had inherited Magnolia Gardens from his father, Thomas Drayton III, left South Carolina when he was named chief royal justice of Florida in 1774. William's uncle, John Drayton, who had built Drayton Hall, then purchased Magnolia Plantation.

I asked Mona what living on an island was like. "Island life requires a bit more planning," she said. "People don't drop in on you so often, and everyone knows everyone else's business. If something breaks, you either fix it yourself or wait for an expensive repair call. An underwater cable brings electricity and telephone lines. Water comes from wells, though most people buy bottled water for cooking and drinking."

Landing at Mona's dock, we could see that an extension had been recently built. We looked through the water, expecting to see a sandy bottom. Instead, the bottom was covered with a viscous black residue. "Decayed water hyacinth," Mona explained. Water hyacinth plagues Florida's rivers and lakes. Even a small piece quickly grows into a large wattle of interlocking stems and leaves, hindering navigation. Florida runs a spray program to control the plant. The plant dies, rots, and sinks to the bottom leaving the surface water clear and the bottom deep in ooze. "The bottom was clear and sandy when I was a kid. We used to swim here, but not anymore. That stuff is a foot or more deep and it isn't going away. We can't get the state to do anything about it either," Mona groused.

Mrs. W. F. Fuller, a native of Brooklyn, New York, snitched a few cuttings of water hyacinth from the 1884 Cotton Exposition in New Orleans and brought it to her home at Edgewater on the St. Johns. The plant thrived in the fish pond and quickly began sprouting spikes of lovely lavender flowers. She thought it would look nice on the water in front of her home, too, and the plant rapidly spread to other rivers and streams. It can double its population in six to eighteen days. Such an innocent gesture, but with such costly and unforeseen long-term detriments. By 1897, hyacinth was considered a pest plant. Jacksonville's *Times-Union and Citizen* reported on water hyacinth on October 8, 1897, "Its introduction was easy and cost nothing. To get rid of this pretty plant may require the expenditure of a million dollars, and its extermination may yet come to appear cheap at that cost." Bartram would not have seen that plant, nor would he have seen hydrilla, which was introduced in the 1970s. But he did see large colonies of waterlettuce (*Pistia*). The plant may have ridden over on trade ships bound for St. Augustine. Waterlettuce disrupts plant and animal communities and hinders boat traffic.

Mona loaded us into her Ford pickup and we rattled off to see Billy Bartram's oak tree on her neighbor's property. An enormous live oak spread over the side yard. Its lower branches rested along the ground; banners of frizzled Spanish moss streamed from every limb, and cool, green resurrection ferns feathered sagging branches. The gargantuan, wrinkled trunk must have been at least ten feet in diameter. Surely, this tree was several centuries old and was probably ancient when William paused here. No reason not to think this was the tree that sheltered him from the storm.

I asked what sort of wildlife lived on the island. Mona recited the same list as Bartram's, sans wolves, and added bald eagles, feral hogs, all kinds of snakes, lots of birds, some goats released by a former landowner, black bears that probably swam over from the mainland, and gopher tortoises. Gopher tortoises? She drove us to an isolated patch of Florida scrub, maybe fifty acres in all. White sandy patches showed between withered scrub oaks and emerald rosemary and, as if on cue, lumbering across the road was a large gopher tortoise. We turned another corner, and saw the brightly colored lantana Bartram had first observed here.

We traded addresses and phone numbers, and drank bottled water after the tour. Mona invited us back and we said we would love to return. She quickly delivered us to *Gator*, skipping the skiff across the water as if she had been born with a tiller in her hand.

Gathering clouds sealed off the blue sky, and we decided to pull anchor and start across the lake. Instead of lunch, we snacked on chips, nuts, and fruit as we motored into a headwind and jittery water. Passing by Silver Glen Springs we thought about stopping, but we were anxious to get back on the river and leave the storms behind. A man in a small motorboat approached. He had become disoriented by that distant circular coast and could not determine his proper direction. Fred aimed him toward a landmark. Thunder rumbled from lightning strikes over the land and we passed through pattering rains. Fortunately, *Gator's* tall mast held no allure for lightning. Even with brief showers and a small breeze, the day was a steambath.

The lake turned choppy. *Gator,* though not nimble under motor power in rough water, was a strong boat. We were not in any real danger, but, once more, I understood how Billy in his small boat had felt his craft seem to shrink around him. The wooden structures marking the river channel appeared through the gloom, and we headed straight through them, toward calm water and sunshine. Agitated weather clung to the lake. We headed for our Lake Dexter anchorage.

We reached the small lake in good time, but calm weather was not going to last. Clouds began merging as we finished dinner and began preparing for a fast approaching storm. Using his stock of bungees and rope fragments, Fred arranged tarps above the mosquito drapes so we could get air and not rain. Cooling showers began as he finished tying knots. Stormy weather kept frog giggers indoors so only natural sounds of frogs and owls carried across the water.

Tuesday dawned clear and the sun quickly heated night-cooled air. After breakfast we made for Idlewilde Point. Anchoring the sailboat well out of the channel, we paddled over and plunged through cobwebs strung across the shrubbery. Wax myrtles grew to the water's edge and there was no telltale alligator-flattened trail. If the creatures used the point at all anymore, it could only have been at the small clearing where the dinghy was tied to an overhanging branch. Cicadas sawed the air and poison ivy lurked underfoot. Lacking the overall height and openness William had described, the point did not look like an inviting campsite to me. We could not go far without hacking away with a machete and the interior receded into an impenetrable maze of greenery. Fred pushed his way inward a few feet at a time while I sifted through shells disintegrating in shallow water. For the first time I found white painted china, bits of glass, and the rusted leg of an old stove mixed with fragments of Indian pottery.

A small speedboat circled *Gator*. Surreptitiously, I watched the three passengers from under the brim of my straw hat. One aimed a camera at the sailboat. Then they headed for the bank and expertly beached the boat. A man's voice boomed, "Did y'all sleep here last night? Did you see any alligators?"

"No, we anchored over in the lake and all we heard were pig frogs and owls," I replied.

The trio climbed out of the boat and stretched their cramped muscles. Fred noisily approached through the undergrowth. The man spoke again in a rather disbelieving voice, "Fred? Gail?" Fred emerged from the woods as I looked up and we answered, "Clay?"

The jolly boatman was Clay Henderson, then president of the Florida Audubon Society. A man so enthralled with William Bartram that he had named his first son after the inquiring naturalist. Clay's companions were a reporter and a photographer for the *St. Petersburg Times*, doing a story on Bartram and the river. We all laughed at the coincidence of meeting at this site and gabbled on about Bartram's adventures for a while. Finally, we parted company and continued our voyage upstream to make Hontoon Island by nightfall. We had to be in Sanford the next day.

By this time, we began feeling the restlessness that comes from being confined. Sailboat fever? Though we had gone ashore numerous times, we could not go far through the thick vegetation. Most of the floodplain land was owned and posted by state or federal government owners. Low, swampy land did not invite rambling. Forests lining the river began closing in, accentuating *Gator*'s limited space. I would not have been a good candidate for a two-month voyage across the Atlantic.

I was barefoot, wearing shorts and a loose cotton T-shirt. A straw hat covered my head, Bullfrog sunscreen glazed my nose, and sunglasses protected my eyes. My skin pricked slightly from mild sunburn. Billy might have worn a hat, but he probably did not have sunglasses to shield his eyes from the sun's glare, and he certainly had no Bullfrog. He worked to make his boat travel, especially on the river where it was unlikely he could sail. Always stopping to observe plants and animals, jot notes, sketch something, William stretched his legs more than we had, but like him, we were weary of heat and mosquitoes. Trying to sleep in the heat with whining mosquitoes hovering and hungry alligators lying in wait must have exhausted him. Unlike Billy, we traveled in relative luxury and I was chagrined at my chafing, but still uncomfortable.

We made the park well before dark on Tuesday and tied up in the end slip, hoping to catch some evening breeze. I headed immediately for a long, cooling shower—the thing I had wanted the most, even though the effects would last only a few minutes. Returning to the sailboat, I slung the wet towel over the boom. Flags on the mast hung dead in the air. Tired from the long day, we ate our last meal on the river and turned in. The towels were still damp on Wednesday morning.

Cold cereal and granola bars sufficed for breakfast. I hurried Fred along, anxious to get off the boat and onto dry land. Although he would not admit he might have a touch of cabin fever, he did agree that his next trip would be shorter.

From this point, Billy had continued upriver to Blue Springs, a few miles southeast of Hontoon Island, then returned to Spaulding's Lower Store, north of Lake George and Mount Royal in June 1774. He left the river and traveled overland to the Suwannee River at a point near Manatee Springs. During August and September he made another excursion to Lake George, then wended his way to Georgia for winter. He collected plants in West Florida in 1775, but he did not return to the St. Johns again.

We motored against the current toward Sanford. There were fewer boats on the river at midweek, mostly carrying dedicated anglers. We passed a small tour boat named *John Bartram*. Then a multi-decked excursion boat elbowed past. Dozens of passengers sat at white-clothed tables eating lunch and admiring the green land from air-conditioned comfort. I was hot and uncomfortable, but I would not have traded places with any of them.

The St. Johns has changed in certain aspects since the Bartrams floated its waters. Some plants and animals have been completely erased from the landscape and will never return. More people now live and travel along the river. William often sought the company of other travelers and residents along the waterway and we grumbled about not finding peace and quiet. The St. Johns is now clouded with pollutants; the Bartrams had drifted over clearer waters. Weather conditions are the same—sudden thunderstorms, heat, and humidity. The river's seductive curves have been sliced for easier navigation. Fortunately, much of the floodplain bordering the river is protected. Managing agencies are replanting native species. If allowed to grow, massive cypress will grace the shore in another century. We hope the river will regain and retain a wilder composition.

Even though we enjoyed better accommodations and food, we had gained a clearer understanding of what William endured. He felt fear and must have sometimes felt a great loneliness. Overpowering those emotions was a sense of freedom, dependence upon himself, a certainty of being in charge of his life, being able to spend as much time as he wanted examining a flower or observing a snake, not quite knowing what to expect each time the river turned, and, possibly best of all, being far from his father's critical eye.

After the biggest adventure of his life, William returned to his family's home. He never married. He helped his brother in the nursery—John, Jr., had taken over the business in 1771—and hosted scores of visitors who felt the same passions for the natural world as he did. John's prediction for his son came true; Billy's love for nature and drawing had never brought monetary wealth, but his life was devoted to what made him happiest and his reputation has lasted these many years.

The power plant's smokestacks came into view and we turned toward the marina. It was five minutes to one o'clock, almost seven days to the minute. Water slid by *Gator*'s hull on the timeless river. I looked behind us and the river flowed on.

CHAPTER 4

The Intriguing Naturalist

André Michaux

(March 7, 1746–November 1802)

As soon as I recovered from my illness I left Charleston, and went to reside in a small plantation about ten miles from the town, where my father had formed a botanic garden. It was there he collected and cultivated, with the greatest care, the plants that he found in the long and painful travels that his ardent love for science had urged him to make, almost every year, in the different quarters of America. Ever animated with a desire of serving the country he was in, he conceived that the climate of South Carolina must be favorable to the culture of several useful vegetables of the old continent, and made a memorial of them, which he read to the Agricultural Society at Charleston.

—François André Michaux, *Travels to the West of the Allegheny Mountains*, 1805

A YOUNG FRENCHMAN sat alone in a room made darker and colder by the sorrow etched on his face. In a short time his small son, just ten days old, would wake and demand to be fed as only an infant can. In another room, the young man's wife, Cecile, mother of the baby, lay in her coffin. The new father stood and walked to the window. Outside, the night sky subtly shifted from dull black to opaque grey as the sun inched relentlessly toward the dawn of another day. Other people moved through the house, their voices mere rustlings of air. The loss of his young wife in 1770 after less than a year of marriage left André Michaux stunned and grieving.

Louis-Guillaume Lemonnier, court physician at Versailles and professor of botany at the king's garden, had become acquainted with André, and worried about the young man's sadness. Michaux's farm lay near the royal palace of Versailles at Satory; in fact, the land belonged to the king. Lemonnier, impressed with Michaux's abilities in improving agricultural plants, drew the farmer into a broader botanical world. The doctor's personal garden became a healing classroom. Setting his grief aside, Michaux directed his passion and considerable intellect to botany.

André had been surrounded by plants since his birth on March 7, 1746, the first son in a farming family, and plants became the tapestry of his life. He gained authority in the scientific field and botany furnished him a reason to travel the world. Alexander the Great had captured André's childhood imagination and he longed to trace the conqueror's trail. Michaux's younger brother had become largely responsible for the daily chores of the family's farm. The extended family shouldered the responsibility of raising his son, François André, leaving the botanist free to follow his consuming interest.

Michaux studied botany under Bernard and Antoine Laurent de Jussieu and then moved to Paris and the Jardin du Roi. Within a short time his capabilities were noted and André was assigned to collect specimens for the royal gardens. In 1780, he joined naturalist Jean Baptiste Lamarck and botanist André Thouin on an expedition to Auvergne. Energetic Michaux dashed ahead, planted seeds of the cedar of Lebanon, paused to chat with shepherds, and collected plants, minerals, and animals. Plants were his primary interest but little escaped his inquisitive eyes.

Upon returning, he petitioned and received permission from Queen Marie Antoinette to collect Persian plants for her gardens. From 1782 to 1785 he journeyed to Baghdad and explored across Afghanistan. As he traveled he picked up Farsi, the Persian language, and composed a French-Persian dictionary. In the desert, he was robbed and held prisoner, but was soon rescued and released. Michaux merely dusted off his hands and began his eternal search for plants. He might have stayed longer but for a family request that he return to France as soon as possible. Reasons for urgency are not clear but likely involved François' need for a father's care.

A large collection of dried specimens and seeds accompanied the botanist on the voyage home. The trip, despite hardships, had been successful for France and for André. He had proven himself capable on all fronts—as a prolific collector, at representing his country, and in his stamina and drive. Michaux returned to Satory to fulfil yet another role.

François was entering his teens, always an erratic time. It is difficult to evaluate the relationship between father and son during the latter's childhood. Little correspondence from that time survives, but there was no hint that the father resented the son or blamed the child for Cecile's death. André's profound depression, his energy turned to botany, and his excursions abroad meant aunts and uncles probably had more influence on the boy's childhood than his father. Nonetheless, François needed his father, and André would prove himself an able parent.

France had lost the forests of Louisiana and Canada in the 1763 Treaty of Paris. During years of conflict with other countries, France had stripped its own limited forests to build ships. Siding with America during that country's Revolution had further strained its economy. With France's treasury and forests nearly empty and the people disgruntled, King Louis XVI vowed to send expeditions worldwide seeking new avenues to restore the country's wealth. Based on Michaux's spectacular experience in Persia, and persuaded by the young scientist's friends, the king named André Michaux as his royal botanist to America in 1785.

The appointment carried an annual salary with all expenses paid by the king, along with several stipulations. A botanical garden would be established near New York for shipping specimens to France. Most importantly, trees with commercial uses, medicinal and edible plants, and, not to be forgotten, ornamental beauties, were to fall under his purview. He was to learn what he could of their care and uses and ship the most economically feasible to France. Also accompanying Michaux were gardener Pierre Paul Saunier, domestic servant Jacques Renaud, and François. Various delays kept Michaux anxious, but finally the ship was underway.

In typical Michaux style, the botanist became a dynamo as soon as his feet touched American soil on November 14, 1785. He first introduced himself to France's minister, Otto. The two met on good terms with Otto promising to receive packages from Michaux and see that they were safely packed on the next ship bound for France. In fact, all of the king's ships had been ordered to give Michaux's botanical cargo preferential service. Less satisfying were farmers unresponsive to requests to supply specimens, expensive commercial growers, and indolent day laborers. The collecting season was drawing to a close and there was no time to lose. France depended upon him. He would have to do the work himself. Well, almost.

Saunier helped, Renaud was pressed into service, and François received a botanical crash course. After a few weeks the first shipment was on its way and Otto and Michaux went shopping for a garden site, settling on twenty-nine acres strategically located near New York's harbor in what is now Hudson County, New Jersey. The tract was ideally situated and contained two excellent collecting forests, a slope, a portion of meadowland, and a swampy woodland.

A small problem arose in that non-Americans could not purchase land. Strings were pulled and on March 3, 1786, the New Jersey General Assembly voted to allow the Frenchman to buy the plot with the caveat that it could be used only as a botanical garden. Michaux paid for the acreage and hired a contractor to build a house. As gardener, Saunier would be responsible for raising plants and for growing food for himself, helpers, and livestock.

Perhaps the greatest hindrance André Michaux faced in his first American years was an unfamiliarity with the English language. From time to time, he hired interpreters and hoped that François could soon take over that role. What he may have lacked in verbal abilities, Michaux made up in charm. He was a down-to-earth man, forthright, honest, comfortable with himself and with people famous and unknown alike. This ease with people was his greatest asset, and it fit with his talent for networking— he knew whom to meet, when to sustain a communication, and how to get what he needed. With the garden well on its way, it was time to begin building a chain of contacts. André placed his son in a minister's home to learn English while he made his first journey southward.

As André traveled by stage through Pennsylvania, his agricultural senses appraised the productive farmlands. In Philadelphia, he met Benjamin Franklin and William Bartram. Michaux returned to Bartram's garden time and time again for rejuvenation and inspiration. Years later, Michaux was the only person who could persuade the reclusive naturalist to leave the garden and adjacent woodlands for a day of botanizing.

Rounds of introductions complete, Michaux left Philadelphia and traveled through Maryland and on to Virginia. This was a collecting trip, but, more importantly, a diplomatic mission. On June 19, 1786, Michaux stopped at Mount Vernon, and dined with the future president and other guests. Washington's diary reveals that seeds brought by the French botanist were sown over the next few days. Like Catesby, Michaux believed in disseminating plants all over the world. Few in that time realized the possible dangers of spreading plants and animals beyond their natural boundaries, for some species survive all too well.

Back in New Jersey by July, Michaux began planning a major southern excursion. But first he and Saunier combed New Jersey's woodlands for plants. Then the botanist tidied up other details, fenced the property, settled accounts, arranged shipments, and took a quick trip to Bartram's garden. On September 6, leaving Saunier in charge, André, François, Renaud, two horses, and their equipment set sail for Charleston. They expected to be gone six months.

The Carolinas were still recovering from Revolutionary War battles. War had been hard on the land. Domestic animals and wildlife had been shot for food or spite, farms and homes destroyed, and forests burned and cut. South Carolina's longer growing season and proximity to southern collecting areas convinced the botanist that a southern garden was needed. Charleston's cost of living was high, so Michaux chose a less expensive site about ten miles from the city with a livable house already on the property.

Michaux planned to leave François behind when he traveled far. Apparently the balky teenaged boy exhibited little of his father's aptitude or enthusiasm for things botanical on the few short collecting trips undertaken by father and son. Longer journeys were necessary if Michaux were to continue his charge. Fortunately, something changed in François' demeanor and he began to show interest in his father's work. Michaux's earlier doubts about his son faded.

The French botanist crossed paths previously explored by John Lawson, Mark Catesby, and John and William Bartram. He hunted the same species, felt relief at finding them, heaved sighs of frustration when they could not be found, and always delighted when an undescribed specimen came to light. Though the ground had been crossed several times over, there was always hope that something had been missed.

Ebenezer, near Savannah, Georgia, was and still is an exceptional place. Ebenezer Creek feeds into the Savannah River just north of Ebenezer townsite. A recent study by the U.S. Forest Service has deemed 1,350 acres of bald cypress/water tupelo/gum floodplain along Ebenezer Creek Swamp an old growth site. Some stands may be one thousand years old and private landowners have agreed to protect the area. Researchers continue studying the site; something might turn up.

Bartram might have suggested that André botanize around Ebenezer. In late April 1787, the Frenchman collected delicate wild orchids and a new species of silver bell there. A short time later, François and two companions explored the Altamaha River while André recovered from an abscessed insect bite in Sunbury, Georgia, a town now faded from maps.

Michaux wrote in his journal almost daily, recounting the miles covered (there were mileposts along traveled roads), plants found, and notable events. He wrote by twilight, firelight, and moonlight, *au clair de la lune.* His field notes were not always detailed and their length depended upon time and light. Written descriptions of plants were secondary to having a specimen in hand, but if a cutting were lost or destroyed such snippets of information would jog his memory. He always meant to write a literary account of his travels one day. Finding and preparing specimens required so much time, and he put off writing lengthy reports.

Most large agrarian landowners were interested in botanicals aside from the crops they grew, and many actively experimented with ornamental plants as well as new cash crops in the early eighteenth century. Planters often visited the French Garden, as the Michaux home was known. When in Charleston, Michaux occasionally strayed from work to return calls on outlying plantations. He was always welcomed at the big homes and visits were a break from routine, a chance to catch up on news. Following his dictum of flowering the world, Michaux nearly always came bearing gifts of seeds or cuttings of native and exotic plants.

The Drayton family took special notice of natural history and Michaux appreciated their interest and hospitality. By nature a generous man, André was attentive to those who supported his work. While he was a guest at Drayton Hall, Michaux's horse died. Dr. Charles Drayton loaned the botanist a mount and after Michaux returned to Charleston he returned the horse to Dr. Drayton. A notation from the doctor's diary of November 12, 1794, reads, "Mr. Michaux returned to his gardens—his horse died by Botts. At night he sent back my horse and 9 genera of rare plants & shrubs."[1] Sadly, little of Drayton Hall's surrounding gardens remain. There is little doubt that the French botanist would have been welcomed by the Draytons of Magnolia; family legend contends that Michaux presented the Middletons with plants said still to be growing in the gardens of Middleton Place.

William Bartram had traversed the Carolina mountains more than a decade earlier and must have praised their beauty to the French botanist. André and François set out with hired Indian guides to explore the sources of the Keowee, Tugaloo, and Tennessee Rivers on June 11, 1787. Using instincts and skill, the guides followed a route over rugged mountains swaddled in mists and dark valleys where sunlight could not penetrate, across cool rock-lined rivers and streams lashing between steep banks. Food ran low and game was scarce. André was disturbed, not by the lack of sustenance, but by the paucity of new plants. Mountain laurel and great laurel were in bloom, but they were familiar. Luck turned for both hunters on the same day; the Indians returned with game and Michaux found a cucumber tree, a type of magnolia.

It was not an easy trip. André wrote, "I was continually in dread of stepping on snakes and terribly frightened when we had to cross over great logs so rotten that they gave way under foot and one was half-buried in the bark and vegetation around them."[2] The difficult journey only whetted his appetite, but there was business to attend to at home.

Back in Charleston, the botanist prepared his collections, oversaw work in the garden, and prepared shipments for France before journeying north to look in on Saunier and share his adventures with William Bartram, who must have warmed to hear the Frenchman's impressions of the Cherokee Mountains. Michaux was anxious to return to the mountains, but the Cherokee were being pushed hard by whites and travel was not safe. Instead, Michaux ventured into Florida, possibly swayed by Bartram's descriptions of his own Florida travels. He would not likely find any plants for his country so far south, but Michaux could not resist the opportunity.

On February 14, 1788, André, François, and a young slave boarded a ship for St. Augustine, but were unable to leave for several days as strong winds kept the ship confined to harbor. Once in St. Augustine, they laid in supplies, purchased a large canoe made from a hollowed-out cypress log, and hired two guides to power the dugout. The conveyance was large enough to hold five men, their supplies, and materials they would collect along the way. Florida was under Spain's control again, and Michaux had to obtain permission from the Spanish governor to conduct a peaceful scientific exploration.

March 12 was a windy day but the group was ready to start. André described wondrous mangrove forests along the shore of Anastasia Island, and he stopped at Fort Matanzas, which means "slaughter" in Spanish. It was stiff going for the men. Michaux botanized among species familiar from Carolina and Georgia—southern magnolia, willow oaks, loblolly pines, and wax myrtles. Showy yellow jessamine vines climbed trees and their fragrant blossoms hung like drops of rich, buttery cream.

Several days later, the men realized they would have to portage the western shore of the Mosquito Lagoon (now the Indian River Lagoon) or retrace their steps. They determined to go forward, but the portage was more difficult than anticipated. They had to cut roller logs to move the ponderous canoe over more than a mile of thickly sown briars, heavy-trunked, razor-sharp palmettos, and scores of rampant mosquitoes. After all that, when they finally reached water, it was nearly six miles wide and so shallow they had to slop through mud and muscle the heavy canoe ahead. Winds too strong for travel kept the party in camp drying clothes the next day. When the weather calmed Michaux found plants he had not seen before: a necklace pod and a new custard apple.

Michaux had planned to travel Florida's full length and though he was finding new plants, they were suited to warmer climates and would not survive in France. His conscience would not let him continue and he turned back at Cape Canaveral, so named by the Spanish because canes and reeds were abundant there. Better weather accompanied the travelers on the return trip and for the first time they saw the small night fires of native hunters. At Matanzas, the party split up, with the guides traveling in the canoe while André and François went ahead by land. The two groups became separated by a large forest fire, doubly frightening as it was burning toward the Frenchmen. The botanists found a way around the blaze and rejoined their guides.

Back in St. Augustine, André again met with the Spanish governor, who was now more suitably impressed since he held letters addressed to Michaux, botanist to the king of France. The party restocked supplies, for it was their intent to explore the St. Johns River, William's old stomping grounds. They reached Lake George on May 5, 1788, and found magnolias and wild olives as Bartram had described. Beyond Lake George stormy weather engulfed the party but soon calmed. On May 8, Michaux wrote in his journal, "We came upon a place frequented by savages. There was a canoe belonging to them on the bank of the river and a cooking pot. I put some biscuits, some beans, and some sweet oranges in this pot, and we went on our way. We heard two shots in the distance which proved that Indians were hunting nearby."[3]

Those few words describing the simple act of sharing food exemplify the French botanist's core. Michaux came upon the empty camp. He could have easily walked away and never made his presence known. He could have waited and made much of his generosity by sharing rations with the hunting party. But he entered camp when the people were away and left food so if their hunting failed they would not go hungry. In his dealings with various tribes, he was honest and never received rough treatment from them. They must have recognized some inner peace in him akin to that lambent light surrounding William Bartram. Michaux searched for plants not so he could boast of how many, but because each one, especially each one that had not been described previously, he hoped would enrich our lives with its beauty, balance, and color, by providing food and shelter, or by possibly saving lives through its healing qualities.

During the cold winter of 1788, Michaux was back in the wondrous Carolina mountains. He gathered bunches of a yellow cucumber tree near the beginning trickles of the Keowee River. This tree was not found again growing in the wild for one hundred and fifty years, when it was discovered farther south, near Augusta, Georgia. On that wintry trip he also collected a "new plant with denticulated leaves spreading over the mountainside."[4] The plant was not in flower and after reaching home, he tucked it away in his herbarium. He never described the specimen or if he did, the paper has not survived. There were other unnamed and undescribed specimens in his collection.

More than thirty years after Michaux's death, botanist Asa Gray was in Paris and came across the unlabeled plant while perusing Michaux's herbarium in the Museum of Natural History at the Jardin des Plantes. Gray named it *Shortia galacifolia* after a Kentucky botanist, Dr. Charles W. Short.

Asa Gray had to find the living plant. A notation on the herbarium sheet led the botanist to Carolina's high mountains in 1840, and though he searched diligently, he could not find the plant. He climbed Grandfather Mountain, Mount Mitchell, Roan Mountain, and all the other high peaks, but not a leaf of *Shortia* was to be found. The quest engaged many botanists, and the plant became a botanical holy grail.

In 1877, seventeen-year-old George McQueen Hyams found some interesting plants growing near the Catawba River around Marion, North Carolina, and took some home to his father, who was an amateur botanist. *Shortia* was thus refound, but not where Michaux had first seen it. Charles Sprague Sargent's party from Harvard, hunting for trees and other plants in the spring of 1887, happened upon *Shortia,* locally known as Oconee bell, in full bloom. Sargent quickly packed a box of the flowering plants and sent them to Dr. Gray, who was then seventy-eight. The site now lies under the water of a reservoir on the Catawba River.

After attending to details resulting from the 1788 collecting trips, Michaux journeyed to the New Jersey garden and then to Bartram's garden. Michaux had been in America for three satisfying years and though he had covered many miles, there was more country to explore. André and his son had grown closer in their personal and professional relationship. The youth was entering manhood and his days of apprenticeship under his father's gently guiding hand were nearing an end. Soon, François would have to return to France for formal education.

On September 20, 1789, François was walking along a road near the Charleston plantation, when a hunter, aiming his gun at partridges, missed and struck the boy in the eye. The accident shook André's world. Michaux had François bled, which, not surprisingly, did not help the injury and the worried father placed his son under a Charleston physician's care. For once, André could not concentrate on his work as he shuttled back and forth between the plantation and Charleston. Luckily, the injury responded to treatment and François recovered. He returned to France in the spring of 1790, and chose to study medicine, but botany was his true calling. André would carry on his work without his son's companionship.

In France, Louis XVI's promises to bring prosperity to the country once again had not been fulfilled, and by 1789 people began pressing for change. The political situation remained in turmoil and an order to sell the Carolina plantation arrived. André sold his home at public auction on March 27, 1792, for about $247 to his friend Jean Jacques Himely who deeded it back to the botanist in a few days. Michaux was also ordered to curtail his travels, but that he could not do. He planned a trip to Canada using his own funds, first stopping to visit Bartram. Michaux left too late to throw in with French traders and began his trip to Hudson Bay on his own, though he was able to engage guides and helpers later. Before the year was out, Michaux was on his way south after a stop in Philadelphia, just ahead of a threatening Canadian winter.

By the 1790s the eastern North American continent had been poked and prodded by outsiders for almost three centuries, if not longer. Roads and settlements pushed the country's frontier into what had once been uncharted territory. Even as wilderness decreased, there were species still to be discovered. Though Michaux might travel coastal lowlands and the Piedmont's gentle swells, it was the interior's ancient and humped, craggy mountains, shrouded in fog that from a distance appeared as smoke, *les hautes montagnes de Caroline,* that called him.

Fresh from his Canadian excursion, however, André grew more fearful that France would end his American mission. Thus, he approached the American Philosophical Society and made it clear that he would forgo the southern regions to undertake an expedition to discover the Missouri River's source and would then proceed to the Pacific Ocean. Thomas Jefferson, whose eyes always turned westward, supported the plan as did George Washington, who pledged $100 in 1793.

Preparations were made, plans drawn up, papers and agreements signed, and then Edmond Charles Genet appeared. His mission, which he undertook with the greatest enthusiasm, was to prepare a commercial treaty between France and the United States. France hoped that America would join them in encouraging the liberation of mankind. The young French minister interpreted that phrase in the broadest sense. His understanding of the government's instructions indicated a military campaign to liberate Louisiana and Florida from under Spain's thumb. Genet was to line up agents in Kentucky and Louisiana for the French cause and persuade the United States to join France in a war against Spain and England. In essence, Genet was given a blank check and free rein to implement the project, and he did so. France wanted to regain access to the rich southern land and felt that this could best be accomplished by sidling up to America for help in driving out the Spanish.

Genet had arrived first in Charleston, not in Philadelphia as America's leaders had expected. The impetuous young man was well received and dropped hints about the planned seizure of Florida. To support his claims he outfitted four privateers in Charleston—never mind that he had not even met, let alone contacted, anyone in the nation's capital. When he finally did set out for Philadelphia, he imperiously left behind orders to raise and train an army.

Ostentatious Genet eagerly stopped in any place of size to trumpet his mission. He was joyously received in Philadelphia. What Genet needed, he confided to America's leaders, was a liaison between Philadelphia and the frontier commanders. What better cover than a botanist, and a French one at that? Calling on Michaux might already have been decided before Genet left France. It was well known that the botanist's loyalty was impeccable and that he would serve his country in whatever role he could.

One wonders about Michaux's personal feelings in this period. He would not refuse to serve his country, yet he would have to withdraw from the far western investigations. Here was Genet, obviously bringing substantial financial backing from France, and André's salary was still in arrears. Prevented from exploring Kentucky in 1789 by Indian hostilities, Michaux was now presented the opportunity to botanize in little explored Kentucky's realm while acting as a spy. He was to spread the word, engage leaders to recruit troops, read the general feeling of the populace toward Spain's ouster, and report back to Genet.

President Washington, however, was not caught up in the zeal surrounding the French envoy and issued a Proclamation of Neutrality on April 22, 1793. The new country was still recovering from its own war for independence and Washington was unwilling to commit America to another war. There was also the not inconsequential matter of financing an army. Obviously, Genet was not happy about this turn of events. Since landing in Charleston, Genet had proceeded without care for diplomacy or protocol and had become increasingly rude, outspoken, and embarrassing. Washington demanded that France recall its minister. Within a few weeks, Genet had been relieved of his mission, sputtering and resentful, but he stayed in the United States rather than face France's uncertain political situation.

Meanwhile, in Kentucky, Michaux had met with George Rogers Clark, Revolutionary War general and hero, who gladly agreed to lead the army. In a few years, Clark's younger brother, William, would serve Lewis? on the ~~Rogers~~ and Clark expedition to the Pacific coast. Five months after meeting with General Clark the botanist was back in Philadelphia and had learned that Genet was out of office and that America had refused to be drawn into a war between France and Spain. Even loyal Michaux must have felt relief when Citizen Genet left office. The botanist applied to his government for reimbursement of expenses incurred on the Kentucky trip and, as usual, received nothing.

In his moving book *Undaunted Courage,* author Stephen Ambrose explained that Michaux did begin western explorations under auspices of the U.S. government but was recalled when Jefferson discovered the botanist's undercover activities. Whether Michaux was playing a double role or acting solely on France's behalf, his mission failed. In any case, it was a few years too soon to launch a western expedition. Jefferson was not yet president and the Louisiana Purchase had not been signed. The country had to focus on organizing its settled lands before thinking about expansion, though Jefferson dreamed of it always. When he became president, discovering a water route to the Pacific and determining the continent's breadth were uppermost in Jefferson's mind. He planned and plotted to see his dream come true, but that would be a few years hence.

Jefferson, a strong supporter of France and very much in favor of liberty and a united country, had tried to rein in Genet, but could not. Chafing under an extended term as secretary of state, Jefferson had been placed in a tenuous position by the Genet affair. He would have been happy to trade Philadelphia, then the nation's capital, for Monticello on almost any given day in 1793.

With a brief romp in political intrigue behind him, Michaux returned to his familiar role in Charleston. He set the garden to rights, caught up his notes and prepared for his next trip. By mid-July 1794, Michaux was riding up the Santee-Wateree-Catawba River valley again. The Catawba River rises in North Carolina's McDowell County in the Blue Ridge Mountains. Its 225 miles pass through the mountains and over the Piedmont to spill finally into Big Wateree Creek, adding its flow to South Carolina's Wateree River. Along the way the Catawba provides habitat for multifarious species of birds, mammals, plants, and fish, as well as water, power, and recreation for upwards of one and a half million people. Though the waters must now wait patiently behind eleven dams, when Michaux ascended the Catawba's watershed it was a free flowing river and had no need of the riverkeepers who now patrol the waters testing for pollution and cleaning up trash that lines the banks and shallows.

Michaux left for the mountains later than usual in 1794 and found flowering plants that he had not seen before, a new *Kalmia* near Camden, a new *Stewartia* between Charlotte and Lincolnton, and he measured a tulip tree twenty-three feet in circumference near Linville. He paused at Martin Davenport's home near the Toe River and the two became friends. Together they climbed Grandfather Mountain on a clear August 30. From atop the windswept summit 5,964 feet above sea level, Michaux and Davenport looked down on waves of mountains and valleys. Exhilarated by the sight and by the climb and memories of his homeland, Michaux sang the *Marseillaise,* France's anthem, and the men's shouts of "Long Live America and the Republic of France, Long Live Liberty," echoed over the peaks.[5] André probably would have sung the *Star Spangled Banner,* but America's anthem was not written until 1814. Michaux declared Grandfather the tallest mountain in America and though it is tall, there are higher peaks in the Blue Ridge. But on that day, it was tall enough and beautiful.

I had traveled up the eastern seaboard of Georgia and South Carolina in May 1999, crossing repeatedly the tracks of Catesby, Abbot, Michaux, Wilson, Audubon, and the Bartrams. As always, I longed to see the country as they had seen it. I wanted a road where there were no people, but, of course, if there were no people, there would be no road. After turning inland and making a one-stop passage through the Savannah River Site, I stopped at a campground built by the Army Corps of Engineers on the South Carolina side of J. Strom Thurmond Lake above J. Strom Thurmond Dam on the Savannah River.

This campground seemed well planned and, best of all on this warm May day, it was almost empty. Long-fingered Thurmond Lake rests along the fringes of the Sumter National Forest. Campsites extend along three high ridges that escaped flooding caused by the dam. Tent campsites have been shunted down one ridge and most other sites are built specifically for RVs and trailers. The best site was set on an isolated toe and had water and electricity. Since the weather was comfortable, I stayed two days and caught up on notes.

On Wednesday morning, I left Thurmond Lake behind for a leisurely drive along Routes 28 and 72, through two units of the Sumter National Forest. Stopping for a snack in an old cemetery, I read tombstones until a light rain began falling. I had a date at the Daniel Stowe Botanical Garden, located near Belmont, North Carolina.

I met Charlie Williams and Bill Hilton at the garden's office, and we shared lunch on the veranda. Charlie manages a branch of the Charlotte-Mecklenburg library system, is active in regional environmental efforts, and volunteers at the garden. Bill was then director of education and research, and explained Mr. Stowe's vision. Daniel Stowe made his fortune in textiles. He liked farms and as they came up for sale, he bought them until he had amassed a sizeable chunk of real estate. He toyed with the idea of a botanical garden, but being a careful planner who thought on a grand scale, he investigated possibilities before the first spade turned the earth. After a year of consideration, he allocated 450 acres and $14 million to make his dream a reality. A ten-acre display garden opened in 1991 and Phase 1 of his grand design was opened in October 1999, with a state-of-the art visitor center and a world of gardens. Stowe Garden expected to raise its visitor attendance from thirty-five thousand in 1999 to one hundred thousand in 2000. As later phases and programs open, the sky is virtually the limit. The garden's mission is to bring together people who appreciate natural habitats and cultivated plantings, with special emphasis on education and research.

The garden had adopted André Michaux as its patron botanist. He crossed the Catawba River near the garden's site in 1795 on his way to the Mississippi and Ohio River country. The royal botanist might have even walked over grounds now occupied by Stowe Garden. Even if he did not, Michaux's name is linked to Carolina's plants and places, and the garden has chosen to honor his many contributions to our botanical knowledge. In fact, an international symposium is planned at the garden for the spring of 2002, the 200th anniversary of the botanist's death.

Bill left for a meeting and Charlie and I ruminated about the French botanist. So little has been written of him in America, and even less in the last fifty years. Charlie became associated with the garden a few years ago while working on a program on André Michaux and *Magnolia macrophylla,* bigleaf magnolia, for the Mecklenburg Treasure Tree Committee. North Carolina's state champion bigleaf magnolia—and size is relative here, for the largest bigleafs are only fifty feet tall and twelve inches in diameter—grew in a Charlotte park and had weathered Hurricane Hugo. The tree comes by its common appellation because its leaves are enormous—twenty to thirty inches long and nine to twelve inches wide—and

FIG. 4. *Magnolia ashei,* a subspecies of André Michaux's *M. macrophylla.*
Photo by Gil Nelson.

in spring it produces soft white blossoms ten to eighteen inches across. Charlie became curious about a reference in the only biography written on the Michaux father and son, by Henry Savage and Elizabeth Savage, which stated that Michaux discovered the magnolia in Tennessee in 1795, but another member of the committee had read that the botanist first found the tree near Charlotte in 1789. A mystery needed solving and a series of coincidences led Charlie to learn where Michaux had first discovered the distinctive magnolia. It was not Tennessee.

Charlie did not speak French, but he had a friend who had worked as a professional translator in Canada. After Charlie obtained a copy of Michaux's journal for 1787–89, she painstakingly translated the botanist's notes written in French, phonetic English, and Latin for him.

On a journey in 1789, Michaux had noticed a new magnolia near present-day Stanley, about eighteen miles from Charlotte. Michaux recorded four additional observations of the tree, but it was unfamiliar and he could not assign a name. A specimen of the same species collected in Tennessee in June 1795 was entered into Michaux's vast herbarium, leading to the conclusion that the plant was first discovered in Tennessee.

As was his habit, Michaux recounted in his daily journal brief descriptions of plants found, miles covered, and places he stayed. Two of the farms where the botanist stayed, about twelve miles west of Charlotte, were owned by Bennet Smith and Christian Reinhardt respectively. André mentioned a new magnolia near Bennet Smith's farm. Another botanist, John Lyon, later stated that he had removed living *M. macrophylla* from *Peter* Smith's farm. Some confusion arose concerning Bennet Smith versus Peter Smith, but Charlie examined county land deeds and found that Bennet Smith had sold his farm to Peter Smith in 1797. One of Charlie's neighbors was named Reinhardt and turned out to be Christian's descendant. Her cousin owns the home built by a son of Peter Smith, and offspring of the bigleaf magnolias transplanted from Peter's farm almost two centuries ago still thrive there. Using the translations of Michaux's journal, period maps, and historical records, Charlie learned the location of Bennet Smith's farm near Little Hoyle Creek. On a subsequent reconnoiter of Hoyle Creek and Little Hoyle Creek, which he determined to be the collecting site for Michaux and Lyon on Smith's land, Charlie found several bigleaf magnolias and satisfied his curiosity at last.

Michaux made six or seven trips up the Catawba River valley following the same general direction through Lincolnton and Morganton. Afternoon was approaching evening when I left Charlotte and headed toward Lincolnton, which was a small hamlet established in 1785 when Michaux passed through so many years ago. I followed Route 27 through Stanley and Alexis. Big Jim's Fence Company and the John Deere Tractor place were closed for the night. It was too late to look for a campground, and a motel seemed a good idea. At last one appeared east of Lincolnton. I had a rendezvous with Grandfather Mountain the next morning.

From Lincolnton, Route 27 led to Morganton and from there Route 18 curled to Lenoir, which cozies up to the Appalachian Mountains' eastern edge. I wandered around town for awhile, searching for a back way into the heights. Narrow, paved Route 90 seemed a likely choice. Immediately the road began to climb and twist and the eight miles to Colletsville took awhile. I was eager to reach my destination, but the journey was equally important. Gradually, houses became farther apart but never entirely disappeared. Sunshine, however, vanished and light rain began falling. At Colletsville, the road turned into the mountains and the Pisgah National Forest. When the pavement turned to dirt and gravel, I was on the right track.

Grandfather Mountain, so named because it resembles a reclining, bearded old man, was somewhere ahead. The rain stopped and I pulled over at a wide spot for lunch, finishing just as rain started again. In the mountains' lower reaches, milky blooms of Fraser magnolias contrasted with their large, soft green leaves. This was another tree Michaux had noted. I had not seen any houses for a long stretch and only one other vehicle, but signs of civilization were evident. Judging from the number of cans, Natural Light was the beverage of choice on this back road. I paused to photograph a bouquet of dwarf irises in a light mist. A tiny creek beckoned, but others had been there before. A cardboard carton dissolved in the damp, a window frame sprouted broken glass, cans, bottles, and other junk littered the creek's banks and bottom. People had tossed out stoves, refrigerators, and water heaters along the road. I ceased noticing trash when the storm finally broke in earnest. Thunder rolled around the hills like the nine-pins in Rip Van Winkle's dream. Lightning flashed, and sheets of rain turned to hail. It was great.

Before the downpour, I had been out in the drizzle, but I could get back into the warm, dry van. André Michaux had no choice. If he and his companions had been caught out in weather like this, and they often had, they could only have gotten drenched. Oil soaked cloth might have been the only thing protecting their powder, food, and specimens from rain and humidity. Their horses would have been restive in the hail and thunder.

These are rugged mountains with steep slopes layered with slick leaves made slicker in the rain. No one should be misled into thinking they are gentle just because they lack the snow-capped ruggedness of the Rockies or the Sierra Nevada. Care had to be taken that the packs did not become loosened or torn when the horses passed through close growing trees. Depending upon the time of year, fast flowing, frigid streams had to be crossed. Mists and rains obscured the sun, disorienting travelers. Though game was plentiful, damp powder or an unlucky day meant the stew pot might be empty. Fortunately, Michaux and his party suffered few injuries and those were minor. Despite the chances for failure, André Michaux pressed ahead and returned with curiosities, increasing his own knowledge and enriching science for all.

There are still few direct routes over the mountains. Roads wander around and up and down and finally reach their destination; the Appalachians pose a formidable obstacle even today. Was Grandfather near, I wondered, and then the mountain's profile greeted me around an open curve. The high land must be viewed from a certain angle or the image is hidden. A few miles later, the graveled road intersected with pavement, the rain dried up, and the sky cleared.

Grandfather Mountain is privately owned and operated by Hugh Morton, who has opened the mountain to the public, paved roads, installed numerous picnic areas, and built two interpretive centers. There are no campsites within Grandfather's boundaries, but camping and motels are available nearby. Of the preserve's 4,000 acres, 2,743 are further protected through an agreement with The Nature Conservancy, a nonprofit land protection organization. I paid my fee and entered. Few people were there, but it was just before the end of the school year and vacation mania was a few weeks away. Resplendent rhododendrons were just beginning to bloom in the lower elevations and would not begin their gaudy mountaintop display until July.

I scanned the gift shop, watched a video at the Nature Museum, and examined exhibits. One is devoted to André Michaux and his mountaintop cavorting. The vision for Grandfather Mountain couples a natural area and a public park. Parts of it welcome the public, but Morton and the Conservancy fiercely protect other sections. The mountain is a refuge for forty-two rare and endangered species, including eleven that are globally endangered. Some 149 avian species have been noted on the mountain. Its biological importance prompted the United Nations to include Grandfather Mountain in its international Biosphere Reserve network.

Pavement leads from the visitor's center to Grandfather's twin peaks. A suspension bridge spans an eighty-foot deep ravine. Much had been made in the introductory video about the small percentage of women who dare cross the short, sturdy bridge. I crossed it with no qualms, but no one was there to see! Cool winds blew briskly at the summit and the view was stunning; 360 degrees of an ocean of mountain peaks. No wonder Michaux had been seized with unbridled excitement. It felt like the top of the world.

One major flaw in the west-facing view immediately draws attention. Across the valley a tall square building rises like an ugly wart near Sugar Mountain's peak—ten-story Sugar Top Condominium. Visitors to Grandfather will appreciate one good thing that came out of that structure. North Carolina passed the Mountain Ridge Protection Act in 1983 limiting future buildings to just three stories above the ridge line.

Daylight was sliding toward late afternoon as I bade Grandfather farewell and headed for the Blue Ridge Parkway and a campsite. The quiet Park Service campground was damp from an afternoon shower and the evening air had a bite. Only a few weeks earlier, parts of the Parkway had been shut down because of snow. I dug out socks and sweat pants while dinner cooked. Distant thunder rumbled and rain started as I finished putting dishes away. Not a good evening for sitting outside, so I did what people used to do when the sun went down, before electricity and television, and drifted to sleep to the sound of softly falling rain.

I was awake and brewing coffee before other campers stirred the next morning. Rain began just as I stowed the stove. Linville Falls was hardly a mile from the campground. Michaux had been near here on his last trip to the mountains in 1795–96, but in his haste to reach Roan Mountain and push on to the Mississippi River had not taken time to stop. I was up for a morning hike, especially because of the cold drizzle, and Linville Falls is worth the walk.

At the first stop, the falls are picturesque. Drifts of small pink-flowered azaleas bloom along the stream. The next level is as spectacular as promised. Here the rapidly moving water squeezes through a narrow, kinked passage. People had thrown coins into the plunging water and some had fallen short and lay precariously on slippery rocks.

On the way down, a small Park Service truck on trash detail passed, going up the wide trail. We waved to each other, me dripping, the rangers dry. Back in the van, I shucked damp sweats and got into dry shorts. Now, to find Roan Mountain.

As the raven flies, Roan Mountain is not far from Grandfather, but on foot or by car it is a smart bit of distance. At 6,285 feet, Roan Mountain surpasses Grandfather. Mount Mitchell, which Michaux also investigated, rises above them all at 6,684 feet, the highest point east of the Mississippi River. North Carolina and Tennessee share Roan Mountain and the Appalachian Trail (AT) passes over its peak.

I stopped at a small country store in Glen Ayre for ice. A cart of cantaloupes by the door smelled scrumptious. This was the only store for miles around and carried lots of local produce. I bought ice and the lady behind the counter said the ice man had just come the afternoon before. He does not make regular stops; she calls him since he comes all the way from Spartanburg. She had had the number in her hand, being down to the last four bags, when the phone had rung. It was the ice man saying he was close by and she was still tickled by the coincidence.

FIG. 5. Beautiful Linville Falls in the mountains of North Carolina.
Photo by author.

The road to the top of Roan Mountain is paved all the way, though it is not generous and should be driven with care. Amorphous fog, comforting in a way, accompanied me to the top. A beagle trotted along the shoulder, no collar, thin, but not poor. I resisted the urge to pick him up. At the fee station—the Forest Service charges a parking fee, not an entrance fee, so a Golden Eagle Pass is of no help—I tried to convince the ladies operating it that they should take in the dog, but they stuck to their story that he was separated from a hiker on the AT. Not likely.

A small kiosk at the parking lot dispenses information and sells T-shirts and books. The lady on duty was quite helpful. She had a heater going because of the cold air and a trap loaded because she worried that the resident mouse would get into her stock. We tried shooing it out the door, but the rodent was determined to stay in warm, dry quarters. She gave me maps, and said she was sorry I had not been here a day earlier when the sky was clear and the weather warm. I said I did not mind the fog or the chill.

Roan Mountain most likely received its name from the colorful catawba rhododendrons described by Michaux. In summer, the plants produce flowers ranging from light pink to cerise and from a distance the mountain appears to have a rich, strawberry-colored sauce ladled over it. Another legend says the name came from a roan horse that Daniel Boone rode on frequent visits to the area. In the 1930s truckloads of rhododendron were dug up, carried away, and sold to nurseries. By 1939 just about all marketable timber had been cut. The mountain became part of the Pisgah and Cherokee National Forests in 1941, so trees and flowers are more protected from commercial ventures. It is harder to protect plants from biological factors. In the 1950s the balsam woolly adelgid appeared in the Southern Appalachians as fir forests were about reestablished. The adelgid feeds on mature Fraser firs and doesn't bother with young ones, explaining why young firs grow so closely under their dead and dying parents.

David Danley, botanist on the Pisgah National Forest, knows about the adelgid, a tiny insect (about 1 mm) that most humans would not notice. No one knows how it got here, but it was almost certainly an unintentional introduction. The insect bores into the cambium layer of Fraser firs, preferring that tree above all others, and eventually kills the tree.

Until the early 1960s, lindane, a caustic pesticide, was sprayed on infected trees. It was expensive, time consuming, did not completely protect the trees, and was quite harmful to other insects. A less harsh insecticidal soap is sometimes used but must be applied yearly to individual trees and still poses problems for some insects. The Forest Service has neither funds nor people to employ such a large-scale spray program, and even if it did other species would be at risk. Prognosis for the firs is not good, though they will probably never disappear from the mountains. Populations of red spruce, however, the fir's strongest competitor, are increasing.

On high ridges and flanks of the Appalachians, grey skeletons of firs nose above healthy trees. Most passersby assume that acid rain has caused their death. Acid rain is a factor; some plants are more vulnerable than others, but the balsam woolly adelgid is the bigger culprit here. So far, the insect has not spread outside the Appalachians.

I was the only person out walking and had there been no pathway, I could have become disoriented with visibility only a few feet. Quietly thickening mist wrapped spruce-fir stands, ghosts of the ice age. Glaciers never sealed and scraped the land this far south, but the ice sheets did have a profound effect on climate. Twenty thousand years ago, Roan Mountain was cloaked in tundra-like vegetation. As the climate warmed, remnants of spruce-fir forests cleaved to the highest peaks. Roan Mountain has been completely logged at least twice since Europeans came to stay. Most components of the ecosystem that were there when André Michaux climbed the ridges are still here, but the altered landscape does not look quite the same.

The trail passed through a treeless bald, which on a clear day would have offered up a spectacular view. There are a few theories on how the balds came to be. It is thought that grazing mammoths kept the areas open and after those large animals went extinct, likely from overhunting, bison and elk took over. Humans got rid of the bison and elk and the balds are still there. Fire does not seem to play a role in keeping them open. During the early 1860s, herders ran sheep on the high mountain balds. If the balds are not maintained by grazing, they do tend to close in, so it is not poor soil or a rock layer near the surface that keeps vegetation from encroaching. Whether the balds have always been there is another question that cannot be satisfactorily answered. Nature is not static. Weather forces maintain and alter landscapes. Throw humans into the equation and who knows what will happen. Maybe a yarn about the Devil walking over the mountains and leaving scalded footprints that stunted growth is correct.

For a few hours the damp cold was novel, but more than a few days of closed-in weather would leave me jittery and short-tempered. Driving down the mountain I noticed roofs of vacation homes peeping over tree-tops. The peaks may be protected, but the lower flanks are up for grabs. From Roan Mountain I wound toward Franklin in western North Carolina, where my family had owned a cabin in the 1960s and I learned to appreciate and love mountains. My ancestors helped settle Macon County and are buried in the Rush burying ground between Otto and Franklin. I always visit them when passing through. On this visit I found their headstones unreadable.

I spent the night in a Franklin motel. The town has changed a little in the last thirty years and plumps up in summer with refugees from Florida's searing temperatures. On Saturday, I walked the dirt road past the cabin my father and uncle built and wished we still owned it. Catesby's trillium, flame azalea, mountain laurel, mayapple,[6] sweet shrub, and false Solomon's seal bloomed along the verge. Great laurel buds were growing fat, but not blooming yet. I marked the flowers in my book and headed back to U.S. 441 and into Georgia.

André Michaux's last journey in America led him through the southeastern mountains again. This time he was gone for almost a year and went as far west as the Mississippi. He still yearned to see the Pacific Coast, but that was not to be. By early summer of 1796 he was back in Charleston. Michaux left no written journals or letters for his last four months in America, or they have been lost. He had not been ordered back to France, so why he left is not clear. Perhaps his own small funds had at last run dry. He boarded the *Ophir* on August 13, 1796, saddened at leaving before he could walk the entire country, with hopes of returning one day.

The ship ran into a furious storm off the coast of Holland. Winds shredded the sails and waves washed everything from the decks. Michaux lost consciousness from the battering and woke up in a room warmed by a fire. All passengers had survived and residents of a little town prepared food, generously gave clothing, and made them as comfortable as possible. Michaux's first concern was, of course, his specimen trunks. He lost only a box of birds, two notebooks, and a small box of writings, which he thought he could recreate from memory. That he lost all his clothes and personal effects mattered little to him.

Settled in France once more, André organized his collections and reunited with François. Michaux prepared two manuscripts for publication, the two-volume *Flora Boreali-Americana* and *Historie des Chenes de l'Amerique Septentrionale*. His finances were exhausted, but his motivation was not. When France asked him to accompany a voyage to the Southern Seas, he worked even harder to arrange his herbarium before departing.

Once again, he approached the interior minister for at least a portion of the salary owed to him. He had previously submitted a request and accounting of his work, but he listed them once more: twenty years of service to his country, collecting in Syria, Babylon, and Persia; eleven years in North America exploring from the St. Lawrence River to Florida and the Ohio River; action as a political agent among the Indian nations, and contributions of more than seventy-five thousand trees and numerous collections of seeds, plants, and herbarium. His personal financial situation was precarious, with no money to have his manuscripts copied, and now that he was about to leave, his works were being copied and printed outside of the country instead of bringing honor to France. In a few years the damage would be irreparable and France would lose prestige. This missive brought apologies and words of praise from the treasury, but no money.

With an impressive send-off, the expedition sailed on October 19, 1800. Before leaving, Michaux had received permission to abandon the voyage, if necessary, to continue his botanical investigations. In April 1801, he decided to remain on Ile de France while the others sailed on. Michaux sailed to Madagascar in June 1802. He explored the area and selected a garden site from where he would prepare plants and seeds to send to France. Heedless of the strength-draining tropical climate, Michaux put in long hours, unknowingly weakening his resistance—after all, he had fought off bouts of malaria in America. He fell ill, probably with malaria, recovered, but fell ill again and died in November 1802 or 1803. News of his passing did not reach France for several months.

After his father's death, François went on to further study America's trees. His work formed the roots of modern forest ecology and he has sometimes been referred to as the Father of American Forestry. François lived into his eighties. The Michaux legacy is well documented in the annals of botany, but their name does not carry the same cachet as Bartram, Audubon, or Muir, who aimed for a popular audience. English translations of portions of Michaux's journals have been published by the American Philosophical Society and in various essays by other authors. Only one biography of the father and son has been published and it is out of print and difficult to find. Their complete journals and writings, outside of François' *The North America Sylva* and *Travels to the West of the Allegheny Mountains*, have not been published in English and made available to modern readers. Copies of the *Sylva* and the *Travels* exist and are for sale, but they cost hundreds of dollars and are too old to treat casually.

According to an article in the *Journal of the Elisha Mitchell Scientific Society* of July 1911, Michaux's garden was still evident in 1910 despite the number of times the property had changed hands. Piles of old brick marked the house site though the building itself was long gone. Ginkgos, mimosas, oaks, magnolias, dogwoods, wax myrtles, red buckeye, smilax vines, ferns and flowers still flourished in the old plot, many planted and cared for by Michaux. At least until 1910, and some time beyond, the property could be reached by taking the train to Ten Mile Station. It seemed out in the country in 1910, but part of Charleston's airport now covers the site. One of the roads leading to the airport is named Michaux Parkway.

Michaux had a reputation as a diligent worker and expected the same of others. His young wife's unexpected death may have reinforced his knowledge that life is fragile; there was never any time to lose. During his eleven years in America, the naturalist gathered, identified, packed, crated, caged, labeled, and wrote observations and instructions for the care of thousands of seeds and plants and hundreds of wood ducks, quail, and other creatures. A rough guess of the ground he covered by horseback approaches ten thousand miles and does not consider the miles on foot and by boat. André Michaux devoted his life to plants. He viewed each seed and shoot as his own offspring, carefully collected and nurtured, and sent on its way to flourish and enrich the world. Along the way, he recorded his travels and observed the natural landscape in detail. I have heard a rumor that someone is translating André Michaux's journals for publication. Perhaps in a few years, we will all be able to read of this extraordinary scientist's explorations through America's wilderness.

CHAPTER 5

A Peculiar Liking for Insects

John Abbot
(June 11, 1751–1840)

In the beginning of the year 1773, I was determined to come
to America, but what part to choose was the only matter to
determine on. A Frenchman & his son come from Orleans,
they praised that very much, but I had met with a hist of
Virginia painted in such glowing Colours, & the Voyage
there being much shorter I determined on Virginia.

—From John Abbot's letters written to Augustus Oemler
before 1834

As MANY LITTLE BOYS DO, John Abbot spent carefree childhood summers capturing creeping, crawling, flying things. Beetles scrabbled uselessly against the clear walls of glass jars he had lined on a shelf in his room at his family's rented country house at Turnham Green. He dropped bits of bread and meat into the jars, hoping the beetles might eat. Leafy limbs leaned against a bureau, each bearing a jewel-like chrysalis of a soon-to-emerge butterfly. Solemnly he watched their miraculous escape from prison. He was dazzled at their colors and the soft powder left on his fingers when he touched their wings. Why did it not all shake loose when they flew? At night, he set a candle outside and captured drab moths. Through their dull colors he discerned subtle designs on their wings. One day he brought drawing sheets, pencils, paints and began sketching their shapes and tried to imitate their colors. He never outgrew the fascination.

Most of what is known about John Abbot comes from a series of letters written to his life-long friend, Augustus Oemler, a Savannah pharmacist interested in natural history. Oemler had entrusted the papers to Thaddeus W. Harris in 1834, with hopes that Abbot would receive some recognition for his work, but they were forgotten until found in the locked files of Harvard University's Museum of Comparative Zoology in 1948. C. L. Remington published the autobiographical fragment as "Notes on My Life" in *Lepidopterists' News* in 1948.

Abbot never sought fame during his lifetime, and in the intervening years, recognition of his outstanding contributions to art and science has been sporadic and short-lived. He left few writings behind, and while he was known to and respected by many in the natural history circle—Thomas Say, William Swainson, John LeConte, Alexander Wilson, and others—Abbot preferred the periphery. His desire to remain in the background has almost come to pass, much to the frustration of modern researchers. John confined himself to a small area of the country and studied it well. Those who are acquainted with his life and work know just about everything there is to know.

John's father, also named John Abbot, was an attorney. The Abbots' first son, Anthony, had been born on January 25, 1750, and was buried on February 7, 1751, a few months before John's birth on June 11, 1751. The family lived on London's west side, where the elder Abbot displayed a large collection of valuable prints and, probably, a substantial library where John acquired a taste for books and drawing at an early age.

Reading between the lines of John's "Notes," I gleaned that he grew up

FIG. 6. John Abbot's self-portrait is the only known likeness of the entomologist.
Courtesy of Georgia Historical Society.

in an open atmosphere where children were invited to follow their natural inclinations. The Abbots indulged their offspring, perhaps because they'd lost their firstborn; young John had enough pocket money to purchase books and supplies on his own.

While hunting insects one day, John met Mr. Van Dest, a well-known flower painter. The man must have been attracted by something in the youngster's demeanor, perhaps enthusiasm in one untested by life. Van Dest had a small collection of insects and invited the boy to visit. John followed up the offer. The artist showed the boy how to make a net and gave him some rare insects. This was just the impetus the budding entomologist needed. John immediately bought a net and studied how to better tend his growing collection.

Mr. Abbot encouraged his son's artistic talents by hiring an engraver and drawing master named Bonneau to give John lessons. The tutor did not paint watercolors, but he had a sublime grasp of drawing and, significantly, he recognized potential. Bonneau was acquainted with Mr. Rice, a grammar teacher who collected insects. Rice, through the insect connection, knew Dru Drury. Drury was to insect collectors as Peter Collinson was to plant enthusiasts, a wealthy devotee and sponsor.

Rice introduced young John Abbot to the illustrious man on Bonneau's recommendation. As past president of the Linnean Society, Drury possessed the best English and foreign insect collections. Abbot was agog at the sight of impressively constructed cabinets housing rows of drawers in which butterflies, moths, and beetles were neatly pinned in regiments standing forever at attention. For his part, Drury saw that Bonneau's assessment of the child had been on the mark and immediately loaned the boy some specimens to draw. It was the beginning of a mutually beneficial friendship.

John must have been giddy from the accolades generated by his drawings and knowledge during the meeting. And he had been encouraged to enlarge his studies. He ordered a mahogany cabinet containing twenty-six drawers, protected by sliding glass covers and betook his net to the woods and hedgerows with renewed fervency. He was drawn to winged and crawling creatures, and readily admitted that he was not fond of strangers unless they shared his interests.

During his teenage years, John honed his skills in capturing, mounting, and drawing insects. One day a young man named Smeathman knocked at the Abbots' door. He had heard through Rice that Abbot was a fellow "flycatcher." John found Smeathman's knowledge to be worthy and bought an English Purple Emperor butterfly from the young collector.

A box of insects from Surinam increased Abbot's personal collection, but it was not enough. For young John, insects were a wondrous array of gems from around the world. He could buy insects from different countries, but wouldn't it be grand to see those places and collect the creatures himself, as his friend Smeathman was doing in Africa?

By this point in his life, John had met a measure of success selling specimens he had collected around London, and his drawings had garnered praise. It was, however, time to think of the future and in 1769 John dutifully joined his father's office as clerk for five years. The young man diligently learned law; his family expected him to follow that staid profession. He recognized his addiction to insect study, but he was not given to rash decisions and bided his time while thinking of choosing a different path.

While following his father's occupation, Abbot continued his avocation. As an artist, he ground pigments and mixed paint, experimenting with recipes to achieve the proper coloration for butterflies and beetles, animals known for their iridescence. Abbot's beetles fairly glow from the page. He did not confine himself strictly to insects, however, but was willing to catch and draw whatever his customers requested. Abbot yearned to follow his heart, and his heart would lead him far from home.

Receiving a gift of Catesby's *Natural History* only whetted Abbot's desire. Virginia's green country and interesting creatures, seen only in books and paintings, were an irresistible attraction. When London's Royal Society asked Abbot to collect natural history specimens in Virginia in 1773, he accepted. His escapade was about to begin. His parents' reaction to his decision is not known. They may have attempted to dissuade their oldest son, but in the end they acquiesced to his wishes. Perhaps they thought John would be gone only a year or so.

How unlike John Bartram's reaction to his son's desires. The elder Bartram, while proud of William's botanical abilities, pushed his son into the world of commerce and trade where he was destined to fail. Had Dr. Fothergill not thrown a despondent Billy Bartram the lifeline which enabled him to cut loose from his father's intruding personality and wander the south for four years, we might not remember William Bartram. Had John Abbot and his wife forbidden their son to go to America and forced him to follow law, today we would probably know nothing of John Abbot, the collector and artist. William Bartram arrived in Charleston on March 31, 1773, on the eve of his great adventure, just as John Abbot was making ready to leave England for his own American odyssey.

In the months before departure, John set about liquidating his large cabinet and drawings. He commissioned smaller cabinets and amassed paper, pigments, and other tools of his trade. He booked passage on the *Royal Exchange,* which was to sail in April, but the ship was undergoing repairs and did not sail until July. Abbot earned extra money by drawing seashells while he waited for the sailing day.

Just before the parting date, Abbot sent his baggage ahead. On the morning of the expected day, John inquired for the boarding time only to find that the ship was already floating down the Thames. With no time to lose, Abbot hired a chaise and with his family sped away to meet the ship at Deal, the last stop before entering the Strait of Dover and the English Channel.

Breathing a sigh of relief, they saw the vessel lying offshore. Abbot quickly took leave of his family, not wanting to chance being truly left behind. His mother cried and his father probably offered emotional words of encouragement. Abbot's younger brother, Tommy, aged seven, excited at his brother's prospective adventures, announced, "he was sorry I was going to leave him, but hang him if he cou'd Cry."[1]

As luck would have it, the *Royal Exchange* did not sail for another three days and though others went ashore, John stuck to the ship. Parke and Mary Goodall were among the eight other cabin passengers on board. Goodall was American, his wife was English, and they were also bound for Virginia. Finally the ship weighed anchor and set sail. As England's coast slipped past, John's parting pangs were eased by his new friends and his excitement over this adventure. As far as can be determined, he never saw England or his immediate family again.

A strong friendship grew between Abbot and the Goodalls during the six-week voyage. The *Royal Exchange* anchored in the James River in early September 1773. Dru Drury had furnished John with a letter of recommendation to a minister in Dinwiddee County, but the young artist decided to board with the Goodalls. Abbot spent two years in Virginia, escaping serious illness, though many were not so lucky. Otherwise, his early years on American soil were disappointing as he did not find the expected variety of insects. Nonetheless, Abbot gathered what he could and saw the packages bound for England, only to hear that the ship was lost.

By 1775, a charged atmosphere lay over Virginia. John was an Englishman residing in a British colony, but it was a country in transition. Politics aside, John's nature was given to peace and he did not wish to choose sides. He must have felt ambivalent about making a decision to leave or stay. If he returned to England, he would surely be expected to give up the insect business and become a lawyer. If he stayed in America, even though he had not achieved his expected success, at least he was engaged in a fascinating career. At last he decided to return to England, but was unable to find passage. One wonders if the irony ever struck him—that he almost missed his passage to America and after two years in Virginia he was stymied in his small effort to return to England.

The day approached when trade with Great Britain would cease. Abbot packed another box of insects, but, again, the ship was lost in a storm soon after putting to sea. Only one of the three known shipments he sent from Virginia ever reached England. This must have been discouraging. It would be difficult to earn his living selling specimens when ships could not last the crossing.

During his Virginia residency, John struck up a friendship with William Goodall, Parke Goodall's cousin. Hearing that Georgia had not yet joined the other colonies in tearing from England, John and the William Goodall family decided to move to the most southern colony. Abbot must have been anxious to leave. He may have had a continued stipend from his family, for he bought the horses and paid for all expenses involving the move to Georgia. He bade a sad farewell to Parke and Mary Goodall and the small party was on its way.

They left in early December 1775, encountered snow and ice, and spent a few days here and there with Goodall's relatives and friends. The overland trip took almost two months. After reaching their destination, they lodged with William Moore, Goodall's brother-in-law, who lived about thirty miles south of Augusta, until a house could be built for them. Abbot ended his notes at that point with a few intriguing words: "the first Years of my living in Georgia, contains much more of Adventure, than the former part of my life, and continued through such bad & terrible time, that I often reflect, upon the goodness of providence, in bringing me safely through them."[2] One wonders just what experiences Abbot faced and what his feelings were as he watched his adopted country wrest itself from the country of his birth.

Judging from the tightly worded account of his early life, it is clear that John was expert at uniting his thoughts. Knowledge of the law may have helped him arrange his contemplations. Though law is not known for practicing an economy of language, this trait stood him well in his future as a student of natural history.

Abbot's steadfast friend, Augustus Oemler, wrung the "Notes" from Abbot. Oemler wanted recognition for his friend, though Abbot appears not to have shared any enthusiasm for the spotlight. In a letter to Dr. T. W. Harris, written on April 27, 1834, Oemler wrote: "I have prevailed on him to furnish me with some notes. I am satisfied that justice be done him, no matter by whom, and as I consider *you* more capable than myself, I surrender these Notes into your hands. They are, as you will perceive, not concluded yet—I will send you the continuation and any thing else desirable that can be procured by me."[3] Perhaps more letters may one day turn up in a forgotten musty trunk.

Abbot had arrived in Georgia in February 1776, and settled near Augusta. William Bartram, unwilling to leave the South just yet, had cut across Georgia toward Augusta in January 1776. The rest of the country headed for war, but these two men, both artists and naturalists, headed toward each other. Bartram spent that spring and summer in Georgia, preparing his last shipment to Dr. Fothergill, which was sent from Savannah. Abbot sent all his orders from Savannah, and surely by the summer of 1776 he would have been filling customers' requests. Did the two men ever meet, pass each other unknowingly on the street, frequent the same shops? It was entirely possible and likely, though we can never know.

I VENTURED INTO MOSS-DRAPED, tidily squared Savannah in early March 1999. My first stop was to meet Dr. Vivian Rogers-Price, a soft-spoken woman who had become intrigued with Abbot after viewing an exhibition of his paintings. He became the subject of her dissertation, and she has spent hours searching fragile records, deciphering faded, spidery writing. We met at a restaurant on a sunny, windy day. Vivian was accompanied by her youngest daughter, who had felt ill, but perked up enough to polish off a gooey dessert. Ah, the resilience of children. Over salads, I asked Vivian to describe Abbot for me—not his appearance, but his personality.

She spoke with the assurance of someone describing a well-known friend. He was a self-effacing man, not given to airs, quiet, keeping to himself and a small circle of loyal friends, she thought.

"What about his military service and those other rumors surrounding him?" I asked.

It was once thought that Abbot returned to England about 1810. Biographers deduced that Abbot was English from his name, though he was thought to have fought on America's side in the Revolution. From the few writings he left behind they also felt he was poorly educated and unable to construct a complete sentence. Spelling and punctuation, however, were not yet bound by rules; even well-educated people practiced creative spelling and sentences straggled on at length. Before the letters written to Oemler were discovered neither the date of Abbot's birth nor when he came to America were known.

"He was quite a peaceful man," Vivian explained. "My goodness, he left Virginia to avoid conflict, why would he join the fight in Georgia? Another man named John Abbot received a sizable land grant for his service in the Revolutionary War and that led people to believe that Abbot fought in the Revolution. But that other man signed the papers with an 'X' indicating illiteracy. John Abbot was perfectly capable of signing his name."

We could have talked the afternoon away, but Vivian had to take another daughter to an afternoon dancing lesson. She furnished directions to the once-vibrant settlement of Ebenezer, where she was sure Abbot had collected specimens and, since it was almost on her way home, she detoured a few miles to show me the less-traveled route to the Savannah National Wildlife Refuge, actually in South Carolina. Unfortunately, the lower bridge was closed for repairs and it was too late in the day to take a much longer route to the refuge, so we could only gaze across the river. Abbot and Alexander Wilson had probably collected in those marshes. They might have scouted the shore from a boat, but surely they beached the craft and stepped onto the mucky land, assaulted by no-see-ums and mosquitoes, up to their knees in mud, wet, hot, filthy, but having a perfectly wonderful time as colorful flocks of birds, busily stalking insects and crustaceans, leapt into the air at the men's approach.

Abbot wrote scrupulous notes about the creatures he studied, but was somewhat vague when it came to his collecting locations—"taken in damp places of yards and edges of water in open ground," for example; "frequents sand islands and salts near Savannah"; "taken off the coast of Savannah"; "taken at night." It was difficult to pair Abbot with a specific place. But he had collected at Ebenezer, so to Ebenezer I went. Along the way, a kind motorist informed me that one of the van's tail lights was out. A worry and an annoyance.

Ebenezer is not far from Savannah, but after turning onto a side road, I saw few cars. Lutheran Salzburgers founded Ebenezer in 1734. The townsfolk commenced silk production in 1736 and even though the industry declined in other parts of the country, the Salzburgers persevered until the American Revolution. Ebenezer embraces a bend in the Savannah River and was a thriving community when the war for American independence began. Continental troops fortified the town in 1776, but it was captured by the British on February 2, 1779, and held until 1782. Citizens suffered under British occupation. On the first Tuesday in July 1782, Georgia's legislature assembled in Ebenezer and it was for a short time the state's capital.

A museum, a church, and a few restored buildings are all that remain of Ebenezer. It is literally at the end of the road and a perfect site for a Lutheran Retreat which blends into the woods across the street from the church and museum buildings. There were a few parked cars, but no people. I walked past the church and peered in the museum's windows. It was not open that day. Following the land's slope, tiers of bleachers nestled in a depression leading to the river and a split rail fence posed a barrier along the high bank's edge. The river slipped below with a soft slooshing sound, freed from upstream dams and hurrying to join the sea at last.

Leaning on the rough wooden fence, I closed my eyes and drew deeply the breath of crisp pine needles, a muted cinnamon bouquet. Myrtle warblers flitted through the underbrush. The howl of a passing jet disturbed the quiet and then was gone. I could have been transported back into Abbot's time. Against closed eyelids I pasted an image of the wooded lower floodplain on the other side of the river. In my mind's eye, a shadow danced through the woods, then a short, rough-clothed man suddenly emerged holding a large net in one hand. Cradling the net in the crook of his arm, he reached deep inside it and withdrew something that he examined closely. Satisfied, he placed the tiny creature into a stoppered jar and added it to a bulky canvas bag slung across his back. He looked across the river and waved at someone I could not see. Then he turned toward the woods and cocked his head as he listened for the minute scuffling of beetles under dry leaves. A sound must have come to him for he briskly stepped into the timber and disappeared from view.

I opened my eyes and nothing had changed, but I was sure there would be footprints in the mud across the river. Afternoon was deepening and it was time to head into Savannah, just in time for the five o'clock rush. I went to the back of the van to get a fortifying Coke from the cooler. That's when the latch to the van's back door broke. Not being able to get into the back was a major inconvenience and I added another item to the repair list.

FIG. 7. Looking across the Savannah River from old Ebenezer where
the Bartrams, Abbot, André and François Michaux, and other
naturalists searched for birds, insects, and plants.
Photo by author.

John and William Bartram had passed by here in 1765 so that John
could observe the silk operation, and I stopped to read the historical
marker that explains their visit to the town. William came through in
1774, looking for the slender tree he and his father had found in 1765, and
collected seeds from the *Franklinia.*

I returned to the van and found that the starter had problems. What
next? With a credit card and a cell phone, I could call for a tow and
charge the repairs if necessary. I would lose some time, inconvenient—
but trifling compared to the hazards faced by early explorers.

It has been decades since I was in Savannah, and even with a city map,
I trusted luck to lead me across town to Skidaway Island State Park, which
was closed by the time I arrived. Several large RVs were ensconced at the
campground, but I found a secluded site. After rearranging the van's interior to make kitchen items accessible, I settled in with a bottle of cool
water at a surprisingly unscarred picnic table to write notes. Immediately,
no-see-ums and mosquitoes homed in on my arms and legs. Long pants,
socks, and a long-sleeved shirt discouraged their efforts. They were both-
ersome, but not so many that they interfered with my work.

Squirrels chased each other through the red bay, live oak, wild olive, sweet gum, and magnolia trees. Stiff palmetto fans formed the undergrowth and thready pines strained to rise above the canopy. The woods were still in their winter doldrums, but in a few weeks new leaves and buds would be sprouting. Darkness and chilled air drove annoying mosquitoes away and me into the van. The warm bed felt good after a long day and I slept peacefully, waking briefly when the bright full moon rose. Dawn came too soon and a hot shower felt good in the sharp-aired morning. Coffee and a granola bar served as breakfast while I gave the map one last look. Time to check out and head for the Georgia Historical Society.

The Society was chartered in 1839 and is housed in ivory-hued Hodgson Hall, built for the Society in 1875, on the corner of Whitaker and Gaston Streets. A broad stairway leads to the entrance doors. The main room is tastefully grand, with high vaulted ceilings, decorative ironwork, and polished woodwork. The decor alone, seasoned with the fragrance of time, would draw anyone into history's alluring maze. A helpful staff person explained their research procedures. Warm oak cabinets held orderly typed cards, their edges worn to velvet by hundreds of searching fingers. Thankfully, they were not on some impersonal computer screen!

Several people bent over books and looked through references and at one point the room was almost full. Somehow the appointments absorbed noise and only murmurs shuffled around the room. I listed several documents and a staff person fetched them. The Society holds an impressive map inventory, but I did not have time to look at them. I had hoped to be gone by noon, but it was after 2:00 P.M. before I could break away.

Interstate 16 begins just a few blocks from the Society and I was soon speeding toward the rural spot where Abbot is buried in a private family plot on the McElveen plantation. Almost every article about Abbot mentions that he is buried there, but none gives directions. Searching online historical societies and posting information requests had led to Smith Banks, who provided Mrs. McElveen's address and phone number. I had arranged for an afternoon visit and didn't want to be too late. Since the site is located on private property, I won't give directions either.

While driving, I thought about Abbot the person. He was brave to have gone against his parents' plans and they had the good sense not to force him into a life he did not want. He lived through a time of great strife, when it would have been easy to become swept up in a fever of loyalty to one side or the other. But Abbot avoided that pitfall and kept to the course for which he was best suited.

By 1777, Abbot was established in Burke County. Georgia had finally joined in the fight for American independence, and though it was probably dangerous to be about in the country, especially since his voice marked his British birth, Abbot had continued limited collecting and also increased his breeding program. Most customers wanted adult specimens, but John needed all the stages of an insect's life for his drawings and notes. In order to successfully breed the animals, Abbot had learned the proper plants required for their food and shelter.

Customers usually provided cork-lined shipping boxes, and Abbot had to carefully pin and arrange the creatures, as damaged animals would not be paid for. Abbot achieved a reputation for expert packaging. His livelihood depended upon his ability to fulfill his customers' requests. If paintings were to be shipped with specimens, he removed the cork linings, inserted the papers, and restored the linings. Not only were the paintings protected, but also hidden from customs officials. Abbot's customers rarely paid duty fees. The boxes were covered with packing material and wrapped in a tar soaked cloth to prevent condensation and water damage.

His earliest set of bird illustrations was sent to his London agent, John Francillon. The only work to bear Abbot's name, *The Natural History of the Rarer Lepidopterous Insects of Georgia,* was published by James E. Smith in 1797. It was mistakenly thought that Abbot did not know of its publication until years later, but the Archives of the Linnean Society contain the manuscript Abbot sent to Smith. Abbot knew of the book, but left the worry of seeing it published to Smith. The volume was well received though not a financial success.

Many of his paintings feature insects stiffly posed, as if mounted in a glass display case. At some point Abbot began to paint insects associated with the plants they depended upon. Admittedly, he did not know botany; Oemler encouraged him to study that science. As he progressed, the plants became as meticulously drawn and colored as the insects. Abbot was one of the earliest entomologists to couple the life cycles of insects with their specific plants, but he did not think of himself as a true entomologist. He was unfamiliar with Linnaeus's system until Oemler explained it to him and he rarely assigned a scientific name, letting those more qualified classify his specimens.

John Abbot married Sarah Warren in 1779 and she bore one son, also named John. In 1784, John applied for a grant of two hundred acres in Burke County, which he received in 1789. With a family to support, Abbot took up teaching for a short time, possibly at Burke County Academy near Waynesboro, and he invested a small sum in a cotton plantation. Now a family man and landowner, John Abbot had entrenched himself in his adopted country. As far as can be determined, he never returned to England though he did correspond with his family there.

For the remainder of his life, Abbot confined his collecting sites to a limited area of the coastal plain between Augusta and Savannah. He favored the Ogeechee River and Briar Creek watersheds and roamed upland pine forests, the shallows of coastal Savannah, and the charm of barrier islands, called the Golden Isles by Spanish explorers, protecting Georgia's coast. Many of the islands are now protected by state and federal ownership. Fertile marshes and estuaries lying behind the islands produce a prodigious amount of small marine life which, in turn, attracts a great variety of birds—herons, egrets, ibises, pelicans, ducks.

The distance between Burke County and Savannah is not great by car, but Abbot must have traveled on horseback or by buggy, camping out or accepting hospitality from scattered homesteads. Most of his work, however, was done on foot, peering into thickets, examining leaves and stems, searching the shallows along riverbanks and tidal marshes.

After America's independence was secured and the Georgia Colony firmly established, more settlers arrived. Farmers began draining swampy areas and clearing land for crops. Abbot noted declining avian populations and predicted that if the practices continued, birds and insects would become rarer.

In 1809, Alexander Wilson, in Savannah selling subscriptions and gathering information for his monumental *American Ornithology,* wrote to William Bartram, "There is a Mr. Abbot here, who has resided in Georgia thirty-three years, drawing insects and birds. I have been on several excursions with him. He is a very good observer and paints well."[4]

Pamela Gilbert, in *John Abbot, Birds, Butterflies, and Other Wonders,* states that Joseph Prentice, who also supplied Wilson with ornithological information and subscribed to his *American Ornithology,* steered the Scotsman to the man who knew more about the region's birds than anyone else—John Abbot. Abbot was happy to oblige. He accompanied Wilson to the best spots and helped him identify southern birds with

FIG. 8. Cotton plant and life cycle of the cotton moth by John Abbot.
Courtesy of Georgia Historical Society.

which Wilson was unfamiliar. Others have said it was Thomas Jefferson who pointed Wilson toward the insect collector. Whoever was responsible for the match, or whether it was a chance meeting, cannot be known for a certainty. Records are too scattered and lost.

Abbot continued corresponding and sending specimens north after Wilson returned to Pennsylvania. To his credit, Wilson generously acknowledged Abbot's contributions to *American Ornithology.* After Wilson died, Abbot continued to send specimens to George Ord, who completed the last two volumes of Wilson's project.

Soon after America declared war on Great Britain in 1812, Abbot retired from studying natural history. He had weathered the Revolution, but at age sixty-one had little patience for another war. He wrote to George Ord, "I have entirely laid it aside, and entered into another line of employment, where I am in hopes the mad and destructive ambition of the rulers of the world can but little interfere."[5] No one knows what his other employment might have been, though it is possible he turned to teaching again. Oemler and LeConte convinced him to return to his first love, collecting and painting insects and birds.

John Abbot, Jr., had attempted a variety of employments, variously listed as a merchant, slave trader, and attorney. Whatever business schemes he tried, the younger Abbot seems to have been something of a wastrel. He defaulted on his taxes in 1808 and his business dissolved. He married Eliza Rawls in 1812, and bought property that he later mortgaged to secure a large financial obligation. The mortgage was eventually paid, and in 1819, his father was a witness at John's debt trial. Abbot may have brought himself close to financial ruin by bailing out his son, but what else would a father do? John Abbot, Jr., died of a liver complaint in 1826, leaving his wife and no children. Abbot gave his daughter-in-law some slaves and probably some money, but she seems to have been little help to her father-in-law, who was then left alone in his old age. Sarah Abbot had died in 1817.

Now that he was growing older, and according to Oemler, had become heavy and less agile, Abbot hired youngsters to chase butterflies. He sent boxes containing 670 insects and about 650 drawings to William Swainson in 1835. He charged $6.00 per hundred insects, large and small, rare or common. William McElveen, Abbot's good friend, built a small cabin at the edge of a pasture dubbed Hudler's field for the elderly entomologist. Abbot's slave, Betsey, cared for him, and the old man continued working until his death in 1840. He left everything to William McElveen and was buried in an unmarked grave in the family burying ground. In 1957, a historical marker bearing his bronze likeness was placed in the cemetery.

When Oemler learned of his friend's death, he set out for the McElveens. Oemler offered to buy his friend's papers at any price, but was told that the "children had used all up."[6] If the McElveens managed to salvage anything, the house later burned and all was truly lost.

Thousands of insects and uncountable drawings passed through Abbot's hands during his lifetime. The specimens have been incorporated into larger collections and it is impossible to ascertain which might have been Abbot's. His artwork is scattered throughout the world, mostly in America and England.

Lost in thought, I almost passed the exit. Mrs. McElveen had given the kind of directions you give when you know exactly where you are going, and assume the person to whom you are giving the directions also knows. Fortunately, the exit, though not far from Savannah, was in a rural area and her directions were much easier to follow than I had expected. In Abbot's time, the McElveens owned a modest plantation. Perhaps it was the same plantation in which John had, in more prosperous times, invested some money.

Unlike many other families, the McElveens did not lose their land after the Civil War, but it has since been divided several times over among descendants, and parts have been sold off. At some point, the land probably supported longleaf pine and wiregrass. By Abbot's time the land was in a continuous process of succession: woodlands were being cleared for fresh fields just as loblolly pines sprouted in worn-out pastures. Now a few acres of shrubby woods alternated between newly planted crops. It was early spring, and many farmers were burning the previous season's stubble before plowing their fields for the year's planting. Some rural residents burned around the perimeter of their homes, clearing underbrush and enriching the soil. The air was smudged with the scent and shadow of smoke.

I drove into the sandy yard of an unpretentious home and knocked on the door. People drive up all the time to visit Abbot's grave, Mrs. McElveen had told me; sometimes the unannounced visits made her nervous. She soon answered the door and invited me inside to see a copy of one of Abbot's prints. Then we walked the short path to the family cemetery in a wooded copse just a few steps from her front door. A rusted iron fence, bent in places from fallen limbs, encloses the graves. Some markers have disappeared and depressions outside the fence reveal unmarked graves. No McElveen has been buried there in almost a century. The cemetery was not as overgrown as Mrs. McElveen had feared it might be. Winter had knocked the stuffing out of some plants, but they would begin growing again as spring progressed. We picked up some fallen branches. She worried about vines and shrubs taking over the graves, and mentioned she'd like to straighten and paint the fence. All her children have moved away and there is no one to help her care for the grounds.

Surviving records show that Abbot's family lived in the town of Jacksonboro, south of Augusta, for a long time. Most of those years were probably spent in relative comfort. When Georgia's original eight counties split, Jacksonboro had dwindled until it became only a memory. Burke County's courthouse burned several years ago and many papers that could have added to our meager knowledge about the English entomologist are gone.

Like Oemler, I want recognition for John Abbot. He was not brash like Audubon or ambitious like Wilson, and he distanced himself from a hub of scientific knowledge and discussion. Abbot painted and was familiar with several birds that were later described by others who accepted credit for their discovery. John Latham, English ornithologist, used Abbot's work to describe the LeConte sparrow, the swamp sparrow, and the barred owl, and Carl Illiger, of Berlin University, used Abbot's specimens in describing Bachman's sparrow, the sedge wren, and the golden-crowned kinglet. Abbot made significant contributions to Alexander Wilson's *Ornithology.* Most importantly, John Abbot's studies and paintings of insects and birds laid a baseline for those who came later. I don't think he realized the treasures he left behind, but as long as we share history, he will not be forgotten.

CHAPTER 6

The Lovely Face of Nature

Alexander Wilson
(July 6, 1766–August 23, 1813)

The general features of North Carolina, where I crossed it, are immense, solitary, pine savannahs, through which the road winds among stagnant ponds, swarming with alligators; sluggish creeks, of the colour of brandy, over which are thrown high wooden bridges, without railings, and so crazy and rotten as not only to alarm the horse, but his rider, and to make it a matter of thanksgiving with both when they get fairly over, without going through or being precipitated into the gulf below as food for the alligators. Enormous cypress swamps, which, to a stranger, have a striking, desolate, and ruinous appearance. Picture to yourself a forest of prodigious trees, rising, as thick as they can grow, from a vast flat and impenetrable morass, covered for ten feet from the ground with reeds. The leafless limbs of the cypresses are clothed with an extraordinary kind of moss, from two to 10 feet long, in such quantities that 50 men might conceal themselves in one tree.

—From Alexander Wilson's letter to Daniel H. Miller from
Charleston, February 22, 1809

"I HAVE HARDLY LEFT THE HOUSE HALF-AN-HOUR; and I long most ardently to breathe once more the fresh air of the country, and gaze on the lovely face of Nature."[1] Alexander Wilson wrote those disconsolate words to William Bartram on April 21, 1813. The Scotsman had been toiling night and day on the seventh volume of his *American Ornithology.* In his lifetime, Alexander Wilson had been a weaver, peddler, poet, teacher, author, musician, and artist, and he would come to be remembered as the Father of American Ornithology.

Others have been draped with that mantle: John Lawson, Mark Catesby, and William Bartram. Each made a significant contribution to the knowledge of ornithology, but no man deserved it more than Wilson. After almost forty years of trying to find his niche in the world, Wilson pursued America's birds—their habits, their movements, their lives. He brought to the study a perseverance and thoroughness not exhibited by anyone up to that point.

Alexander Wilson was born July 6, 1766, in Paisley, Scotland. His father, Alexander Wilson, Sr., nicknamed Saunders, was a former smuggler who had given up that tantalizing trade for legal employment as a weaver to please his wife. Paisley was one of Scotland's fast-growing towns and one of Great Britain's first manufacturing centers. Weavers wore fashionable styles made of cloth woven from their own designs, and they organized societies based on their common interests: hunting, fishing, literature, and, of course, golf.

Young Alexander, or Sannie as his family called him, grew to be a lighthearted lad tinged with sensitivity and given to deep reflection. He enjoyed the outdoors and was quick to learn. His parents groomed him for the ministry, but he never wanted that profession for himself.

Paisley was a prosperous town during Sannie's childhood, but America's Revolution reverberated through its financial stability. Seventeen seventy-six was also a tumultuous year for the Wilson family. Mrs. Wilson died of tuberculosis and Saunders returned to smuggling. On Sannie's tenth birthday, July 6, 1776, Saunders married Catherine Brown.

Family life changed drastically for Sannie. All thoughts of the ministry were dropped, as was schooling of any kind. Worse yet, he was sent out as a herd boy to a farm a dozen miles from his home. Did the new Mrs. Wilson banish the boy? Maybe. She was already expecting a child when she married Saunders. Life might have been less complicated with the youngster out of the way. The boy missed his mother and sudden expulsion couldn't have been easy for him.

Fences were uncommon at the time, and the herd boy's duty was to keep cattle from straying into cultivated fields. Sannie's charges often found their way into the corn rows as he forever had his nose in a book or lay against a mossy rock watching the sky, oblivious to the animals. At age thirteen he returned home and apprenticed as weaver to his sister Mary's new husband, William Duncan. The Duncan's first son, also named William, had just been born.

As Sannie's apprenticeship ended, Saunders Wilson found himself ostracized by the town, for the tenor of the times had changed and smuggling was no longer looked upon with a benign eye. Saunders moved his family from place to place, settling at last in the Tower of Auchinbathie at Lochwinnoch. The imposing tower was a remnant of one of Scotland's oldest castles, once home to the country's greatest hero, William Wallace, and offered an unimpaired view of the countryside. A plus for one involved in illegal trade.

Land around Auchinbathie was owned by Colonel William M'Dowell. Unlike others of his class, the colonel was indifferent to trespassing and poaching on his land. Sannie spent many hours roaming the great estate, hunting game, exalting in the forests and glens. He was charmed by each new discovery and developed the deep curiosity that would define his ornithological career. Sannie began writing poetry, hoping it would lead to a respectable life far from the loom. M'Dowell grew fond of the boy and supported his poetry.

The young poet worked as a journeyman weaver in Lochwinnoch for a short time, but a youthful fling with a young girl employed in the household ended in his being banished from home again. He found a position in Paisley and discovered kindred spirits in the well-read weavers. David Brodie remained Wilson's lifelong friend and encouraged his comrade's poetry. Alexander had difficulty finding his own voice, tending to write in the style of his favorite poet of the moment. In 1786, Robert Burns's first book of poetry was published and, written in the earthy Scots dialect, set the literary world on its ear. Many emulated Burns but few attained his popularity. Wilson admired Burns and reportedly tried to meet him, but probably never did.

Restless and disappointed over his failure to attain success and acceptance through poetry, Wilson took to the road with packs of cloth on his back, traveling far afoot to sell what he could, free from the demands of weaving. He published a volume of his own poetry in 1790. Two hundred copies sold, but Alexander felt the book a failure. The youthful silk peddler had no educational advantages other than his own inclination to learn. Despite his humble beginning, Alexander Wilson wanted more for himself. He loved his father and had come to accept Kate as his stepmother, but he must have felt the town's disapproval of his father's chosen profession. Pushing cloth by day and writing poems at night, he tramped the countryside, frustrated at his inability to gain success. The salesman was drawn to a Paisley lass, Martha M'Lean. Wilson could not yet provide for a wife but expressed his longing in romantic stanzas. About this time he began work on a comic verse, *Watty and Meg*.

The French Revolution erupted in July 1789, and it was not long before the winds of reform were blowing over Scotland. Some mill owners were suspected of deliberately shortening the measurements of cloth, thereby cheating the weavers, who soon demanded change. Wilson wrote a poem in 1790 entitled "The Hollander," a thinly disguised attack on a local mill owner for unfair practices. The man called for Wilson's arrest, but Wilson was away collecting subscriptions for his book of poetry. When he returned the sheriff was waiting, but Wilson was ill with a chest inflammation and remained at home cared for by his family. Fortunately the court was lenient and the matter quietly faded away.

In the spring of 1792, William Sharp, owner of Long's Mill, received a copy of a derogatory poem entitled *The Shark, or Lang Mills Detected* along with an anonymous letter demanding money. Sharp was certain Wilson had written the poem. As soon as the weaver returned from an errand in Glasgow, he was arrested and brought before Paisley's sheriff. When shown the letter and poem he readily admitted he had written them, but denied being the author, implying that he had either copied them or written them while someone else dictated the words.

A new law against seditious writing had recently been enacted. Those found guilty could be expelled to a penal colony or put to death. *The Shark* was considered seditious. Wilson was out of jail when ordered to appear and pay a fine and damages to Mr. Sharp. For some reason, he was not present at the hearing and was again arrested and charged with contempt. The case dragged and Wilson was set free once more. He wandered the countryside, for he felt himself a pariah in Paisley. *Watty and Meg* was published anonymously and hawkers attributed it to Burns. Of course, his relationship with Martha had been terminated.

Months crept by. The poet was back in jail and ordered to publicly burn copies of *The Shark* and write a letter to Mr. Sharp. Wilson burned the poems and refused to write the letter. Out of jail again, he set off on a peddling trip and reflected on his bleak future. He had survived two run-ins with the law and his poetry was not a roaring success. He decided to emigrate to America and bury the past. Wilson's sixteen-year-old nephew, William Duncan, also elected to go. Alexander Wilson never returned to Scotland.

His ship had cast off from Belfast Loch on May 23, 1794, and coasted through unremarkable seas until she picked her way through a flotilla of ice islands on June 18 and 19. Wilson counted thirty-four, several more than twice as tall as the ship's main mast. Strong storms and fog roiled the waters for the next week or so. During the entire trip an old woman and two children were buried at sea; two sailors drowned, one just as the ship reached Delaware. Wilson had not told his parents of his plans and his first letter to them began with apologies; he had not wanted to worry them, but feared he had caused more concern than ever. He went on to recount the voyage and asked that letters be sent to him at a Philadelphia bookseller.

Finding small demand for weavers in Wilmington, the pair made their way to Philadelphia. Yellow fever had killed 4,044 Philadelphians in 1793 and residents had swarmed away from the city to escape the disease; they were just returning and the town was booming. Wilson found employment at an engraving shop, a trade about which he knew nothing. Homesickness settled on the Scotsman and he and Duncan traded Philadelphia for a smaller community, where they were hired as weavers once again.

Soon, Alexander was off on selling trips. When he tired of those, he found a teaching position. Teachers being in short supply, scant attention was given to qualifications; Wilson had to study to keep up with his students. He liked teaching more than weaving and he enjoyed learning much more than he liked teaching. In 1796, the former weaver moved to a school at Milestown, Pennsylvania, and remained there for five years.

While in Milestown, Wilson boarded with a family and kept to himself, walking in the nearby woods every morning and afternoon. The teacher sought the woods when he could, for his pensive soul had always found nature a ready companion. Evenings were devoted to studying math and American history.

Pennsylvania's changing seasons were defined by the passages of birds. Great clouds of ducks on their way south heralded fall. First to alight were blue-winged teal, followed by geese, canvasback, buffle-heads, mallards, widgeon, and pintail. Wilson hunted at Duck Island, entranced by the variety of birds. After cold, confining winters, spring fever hit hard and it seemed more of an ordeal for the teacher to remain in the classroom than for the students. Choruses of bird songs floated through the schoolhouse windows and their brilliant colors flashed through the trees as they performed courtship rites and defended their territory.

By 1798 or 1799, Wilson, slowly emerging from his self-imposed exile, became attracted to a young woman named Sarah Miller, daughter of a property owner of local standing. Wilson remained aloof when two Scots immigrants, Charles Orr and Alexander Lawson, tried to establish friendships. In a few months, however, he renewed contact with the two men and began openly to court Sarah. The poet in Wilson wrote to Orr of his romance, but he was poor and possessed no social standing and could not commit himself to the young woman.

Another yellow fever outbreak hit Philadelphia in 1798 and everyone who could, left the city. Wilson heard of rich land for sale between lakes Seneca and Cayuga in New York State's Finger Lakes region. Cayuga and Seneca are the largest and deepest of the glacially formed lakes. Their waters could be rough and inhospitable, the surrounding landscape marvelous, intimidating. Cold winds swirled across fields except for a few precious warm days each year. Duncan set out on foot for the area and returned to describe the land as the richest he had ever seen, full of deer, bear, turkeys, and all sorts of waterfowl. The choicest plot was five dollars per acre and Wilson determined to buy 150 acres on the edge of Seneca Lake not far from the town of Ovid, New York. Duncan moved to the property, built a small cabin, and began clearing the land. It was hard work and winter was achingly long. Wilson held onto his teaching position for steady income. Duncan opened a distillery to augment their finances.

By 1799, Wilson had tired of teaching and wanted to assist his nephew on the farm. He resigned, but school trustees did not want to lose their teacher and counter offered. Wilson agreed to remain another year. Thomas Jefferson was elected President of the United States and Wilson, already a Jefferson admirer, was asked to make an inaugural day speech at a Milestown patriotic meeting. His oration was a success and, at last, he felt he had earned respect and a good reputation. He regained his confidence and, in 1800, tried again to break from the school. Promises had not been kept. Repairs had not been made to the small schoolhouse, teachers were paid by the number of pupils but attendance was down, and he wanted time away. A prospective successor revealed he had made more at his previous school. Negotiations resulted in the trustees agreeing to repair and enlarge the school, increase Wilson's salary, and extend his vacation leave.

In the middle of 1801, the bottom dropped out of Wilson's secure life. On a dark night, he hastily left his lodgings, deserting his school and destroying in a few hours the good name he had built over five years. He wrote secretive, enigmatic letters to Orr, hinting at a love affair with a married woman, or it could have been the awful secret about his arrests in Scotland that had followed him across the sea. Whatever the reason, Wilson disappeared.

Losing himself in New York City, Wilson soon began teaching in Bloomfield, New Jersey. Despondent, he saw no one, only making clandestine demands on Orr and never returning to Milestown again. He could not earn enough in New Jersey and returned to Philadelphia in late 1801 or early 1802, contacted Orr, and received a chilly reception. Apprehensively, he agreed to a position at the Union School of Kingsessing, which paid more than he had ever received.

When he was not teaching, Wilson immersed himself in nature during periods of melancholia, and he was often given to melancholia. Streams bracketed Wilson's boarding house and he passed many hours perched on lichen-clothed rocks surrounded by birds and lost in deep, searching thoughts. The variety of avian sounds and colors impressed him as never before. He strolled the paths of a famous nearby refuge, for Bartram's garden lay just down the road. Many people wandered through the open garden, attracted by plants strange and familiar and by the kindly man who tended them. Wilson met William Bartram about this time. Perhaps their romantic souls and mutual appreciation of nature's beauty helped forge a bond.

A letter from Scotland arrived in the summer of 1802. At last, Wilson's brother-in-law, William Duncan, had decided to bring the rest of the family to America. Wilson hurried to the Ovid farm to share the news and help his nephew prepare. Working alongside young William restored Wilson's spirits. He hunted and made notes for future poems. However, the family did not appear and Wilson returned to Philadelphia to open school. There he found his sister Mary and six children. The elder Duncan had left ahead of his family and, unbeknownst to them, had stayed in Belfast while they boarded the ship for America. The Duncan marriage had not been good for years. William Duncan was shed of his family at last, for he had no intention of coming to America. Frantically, Wilson moved the family to the Ovid farm before winter set in.

All was not idyllic. Mary was dismayed at the rude cabin and the incarcerating winter. Wilson's nephew wanted to come back to Philadelphia and return to weaving; money was in short supply and his life had changed abruptly with the arrival of his family. He had lived a singular life for four years and suddenly he was surrounded by six siblings and his mother, suffering from uncertainty in a strange land and embittered at her husband's desertion. Wilson urged his nephew to stay on the farm and keep the family together. For his part, Wilson tutored night classes, sending every spare penny to the family in Ovid in a constant stream of encouraging letters meant to keep their spirits from flagging, drumming in the benefits of hard physical work gained in clearing land and sowing crops. Above all, he stressed education. By 1803, with the family settled, Wilson had begun sketching birds and wrote to a friend in Scotland of his intention to draw all of America's winged creatures. His plan was twofold. Not only would he relate all he could learn about birds' habits, he would paint their likeness in the greatest detail.

A small, brown owl, which Wilson had shot, stuffed, and mounted, was his first model. His initial artistic efforts were awkward. Attempts at drawing the owl made him realize that he needed help and he shyly approached Charles Willson Peale and William Bartram. Both men encouraged the teacher to continue drawing. Meanwhile, Meriwether Lewis came to Philadelphia in 1803 to prepare for his part in President Jefferson's great western expedition, and became acquainted with Wilson.

The art student spent his free time in Bartram's garden, discussing birds with William and practicing drawing. William's niece, Nancy, a fine artist in her own right, offered inspiration and advice. In March 1804, Wilson wrote to Alexander Lawson about his scheme of publishing his drawings and observations of America's birds, adding, "Now don't you to throw cold water."[2]

Lawson, of course, did. It would be difficult for a rich man to produce such a work, he replied. Engraving cost from $50 to $80 a plate; the copper for each plate alone cost $5.66. Coloring impressions by hand would cost twenty-five cents per page. The cost of printing five hundred copies of one hundred birds would amount to more than $500 for copper, $5,000 to $8,000 for engraving, and $12,500 for coloring, not to mention paper, binding, and printing. Was he off his head? But Wilson was supremely confident that he could complete the work and that it would be worthy.

Every spare minute went into drawing. A student provided a live mouse. Wilson intended to kill it and place it in the owl's talons for a more realistic picture, but first he leashed the trembling creature with a bit of string and set about drawing it, finding that it was more exciting to draw something living than dead. The frightened animal's heart beat furiously. Alexander spilled a few drops of water near it and the tiny creature lapped the liquid while looking pleadingly at Wilson. Wilson freed it. The finished drawing seemed more accomplished than that of a stuffed animal.

His students supplied a variety of active creatures. Instead of apples, the teacher received crows, hawks, owls, snakes, lizards, until the room resembled Noah's Ark. Wilson paid ten cents for each live bird, and that motivated students more than anything else, but they were delighted to be part of the project. Wilson felt the exhilaration that poetry had once stirred. During the years he spent compiling the *Ornithology,* periods of doubt intruded on his soaring confidence now and then, but he would not, could not fail again. America's birds would bring greatness.

Once he began serious attention to the project, little distracted him, but he did have one task to accomplish. After recessing school for the summer, Alexander Wilson renounced all fidelities to any foreign sovereign and became a United States citizen in June 1804.

William Duncan had been struggling on the Ovid farm for six years and needed a break from routine. Wilson needed to travel farther afield to find new species and proposed a vacation journey. William, Alexander, and a young friend named Isaac Leech set out from Philadelphia for Niagara Falls in October 1804.

They hunted and fed well on fat ducks and geese migrating southward, pheasant, and quail. Cougars snarled and wolves howled in the night and a bear snuffled across their path. They tramped through woods and fields, stopping at farmhouses that were becoming a common part of the landscape. One day a coiled rattlesnake blocked the track. Wilson took up his gun, but Duncan said no, snakes were not the aggressors. The trio waited quietly and the serpent silently glided into the underbrush. Wilson shot a tiny bird marked with a scarlet spot on its head. It was new to him, a lesser redpoll, but it proved to be a fairly common bird. Like small boys, they rolled rocks into the Susquehanna River and watched them splash into the water below, giggling and guffawing, shouting as their rock produced the biggest splash. Stripping and jumping into the cool water, they dried themselves and their clothing on sun-warmed rocks. They traveled unfettered by time, speaking with people along the way, stuffing their bellies when hungry, through a country beginning to fill up, but still wondrous in its wildness.

The three probably splashed through marshy land surrounding the northern tip of Cayuga Lake. Montezuma National Wildlife Refuge protects those marshes today. Wilson could not have known that the Erie Canal would be coming through in a few years and limited marsh drainage would begin in 1826. A dam and lock were constructed at the northern end in 1910 and more water drained from the marshes. The Bureau of Biological Survey, precursor to the U.S. Fish and Wildlife Service, purchased 6,432 acres of former marshland in 1937, and the Civilian Conservation Corps began building a levee system to restore part of the wetlands. The refuge was established in 1938, and today, seven thousand marshland acres have been restored.

Purple loosestrife, a striking plant, blooms over Montezuma in spring. The plant emigrated in the early 1800s to the United States from Asia and Europe where it is a minor player among wetland plants. It appeared on the refuge in 1951 and by the late 1990s had established itself as an invasive pest, infesting thirty-two hundred acres. Having no natural enemies here, aggressive loosestrife shoves native species out of the way. The plant grows in thick, decay-resistant clumps, with stems too stiff for nests and unappealing to muskrats' taste. Specialists from Cornell University's Biological Control unit introduced two leaf-beetle species in 1966 that feed exclusively on loosestrife. Regaining the marshes using this method takes years but is less damaging to the environment than enormous doses of herbicides.

The land protected by Montezuma, altered since Wilson's time, still remains an important haven for migrating and resident animals. Thousands of waterfowl, wading birds, warblers, and shorebirds pass through the area during twice yearly migrations. Bald eagles, osprey, herons, Canada geese, and several duck species nest within the refuge's boundaries. There are a few walking trails, but the best way to see wildlife is by car on the Wildlife Drive. A vehicle acts as a mobile blind on the exposed road and birds do not seem to mind. On a visit a few years ago, I stopped near a great blue heron that had just caught a large fish. The bird tossed the fish like a slow motion juggler, getting it into just the right position to slide down its long throat. It looked as if the heron would surely strangle, but the massive lump slowly descended as the stately bird stood like a statue.

When the trio reached Niagara, Wilson herded them down a path behind the falls where the suction almost pulled them into the plunging waters. It was an awesome experience. Wilson returned from the journey invigorated, tattered, and tired; he walked forty-seven miles the last day. School opened late, slightly tarnishing his reputation as a steadfast teacher. After the trek, William Duncan decided to follow his uncle's vocation and became a teacher in Milestown.

The 1805 winter was particularly severe. Many families could not afford to send their children to school and that meant less income for him. But for perhaps the first time, Wilson was primarily concerned not with money but with the best way to proceed on his project. Lawson's admonishments had deterred him not a whit. Letters to William Bartram revealed that Wilson yearned to live as a wilderness explorer. Admittedly ignorant in botany and drawing, he asked the gentle naturalist for advice. Long hours of drawing practice paid off and Wilson's sketches and paintings improved remarkably. Once again, he tried to leave the school, which demanded too much time, and, once again, trustees raised a sub-stantial amount of money to keep him.

A new idea came to the budding artist. He borrowed some of Law-son's tools and began engraving his own plates, just as Catesby had done. By February 1806, Wilson had completed one hundred colored plates. In the same month he wrote to Jefferson asking to be attached to the Red River expedition, requesting Bartram to forward the letter with a personal recommendation. This was the expedition that Bartram had declined in 1805. The record runs murky here, for the expedition was secret since it would cross Spain's holdings, clearly trespassing with the possible intent of future invasion. Jefferson never replied to the letter and later professed no recollection of it. The correspondence probably never reached Jeff-erson.

Wilson, dismayed at Jefferson's silence, finally left teaching in April 1806. Samuel Bradford hired Wilson as the editor for his new edition of *Rees's Cyclopaedia.* At some point during discussions with Bradford, Wil-son mentioned his *American Ornithology.* Bradford liked the idea and agreed to publish the work—after the *Cyclopaedia* was completed. Wil-son now had a reliable income and another friend who believed in his undertaking.

Wilson's travels and observations resulted in deepening concerns about birds. He noted many aspects of their behavior that were beneficial to humans besides their sweet songs, tasty flesh, and interesting antics. Some species were detrimental to crops but others daily devoured insects by the pound and distributed seeds. Every spring thousands of robins were shot and sold for food. One hunter could easily shoot a few hundred birds in a day. Wilson saw that the birds ate berries in addition to insects and worms, a trait worthwhile to farmers. He had dissected birds and studied their anatomy and the food in their stomachs. Pokeberries stained a robin's stomach red. A newspaper story appeared stating that pokeberries made the robins' flesh unwholesome. That was not true, but the market demand for robins dropped, saving the birds from continued slaughter. There was little doubt that Alexander Wilson was behind the article.

Throughout 1806 and into 1807 he worked on the encyclopedia and engravings for his book. He hired colorists for the plates and oversaw their work. Wilson continued to comb the nearby forests for new birds, but there were few to be found. He would have to search unbeaten regions. Meriwether Lewis arrived in Philadelphia to prepare his accounts of the Lewis and Clark expedition for publication and gave the birds he had secured on that trip to Wilson. In addition, Wilson, using Lewis's observations, was able to report the ranges and habits of those birds. Among the new birds, the ornithologist named two after the intrepid explorers: Lewis's woodpecker and Clark's crow, now known as Clark's nutcracker.

Months spent as a wandering peddler had prepared the birdman for what lay ahead. By late 1808, he had milled around his own territory long enough. Wilson initiated trips up and down the east coast and into the settled interior. He covered more ground than Banister, Lawson, or Catesby. The traveler wrote wry, witty, informative letters full of observations of people and places. Wilson had no patron for this endeavor; he collected specimens and sketches for his own information, and set up a network of correspondents and observers "so that scarcely a *wren* or *tit* shall be able to pass along, from New York to Canada, but I shall get intelligence of it."

In December 1808, Wilson secured sixteen subscribers in Baltimore and confidently rode into Annapolis where he presented his prospectus to the legislature. "The wise men of Maryland stared and gapt, . . . The *Ayes* for subscribing were NONE & so it was unanimously determined in the negative. Noways discouraged by this sage decision, I pursued my route through . . . this illiterate corner of the State, to Washington, distant 38 miles; and on my way opened 55 gates!"[3] The once open land was quickly becoming enclosed by fences.

Soon after arriving in Washington, Wilson was received by President Jefferson, who immediately placed a subscription for the *Ornithology,* one of seventeen pledges Wilson gained in the capital city. After a few days respite, Wilson was astride his horse bound for Savannah, Georgia. He passed through Norfolk, Virginia, which was semisubmerged following an extraordinarily wet winter. Then on to Suffolk, Jerusalem, and Halifax, through solitary pine woods and swamps, his strong horse swimming swollen rivers and plodding through viscous mud into North Carolina.

Immense pine savannahs, broken by creeks and swamps, spanned eastern North Carolina. Turpentiners stripped bark from one or more sides of nearly every pine tree, and the wounds bled sap into collecting buckets. Such trees were commonly called cat-faced. A small, unfamiliar, black and white striped woodpecker was discovered in the piney woods.

Only the male sported a tiny red patch on each side of its head, invisible from any distance. Wilson named it the red-cockaded woodpecker. Especially partial to longleaf, or yellow, pine forests, the bird has since been added to the endangered species list as its habitat has fallen under intensive logging. Approximately fourteen billion board feet of yellow pine were cut from Louisiana, Mississippi, Texas, North Carolina, South Carolina, Alabama, Arkansas, Florida, Virginia, Georgia, and Oklahoma in 1915 alone.[4]

In the southern swamps, Wilson found many birds that never wintered in Pennsylvania, and though he had heard a passel of alligator tales, he never ran into a gator. That would have been unlikely in winter's grip when the reptiles were snoozing in their holes. The main products of the state, he wrote, were hogs, turpentine, tar, and apple brandy, which seemed to be the first nourishment taken upon rising.

Savannahs and flatwoods continued around Wilmington and southward. Crossing ice-capped streams had lacerated his mount's legs and chest and Wilson traded for a big, elegant, sorrel horse that took off at a canter for some fifteen miles before slowing and covered, in all, forty-two miles that day. The horse carried not only Wilson, but his clothing, books, gun, and implements of his craft. Though an easy keeper and strong traveler, the horse was prone to skittishness and had to be ridden with a tight rein and close attention. Wilson's route through South Carolina hugged the coastline below the Santee River following the King's Highway to Charleston and Savannah.

Because England's king ordered the roads be constructed (another one ran from Florida to California), those early roads were known as the King's Highway. Sometimes called the Post Road, the highway was first used for delivering mail; travelers and freight soon followed. Many of Colonial America's roads followed existing Indian trails—why forge a new path when an existing one could be more easily widened? U.S. 17 up the coast of the Carolinas is a shadow of the old King's Highway; the Bartrams, Michaux, Wilson, and others traveled this same route.

I HAD COVERED PART OF Wilson's route around Savannah, but wanted to visit South Carolina north of Charleston. Spring was declining when I began a northward trip from Tallahassee in early May 1999. Interstate 10

carried me toward the Atlantic and a meeting with a smaller road. U.S. 17 snuck inland for a way after crossing the St. Marys River, darted for the coast, and then lazily crawled alongside Interstate 95. Georgia's Department of Natural Resources, for purposes of commercial and sport fishing activities, has decreed U.S. 17 as the demarcation line between salt and fresh water on certain rivers: St. Marys, Satilla, Altamaha, Champney, Butler, Darien, Little and Big Ogeechee, North Newport, Medway, and Savannah. Water seaward of the highway, except for freshwater ponds, is salt. Water to the landward is fresh. Smaller, shorter rivers—Crooked, Little Satilla, South Brunswick, Turtle, Sapelo, South Newport, and Salt Creek—are deemed salt water for their entire length.

As usual, I had gotten a late start, and had no clear idea of where to camp for the night, so it was after dark when I found Georgia's Fort McAllister State Historic Park near the Ogeechee River's mouth. General Sherman ended his March to the Sea here and after capturing the fort went on to take Savannah. Wilson had ended his land journey in Savannah though he probably wandered around the Ogeechee region and coastal outposts with John Abbot.

The Ogeechee River rises in Georgia's Piedmont and accepts most of its flow from the coastal plain in a drainage basin of seven thousand square kilometers. Although the Ogeechee is classified as a blackwater river, Magnolia Springs contributes a large amount of carbonate-rich water, giving the Ogeechee a high pH. Large homes line the Ogeechee's banks on the last few miles to the park. Some stand on tall, heavy pilings in awe of storm tides. The park was quiet when I arrived. There was not much ambient light from the night sky because the campground is situated in a thick grove of leafy magnolias. As I called home from a dimly lit phone booth, a gray fox trotted past, casting furtive looks over its shoulder to make sure I stayed away. Following the barely discernible asphalt strip leading back to the campsite, I felt as if I were walking through a dimly lit tunnel. Back in the van, I wondered if John Abbot had visited this spot. Perhaps he brought Wilson here. So long ago, so difficult to know exactly where they were.

I worked my way north the next morning, driving just a few miles on Interstate 95 before I left that busy road behind. When visiting here the previous March, I had found the bridge over the Savannah River on State Route 170 closed for repairs, but it was open now and provided a back way to Charleston through the Savannah National Wildlife Refuge.

Refuge managers had made good use of old levees left from abandoned rice fields, using them to impound twenty-eight hundred acres of
pools for wintering waterfowl. The refuge was established in 1927 and
covers more than twenty-six thousand acres, including thirteen thousand
acres of cypress/tupelo swamps. That seems like a lot, but is hardly a
shadow of the forests that shaded the coastal rivers of Georgia and the
Carolinas before Europeans arrived.

A one-lane road over some of those levees is open to traffic. About 260
avian species use the refuge during a year and on a warm May morning I
counted twenty different kinds of birds without even trying. A yellow-
throated warbler flicked through the grasses next to a water control structure. Mobs of bobolinks, Catesby's rice-birds, worked over nodding
seedheads of lanky grasses. Two Mississippi kites lazily twirled overhead.
I stopped in a shady spot for a tailgate brunch while a nighthawk looped
above and through the trees in hot pursuit of insects. Stooping and div-
ing, the bird boomed the sound that had earned it another common
name, bullbat.

Time to move on, following Route 170 over a long bridge across Port
Royal Sound where anglers fished from boats lined up like horses in a
starting gate. A two-lane road that already carries a fair amount of traffic,
Route 170 will carry much more if plans for its widening go through.
Billboards announce golf course homes designed for retirees. From Beaufort, Highway 21 took me back to U.S. 17 and through Charleston's diminished Sunday traffic. Two wide bridges spanned the Cooper River's
grand entrance to Charleston harbor and the sea. Tall, steel cranes
awaited their orders to lift cargo from incoming ships along the industrial wharves. Progress has followed U.S. 17. Chain stores and restaurants
abound. Most of the traffic had turned toward sunny, coastal beaches
before I saw a familiar brown and yellow sign announcing the entrance to
Francis Marion National Forest. The solid green thumbprint on the map
indicating public land was misleading, for private homes hugged the
highway. In reality, most public lands are honeycombed by the properties
of private landholders.

A few miles up the road a new visitor center invites passersby to stop.
The center is a joint operation for Francis Marion National Forest and
Cape Romain National Wildlife Refuge, and was built after Hurricane
Hugo took the original offices and exhibits in 1996. The new center con-
tains exhibits on the land, wildlife, and first people in the area. Friendly

volunteers and staff answer a variety of questions from visitors with a purpose and from those who stop not knowing what to expect. Cape Romain is one of several sites around the country that participates in the red wolf captive breeding program.

Outside the center, a short amble over a boardwalk led to an enclosure where some red wolves rested in the shade. Their buff and brown mottled coat burnished with black and chestnut shadows enables them to blend in with the forest and it took several slow visual passes before my eyes picked them out. The wolves in this enclosure had been exposed to human scrutiny several times, but they looked distinctly uncomfortable at being the object of attention. If this had been a true wilderness setting, they would have slipped into the forest long before I knew they were there. They are small, shy animals, only slightly larger than a coyote, though they were once one of the region's top predators. The southeast's native wolf population was nearly exterminated by loss of habitat, poison, bullets, trapping—you name it—and by 1970 numbered only about a hundred survivors in coastal Texas and Louisiana.

The U.S. Fish and Wildlife Service implemented a campaign to save the wolf and captured as many as possible between 1974 and 1980. Wolves, dogs, and coyotes are capable of interbreeding but social structure and territoriality usually preclude mating. By the 1970s, such natural controls had broken down and wolves had mixed with other canids. Genetic testing found only fourteen animals capable of meeting the purebred criteria and that small pack formed the crux of a captive breeding program. Breeding pairs were settled in zoos and nature centers around the United States and, beginning in 1987, young wolves were reintroduced into their former habitat. Released wolves have been fitted with radio transmitters so their movements, or lack of movement, can be traced.

Coastal islands are perfect places for breeding pairs. The lands are isolated and offer some protection from those whose fear of wolves blinds them to the animals' true nature. Although wolves are capable of injuring people, in five hundred years of coexistence there has never been a documented case of a red wolf attacking a human.

Red wolves prey on white-tailed deer, raccoons, and small mammals, rabbits, mice, rats, and nutria. A wolf requires about two to five pounds of food a day—not a conspicuous consumer. Domestic pets and livestock account for less than two percent of its diet. The south's deer population

FIG. 9. The endangered red wolf, *Canis rufus.*
Courtesy of St. Vincent National Wildlife Refuge.

is hardly declining, and wolves serve as a natural check on deer and small mammal populations, which can be pests for farmers. A red wolf pack, comprising a close-knit assemblage of the alpha pair and offspring from previous years, deters encroachment from coyotes, which are more inclined to prey on small domestic animals. It would seem, therefore, that people should be happy to have a wolf pack nearby but fear and old ingrained stereotypes are hard to overcome. While most eastern North Carolina residents support the program, there is a minority who emphatically opposes it.

Few wolves have been released into the wild. For their own protection, they are set free only into large expanses of land, such as Great Smoky Mountains National Park, but the majority are held in captive breeding facilities. Red wolves will never freely roam the southern states as they did when the first naturalists explored the land, but the fact that they are hanging on means a tiny part of essential wildness remains.

An unpaved remnant of the King's Highway runs through Francis Marion National Forest from Hampton Plantation State Park on the Santee River to near the Buck Hall campground, a short distance northwest of modern U.S. 17. Hampton Plantation was built in the 1750s, and a few miles down the road devout colonists built St. James Church in 1768. Wilson must have passed by these harbingers of civilization on a track considerably less stable than the solid crushed limestone that now paves the passage. Across the Intracoastal Waterway to the east lie the barrier islands of Cape Romain National Wildlife Refuge—Bull, Lighthouse, Raccoon Key, and Cape—and unnamed marshes segmented by waterways such as Horsehead, Five Fathom, and Little Papas creeks. Catesby might have explored this region, though he seems to have kept to the area between Charleston, South Carolina, and Augusta, Georgia.

Francis Marion National Forest offers four less developed campgrounds and several hiking trails. Buck Hall campground, located on the Intracoastal Waterway, has fourteen open sites, a boat ramp, and bath house. The grounds are nicely mowed, leaving not a twig to shield you from your neighbor. There are few shade trees, but there were probably more before Hugo. The showers rank among the oddest I've ever encountered. There were no faucets and I fiddled with everything I could find but nothing seemed to work. Then I noticed a button and pushed it. Luckily, the water came out warm, but with a force only slightly less than the power needed to project water to the third floor of a burning building. I can't speak for the men's showers, but if they were the same I'd bet good money that a grown man with a sunburn would howl when the first blast hit.

Alexander Wilson had ridden through tall pines in the area now encompassed by Francis Marion National Forest, and skirted and waded through coastal wetlands around Cape Romain. There were few bridges over the rivers; travelers swam or paid for dry passage on a ferry. Wilson's sorrel threw a boatman into the river at the Georgetown Ferry, then shied at a shadow and landed himself in the Savannah River while crossing at Two Sisters Ferry. Wilson jumped into the cold water and caught the reins before the horse was swept away. On his southern tour, Wilson had little good to say about Southerners, but nevertheless signed 250 subscribers and found his most reliable and knowledgeable collector and correspondent in Savannah—John Abbot.

Wilson did not continue beyond Savannah but spent a few days in the town resting from his journey and exploring with Abbot. On March 8, 1809, Wilson wrote to his publisher a quick letter from Savannah relating his travels. He would have written more, but he was not yet well, having caught a chill when rescuing the sorrel from the river. He planned to return by ship, faster and safer than overland travel, and hoped the sea air would cure him. Before leaving, Wilson sold the horse, expressing neither regret nor joy at separating from the steed.

Wilson remained in Philadelphia for the remainder of 1809 and, at the end of January 1810, set out on a westward journey over the Allegheny Mountains to Pittsburgh. He bought a rowboat and made his way down the Ohio River to Louisville. This trip was a poignant one for Wilson. He searched the forests, waters, and skies for new birds, but his ultimate goal was a cabin on the Natchez Trace where his friend Meriwether Lewis had died under mysterious circumstances on October 10, 1809.

Lewis, waiting for the government to honor bills still pending from the Lewis and Clark Expedition, had paid the debts from his own funds. He was serving as the territorial governor of northern Louisiana when he decided to go to Washington and settle financial matters himself. He stopped for the night at Grinder's Stand on the Natchez Trace but did not leave the place alive. At first his death was kept secret. When the news was released, rumors circled like hungry vultures. Days passed between communications; Lewis was buried without being fully examined by any save the man who dug his grave. There was no inquiry into his death and it was reported as a suicide, though others believed he had been murdered. Wilson hoped to learn the truth about his friend.

The ornithologist, therefore, had more on his mind than subscribers and species when he arrived in Louisville and rented a room at the Indian Queen Tavern. He left four letters to prominent citizens about his book and wandered the town. On Tuesday, Wilson entered a store called Audubon and Rozier. The young man behind the counter, in an otherwise empty store, was John James Audubon. Wilson introduced himself and stated his purpose. The storekeeper looked over the *Ornithology* and was about to subscribe when his partner, dour Ferdinand Rozier, appeared. Speaking in French, Rozier admonished Audubon for thinking of spending so much money on a book when his own talents were so much better. Instead, Audubon pulled out his portfolio. When Wilson asked if he intended to publish, Audubon replied that he had no thoughts on the matter. The merchant was recently married and a new father and the store was not doing well. The young Frenchman probably would not have been able to meet his obligation to Wilson had Rozier not discouraged him from signing up.

The Audubons were also lodged at the Indian Queen Tavern and Audubon invited Wilson to meet his wife, Lucy, and the couple's infant son. The two men did go on a few collecting trips together. Although the meeting seemed insignificant, it later sparked controversy between camps supporting the two bird artists.

What really happened cannot be known. After Wilson died, George Ord took over as self-appointed biographer and altered Wilson's journal so that it cast an unfavorable light on Audubon. Ord later accused Audubon of copying Wilson's work. In return, Audubon fired back that Wilson had done the stealing. Anything is conjecture at this point. Audubon, who had been drawing almost since he could hold a pencil, may not have had aspirations to publish until he saw Wilson's work. Wilson's paintings were above average and greatly detailed, but lacked the vibrancy Audubon brought to his art.

Wilson did not find much to keep him in the Kentucky river town and he was anxious to reach Grinder's Stand. Louisville was a boat-building town and the ornithologist was disappointed to receive a low price for his rowboat. The journey to Natchez and New Orleans would be on foot and by horseback from that point. He searched for a large passenger pigeon roost near Shelbyville. The birds were away foraging and Wilson estimated that the forest of dead trees stretched about forty miles with roughly ninety nests per tree. Later that afternoon the birds returned in a stream that darkened the sky with whistling wings. He estimated the flock contained two billion birds. The last wild passenger pigeon was killed on March 14, 1900—less than a hundred years later—and the last captive bird, Martha, died at the Cincinnati Zoo on September 1, 1914.

The ornithologist purchased a horse in Lexington, of a much better temper than the South Carolina sorrel. For the rest of his short life, Wilson praised Kentucky-bred horses as the finest to own. He rode slowly through a landscape tumbling with birds, streams, and caves. Droves of warblers flitted through the woods, feeding their way to the northern ranges; among them, Wilson named a new bird, the Tennessee warbler.

The path south of Nashville, the Natchez Trace, was a long-used route for Natchez, Chickasaw, and Choctaw Indians, and later the French and Spanish. Hernando de Soto was the first European to describe the area when he camped nearby in 1540–41. Wilson now rode into the nation's heart. At that time, the Trace was one of America's most heavily traveled roads.

Wilson found Grinder's Stand and interviewed Mrs. Grinder, who had been nearby when the shots that killed Lewis rang out. She related that Lewis and his servants had appeared at dusk, asking for a room for the night. Lewis appeared deranged, alternating between agitation, muttering to himself, and polite calm. Her husband was away on business and Mrs. Grinder, alarmed at Lewis's behavior, locked herself in a nearby cabin for the night. A shot boomed in morning's early hours, a cry, "Oh, Lord!" and another shot. Peering through chinks in the cabin's wall, the woman could see movement in the shadowy woods, then Lewis attempted to open the cabin door, begging for help for his wounds. Mrs. Grinder stayed inside and Lewis staggered away. As the sky lightened, she opened her door, roused the servants, and found Lewis in his bed, still alive. Part of his forehead had been blown away and his brain exposed. Another wound gaped in his chest. He pleaded for death, offering her money to kill him and end his misery. He lingered a while longer, murmuring that he was so strong and it was so hard to die.

Wilson became convinced that his friend had been murdered and, before departing, left money with the Grinders to build a fence around Lewis's grave so that it would not be disturbed by rooting animals. His was the only published account of Lewis's death.

Stephen Ambrose, in *Undaunted Courage*, provides a good account of Lewis's last hours. Although a gifted military man and explorer, Lewis was unsuited to political office. Throughout his life he suffered bouts of extreme depression. Traveling down the Mississippi River on the first leg of his final trip, he apparently tried to kill himself twice, but was restrained by the crew. After learning of the suicide attempts, friends at Fort Pickering, today's Memphis, Tennessee, held Lewis until his rational self reappeared. Ambrose states that Lewis admitted trying to kill himself at Fort Pickering. His friends thought his spirits were restored when Lewis mounted his horse and set off on the Natchez Trace.

The National Park Service has constructed a highway paralleling the old Trace and preserved parts of the original path worn several feet deep by moccasins, hooves, and boots. The modern highway is a two-lane road with a slow speed limit, a quiet way to travel from southern Nashville to just north of Natchez. Drivers should stop and walk parts of the historic track, letting their senses carry them back in time. A monument at mile 385.9 marks Lewis's grave.

Much saddened, Wilson continued to the Gulf. He crossed dozens of streams and rode through heavily canopied forests. The trip tired him and he rested in Natchez, taking advantage of the stay to scavenge for subscribers. He sailed from New Orleans armed with a letter to Florida's Spanish dignitaries, though his ship only stopped at a few barrier islands. He landed in Philadelphia in August 1810, having been gone eight months. The trip cost $455.

He gave up editorship on the encyclopedia to concentrate on the *Ornithology*, and stayed close to Philadelphia until May 1812, when he spent a month in Cape May. During August and September of that same year he made a circuit through New England. When in Philadelphia, Wilson visited Bartram's garden and the friends compared travel tales. Wilson checked on progress on the copper plates and those hired to lay on the colors. He sifted through reports sent from his field correspondents. Having studied enough to know that birds exhibited recurring habits, he nevertheless discovered a new bit of behavior every now and then.

By the time Alexander Wilson launched his studies, the country was a good deal more settled than it had been in Catesby's time. Wilson often stayed in private homes, trading drawing lessons for his board. He encountered native people, though he wrote little of them. Wilson lived for his birds. Like Catesby, Wilson was a self-taught artist but he introduced carefully documented science to his publications. His paintings were not great works of art, but coupled with his narratives, they were the means to familiarize people with America's beautiful birds. It was not enough to capture the likeness. He agonized over the smallest detail until the feathers were arranged just so, the plates on the diminutive legs perfect, and the coloration patterns exact.

His drive to complete his work led him to labor long hours, with little time for entertainment. Collecting trips through adverse weather and attendant chills and fevers, the strain of seeing his work rejected more often than it was accepted by subscribers, worry over whether those subscribers would come through with payment, constant concern over the state of his personal finances all served to weaken his constitution. Then, during the winter of 1812–13, the colorists became dissatisfied and left a mountain of unfinished work.

As the seventh volume was poised for release, he wrote the words that began this chapter. There can be no doubt that he was tired and restless from his enforced confinement and within a few weeks of his letter to Bartram, Wilson and George Ord left on another collecting trip to Cape May for the eighth volume. The ornithologist hoped a good dose of nature would restore his strength. The eighth volume was due in November and then he had only to complete the final book due out in 1814. Back in Philadelphia, he knew that his health had worsened. He filed his will on August 16, 1813, and collapsed later that day. A doctor was summoned, but Wilson's condition was beyond the powers of nineteenth-century medical knowledge. A severe bout of dysentery quickly depleted his strength. Alexander Wilson died on August 23, 1813.

Had he lived longer than his forty-seven years, he would not have sat back, admiring the laurels hung on his work. America had many more birds to be discovered and described. Wilson knew that, just as he surely knew that in his few years of study he had not even learned all there was to know about the birds with which he was familiar. He would have continued traveling and learning, and he might have become more famous than his successor, John James Audubon.

In 1839, Thomas M. Brewer compressed Wilson's *Ornithology* into a single, affordable volume that included new species described by Bonaparte, Audubon, Nuttall, and Richardson. Brewer hoped the book would appeal to more people and revitalize some memory of the man who sought to awaken an appreciation of America's birds. In this volume, the black and white plates are greatly decreased in size. Discussions of each bird vary in length, packing in all that Brewer could reap from his own and others' observations. By that time, Audubon's *The Birds of America* had been published as had his *Ornithological Biography.* Audubon's dramatic presentations of birds, his flamboyant persona, and the fact that he lived after the appearance of his works, guaranteed that his name would outshine that of Alexander Wilson.

The Wilson Ornithological Society was founded in 1888 for people who are curious about birds. Today, membership totals about twenty-five hundred people worldwide. The Society publishes a quarterly bulletin as well as a bimonthly newsletter. Much smaller and less known than the Audubon Society, the Wilson Ornithological Society nevertheless awards a few small research grants each year, in an effort to cement partnerships between serious amateur and professional ornithologists carrying forward Wilson's ideals.

As the southern Atlantic coasts became more populated, forests were cut and cut again. Lumber went for construction and tens of thousands of trees were squandered as land was cleared for agriculture and towns. It was easy to justify the waste in the face of millions of trees. Understory grasses and shrubs were destroyed and longleaf pines no longer dominated the horizon. Forests reappeared in a few years, but they were different from the land Wilson had ridden through. After the War Between the States, loblolly pines, fast-growing trees partial to disturbed land, began repopulating untilled fields.

That the forests needed to be managed had been recognized by the late 1800s, but the need for such measures would not be fully acknowledged until forester Gifford Pinchot allied with President Theodore Roosevelt in 1905. When Alexander Wilson rode along the Carolina coasts, he heard the voices of forest denizens and must have stopped often to follow a darting bird or examine a nest. The forest I drove through was not what he had seen, but more than that I didn't hear the sounds he'd heard or have his opportunities to learn.

What would have happened had Wilson lived? If he had never walked into that Louisville store, would Audubon have thought to publish his own paintings? Such questions, of course, can never be answered. Wilson's pioneering observations furnished Audubon and subsequent ornithologists a platform upon which to further the study of ornithology.

CHAPTER 7

The Man Who Painted Birds

John James Audubon
(April 26, 1785–January 27, 1851)

Twenty miles our men had to row before we reached "Sandy Island," and as on its level shore we all leaped, we plainly saw the southernmost cape of the Floridas. The flocks of birds that covered the shelly beaches, and those hovering overhead, so astonished us that we could for a while scarcely believe our eyes. The first volley procured a supply of food sufficient for two days' consumption. . . . Rose-colored Curlews stalked gracefully beneath the mangroves. Purple Herons rose at almost every step we took, and each cactus supported the nest of a White Ibis. The air was darkened by whistling wings, while, on the waters, floated Gallinules and other interesting birds.

—John James Audubon, "The Florida Keys," essay on
a trip taken in 1832

THE NUMBER OF PUBLICATIONS written about the charismatic artist/ ornithologist, John James Audubon, could fill a wall of bookshelves. Almost every American as well as people around the world recognize the name, even if only as a man who painted birds. Mystery accompanied him during his life. Subsequent research revealed the facts surrounding his birth and details of the multi-faceted, complex personality of the man.

Audubon wrote that his mother was a beautiful, wealthy Spanish Creole lady and that he was born in Louisiana. Of the three sons and one daughter she birthed, he was the only son who survived. Soon after his birth, she accompanied her husband to his estate in Santo Domingo where she died in a slave uprising. Audubon apparently penned this reminiscence for his sons; it was found inside an old book in a Staten Island barn in the 1890s.

It is generally accepted that Audubon was the issue of a union between a successful sea captain, Jean Audubon, and an attractive young woman, Jeanne Rabine. She was on her way to a position as a servant girl in Santo Domingo when she met Captain Audubon aboard ship; she quickly became Audubon's companion instead of taking the servant job. Though he had left a wife in Nantes, France, Audubon had a quadroon mistress, Catherine Bouffard, at his Santo Domingo plantation; they had already produced a little girl before lovely Jeanne arrived. Audubon later fathered another daughter named Rose with Catherine, but for the moment he was infatuated with Jeanne, who soon became pregnant.

A son named Jean Rabine was born on April 26, 1785. Jeanne never recovered her strength after the baby's birth and died seven months later. Catherine raised the little boy until 1790, when whites began fleeing the island to escape a slave uprising. Before leaving, Captain Audubon made arrangements for son Jean and daughter Rose to follow.

Donald Culross Peattie, in *Audubon's America,* mentions that Jeanne bore Captain Audubon four sons altogether, but modern historians accept that Jean Rabine, whose name would later be changed to John James, was her only child. Researchers continue quarrying records, going over old ground with hopes that more information will turn up some day. Not only has time clouded the records, but Audubon and his father and stepmother shielded and covered up the truth as much as possible so that the real story may never be known.

Captain Audubon and his wife, Anne Moynet Audubon, were childless and Madame Audubon legally adopted Jean and Rose. Young Jean was baptized Jean Jacques Fougère Audubon on October 23, 1800. Madame Audubon, several years older than her husband, watched over the two children as if they were her own when the Captain resumed his seafaring life. Jean Jacques was the spitting image of his father and cared little for lessons; he would rather draw and spend his time outside. Madame Audubon indulged him. He was altogether charming, willful, restless, vain, stubborn, handsome, intelligent, conceited, energetic, thin-skinned, talented, rebellious, entertaining, quick to anger, quick to laugh, and totally lacking in shrewdness or business sense.

Before losing his fortune in Santo Domingo, Captain Audubon had invested in an estate called Mill Grove near Valley Forge, Pennsylvania. He sent eighteen-year-old Jean Jacques to manage the land in 1803, for several reasons: both he and his wife wanted to blur Jean Jacques' illegitimate birth; the young man could not be drafted into the French army if he were out of the country; and perhaps responsibility would bring maturity to the flighty young man.

Soon after landing in the United States, Jean Jacques came down with yellow fever and was nursed back to health by two Quaker women. During his recovery, he became more familiar with the English language, but "thee" and "thou" forever peppered his speech. He never mastered English and, truth be told, he did not manage French very well either. His written and spoken language was a zesty blend of French and English, formal and colloquial.

Audubon did not exactly take to his duties as master of Mill Grove like a duck takes to water. He spent most days hunting in the woods and evading visits from an English family named Bakewell who had moved into a home nearby. As a loyal Frenchman, Audubon disliked the British, but one day by chance he met the Bakewell men hunting and could avoid them no longer. Polite manners demanded that he pay a call. When he did, the men were out, but the eldest daughter, Lucy, was home. Audubon fell head over heels in love with her on the spot. Though he was prone to tumble head over heels into many ventures, his love for Lucy proved to be one of his better choices.

Lucy returned his affections and the couple decided to marry. Neither family approved. Captain Audubon was sure Lucy was after the Audubon fortune, which had dwindled considerably; Lucy's family, while they liked the young man well enough, had no faith in his ability to earn a living. Jean Audubon was wrong about Lucy's intentions, but Lucy's parents were, unfortunately, correct in their assessment of the dashing Jean Jacques. As it turned out, over the years Lucy or Audubon called on one or another of the Bakewells for several loans.

Audubon returned to France in 1805 to discuss Mill Grove's management and his marriage plans with his father. They reached a compromise but things were heating up in France. Napoleon Bonaparte had crowned himself emperor in 1804; by 1805 he was amassing an army to expand the French empire in Europe. Jean Jacques, along with Ferdinand Rozier, the son of an Audubon family friend, hurriedly left the country to avoid military service.

Ferdinand and John James, as he was now known, decided to divest themselves of their Mill Grove holdings and move to Kentucky where they would open a store. Once established, John James would return to Pennsylvania and marry Lucy. Audubon probably instigated this enterprise; he would have found adventure on the frontier infinitely more appealing than farming or working in Uncle Benjamin Bakewell's counting house, and the young couple would be far from Lucy's disapproving family.

Rozier and Audubon opened their Louisville, Kentucky, store in 1807. Ferdinand readily took to shopkeeping, but Audubon spent his time exploring the Ohio River's banks and woodlands. The venture should have been successful, but the Embargo Act cut off all imports in December 1807. It was rather difficult to conduct business without merchandise on the shelves. John James returned to Pennsylvania, where he and Lucy were married on April 5, 1808. He brought his bride to Kentucky via coach, flatboat, and horseback.

With the business floundering, the family suddenly grew on June 12, 1809, when Victor Gifford Audubon was born. It was just a few weeks later that ornithologist Alexander Wilson stepped into the mercantile establishment. In a few years Wilson would be dead and almost forgotten; Audubon's mystique has continued for nearly two centuries. Neither man knew what the future held for them at that 1809 meeting.

Rozier and Audubon eventually moved to Henderson, Kentucky, with short-lived hopes of improving business. Next, the pair moved to Sainte Genevieve on the Mississippi River. Lucy and Gifford stayed in Henderson. The Audubon-Rozier partnership was, however, fading and finally dissolved in April 1811. Lucy had never cared for Rozier and probably shed no tears at his departure. The Audubons now had very little money and Lucy, for the first time, offered her services as a tutor.

John James tried an unsuccessful business partnership with Lucy's brother, Thomas. A second son, John Woodhouse Audubon, was born on November 30, 1812. While on a visit to Pennsylvania in that same year, Audubon contacted Alexander Wilson, who invited the Frenchman to view Rembrandt Peale's studio in Philadelphia. If there had been asperity between them at this stage, the two probably would not have willingly met. Wilson, remember, kept a busy schedule that year with trips to Cape May and New England when not hard at work on the seventh volume of the *Ornithology.*

Lucy bore daughters in 1815 and 1819 but both died in infancy. In 1819, John James Audubon was jailed for debt in Louisville and released when he declared bankruptcy. Lucy and John James sold all their household goods—the Bakewell family china, linens, furniture—to pay their debts. The experience was deeply humiliating for both.

Audubon later wrote that he paid as many of the debts as he could. The family left Henderson miserably poor. It was the only time in his life when wild turkeys and all other birds "looked like enemies, and I turned my eyes from them, as if I could have wished that they never existed."[1] He could be melodramatic at times.

The Western Museum in Cincinnati hired Audubon as a taxidermist in 1820. Lucy stayed in Kentucky with the children, but soon the family was reunited in Ohio. She took up teaching again and hoped for financial stability. Audubon, however, left the museum. They could not meet his salary and his wanderlust could not be confined. More than a decade after the brief meeting with Alexander Wilson, Audubon began to seriously consider publishing his own work.

The artist took to the road, looking for new birds, practicing his painting and drawing. He traded art lessons for food and board, trying his own hand at teaching for a spell. In those years, children of well-to-do parents studied art and music whether they showed any inclination or not. Audubon did not have the patience for teaching, being too critical and unsympathetic with his students. Lucy and the two boys moved to West Feliciana, Louisiana, where Lucy ran a private school at Beech Woods plantation for five years. Beech Woods' widowed mistress did not approve of Lucy's here-and-gone husband and on at least one occasion had him literally thrown off the premises.

During those years, Lucy was virtually solely responsible for raising their sons and earning their daily living. Her family helped but they did not have a limitless vault of money. Audubon himself bounced between elation and discouragement, anger and depression. He sent money home when he could, but resented Lucy's letters enumerating gaps in their finances. When Audubon was home, his wife and sons received his bountiful adoration and attention. When he was gone, his letters spoke words of affection but his actions implied otherwise. He seemed a man not so much committed to his work as he was pledged to not staying in one place for long, especially home. Like his father, John James was obliged to roam. Always bounding between two worlds—that of the model family man, and that of the robust, rollicking woodsman and hunter—Audubon was unable to find total satisfaction in either.

In 1824, the bird artist packed his portfolio and went to Philadelphia to find a publisher for his work. An exhibition of his paintings drew favor, but George Ord, who supported the late Alexander Wilson and found no redeeming qualities in the upstart Frenchman, discouraged any help for John James. Audubon then took himself to New York where the reception was much the same. His paintings were appreciated, but no publisher could be found.

After his initial disappointments in the north, Audubon made a decision to look for a publisher overseas. He left New York with a goal of saving his money, something that was not easy for him, in order to travel to London. He sailed from New Orleans on April 26, 1826, his forty-first birthday, and reached Liverpool sixty-five days later. The ship was becalmed in the Gulf of Mexico for nearly a month. He must have been itching to be in Florida, somewhere in the eastern distance, rather than sitting on the water in the breezeless air.

In all the writings about John James Audubon, he emerges as a hugely talented, terribly insecure man. His family's machinations to hide his illegitimate birth, his many business failures, and his inability to gain acceptance from the American scientific community haunted him. Through it all, Lucy stood by him. She, more than anyone else, knew and understood him.

Researching Audubon, I felt a gamut of emotions: he was a genius, he was a cad, he was to be admired, he was loathsome. He certainly did not accept criticism with good grace. Audubon can be best appreciated for the work he left behind, for the true man is elusive. After Maria Audubon edited her grandfather's journals for publication, deleting anything she felt to be detrimental to his memory, or indelicate, she burned the originals. His surviving journals must be read with caution; he was inclined to embellish the truth in his favor.

Audubon stood about five feet ten inches tall and wore his hair long. He dressed in finely cut clothes when he could afford them or opted for an ensemble of animal skins and furs. Well aware of his imposing figure and striking features, he always stood out in a crowd.

England's reception of him was favorable and he was soon writing to Lucy of wearing elegant clothing and being swept up in the social swirl.

FIG. 10. Portrait of John James Audubon by Frederick Cruickshank.
Courtesy of Florida Archives.

Surely her patience must have been tried at reading those letters. She was still teaching, still pinching pennies, while her husband danced in the arms of beautifully coifed and expensively dressed women.

He hinted at bringing his family to Europe, but the time was not quite right. Reading of Audubon's success without being allowed to participate brought Lucy the closest she ever came to breaking with her husband. She had been faithful and supportive through his many failures and absences. If he wanted her to join him in England, he would have to come and get her. While Lucy was simmering in Louisiana, fortunate events showered on an ecstatic Audubon in Europe.

Riding a crest of exhilaration, John James wrote that a publisher for *The Birds of America* had been found. William Lizars was positively bowled over by the paintings. Audubon gathered his portfolio and made the rounds of Great Britain's cities, signing subscribers. Because of labor problems, Lizars had to break his contract but another publisher, Robert Havell, was soon found. His son, Robert Havell, Jr., was a master of engraving; his expertise in executing Audubon's paintings sealed a lasting reputation for both.

Audubon returned to America in 1829, reconciled with his family, and returned to England with Lucy in 1830. He began work on the *Ornithological Biography*, a separate volume that would complement *The Birds of America*. August of 1831 found Lucy, Audubon, and Henry Ward, hired as Audubon's taxidermist, sailing for America, where the artist would hunt for new birds. He would penetrate Florida to the tip where neither Wilson, Bartram, nor Catesby had gone. Western travel over the Rocky Mountains to California appealed to him, but for now he would be satisfied with Florida.

The Frenchman who had left America—feeling a scorned interloper—returned victorious. He held a coveted membership in England's Royal Society and could almost feel banners of praise trailing behind as he proceeded to Washington, D.C., where he asked for and was granted permission to travel on a government revenue cutter, the *Spark*, that made regular visits along Florida's wilderness rivers and coast.

Lucy left for Louisville, where she would join her sons and stay with her brother's family, while John James and Henry started overland for Charleston, where they would meet the cutter. Audubon voiced the same complaints as others traveling in the South—monotonous pine forests devoid of life, filthy inns, and inedible food. Upon arriving, they found that the *Spark* was undergoing repairs. While waiting, Audubon became acquainted with John Bachman, a Lutheran minister who had also befriended Alexander Wilson. During the chafing stay, John James taught Bachman's sister-in-law to draw. The Audubon-Bachman friendship became stronger over the years and the Audubons would stay at the Bachman home whenever they were in Charleston. Gifford and Woodhouse Audubon later married two of Bachman's daughters.

The group left South Carolina in mid-November and arrived in St. Augustine a few days later. Audubon wrote to Lucy describing the city as "doubtless the poorest village I have seen in America."[2] Sandy streets were lined with thousands of orange trees and fruit sold for two cents apiece. Daily submersion in the salt marsh ruined his socks, could she send more? He saw few new birds, it was 82° and a few days later a frigid 29°. She should write to him in care of the garrison's commandant and Indian runners would carry the mail on—there was no regular delivery farther south. In a later note he criticized the town again. If it were not for fish and oranges the inhabitants would starve as they were much too lazy to farm the bare sand hills. The seesaw weather continued hot one day and cold the next.

Audubon found little to recommend Florida from his point of view. Unpredictable weather and fleets of insects did not amount to the paradise that Bartram had described. "My *account* of what I have or shall see of the Floridas will be far, very far from corroborating of the *flowery sayings* of Mr. Barton [Bartram] the Botanist." But he was there to explore the St. Johns and down the river he went, following Bartram, finding fault.

Delays plagued the *Spark*. In a letter to Lucy, he complained of finding nothing to draw, so passed the time by shooting five bald eagles in twenty-four hours "more than most Sportsmen can boast of."[3] They progressed a short way down the St. Johns River when a crewman was wounded and had to be transported across forty difficult overland miles to a hospital in St. Augustine. Restless Audubon hired a boat to Fort Picolata and explored the surrounding country during the *Spark's* enforced idleness. He stopped at a small island that for a time came to be called "Audubon's Island," covered with dozens of cool, fragrant, wild orange trees. "Under the shade of these beautiful ever-greens, and amidst the golden fruits that covered the ground, while the humming birds fluttered over our heads, . . . I refreshed myself with the bountiful gifts of an evercareful Providence."[4] The skeptical woodsman seems to have fallen under the spell of Bartram's flowery pen. Audubon's Island is a landmark unlikely to be found on modern maps, but is thought to be the spot known as Idlewilde Point where William Bartram experienced a heart-thudding alligator encounter.

After two days of recuperating from the journey, the captain returned to the *Spark.* By then, Audubon had decided he was getting nowhere fast and caught a return ship to Charleston where the party could find passage on another vessel. Once again, the Bachmans warmly offered their home to the weary travelers. Audubon enlivened Bachman's fledgling interest in birds and the minister later discovered two new species that are named for him, shy Bachman's sparrow and North America's rarest songbird, Bachman's warbler.

Luckily, another revenue cutter, the *Marion,* happened to be heading down Florida's east coast to check the Dry Tortugas lighthouse. The schooner took a leisurely cruise, allowing the artist to explore the Keys. Now he had what he had come for, Florida's fabulous waterbirds.

Few people lived along those islands, suspended from Florida's southern mainland, at that time—mainly those hiding from the law or living on the fringes of it, one way or another making their living from the sea. The narrow shorelines were known as the beach store. Who knew what treasures might wash up in the night—crates of food, trunks of clothing, bodies. Wreckers made a shady living ignoring or bending salvage laws, but they knew the inlets like no one else and gladly guided a bird-hungry Audubon.

SINCE THEN, THE KEYS HAVE BEEN DISCOVERED. Plants and animals, land and marine, are disappearing, the once turquoise waters are muddied, the reef has been scarred by careless boaters and is dying. About the only thing that has not changed is that the Overseas Highway, also known as U.S. 1, is the only road to mainland Florida. Henry Flagler began building an extension of his Florida East Coast Railroad to Key West in 1905. Seven years and $50 million later, the 106-mile long road linked thirty-one islands to the peninsula. Key West was a deepwater port and Flagler realized its potential for profit. The Labor Day hurricane of 1935 ripped away the rails with two hundred-mile-per-hour winds and an eighteen-foot tidal wave. More than eight hundred people were killed. For three years boats were again the only mode of travel, but engineers used Flagler's old roadbed and bridge structures to build the Overseas Highway that opened in 1938.

In the early 1960s the Keys were quiet and not overpopulated and they were often my family's vacation choice. My father fished, my mother sunbathed, and I was always ready to go on the boat, though I never developed a liking for fishing. Mostly I stayed too long in the sun and paid for it in sunburned misery. Two decades before the Mariel boatlift of the early 1980s, boatloads of Cuban refugees fleeing Castro's regime landed along the Keys. I remember watching one such boat tie up at the dock. The people's faces measured relief and fear; would they be allowed to stay, or be sent back?

I could not bring myself to follow John James to the Keys. It has been about thirty-five years since the last visit and I do not want to disturb or replace the memories of quiet beaches, beautiful water, and real Key lime pie made by someone who knew how.

Audubon took another brief trip to Florida in 1837. He wanted to explore the Gulf coast, but the Seminoles were at war and Texas was having its own revolution. John James sympathized with the Indians' plight, but he was not about to traipse through country where angry natives neglected to learn a person's political leanings before taking aim. Before leaving England, Audubon wrote to his old friend Bachman for advice. The minister thought the uprising would be quelled by the time the artist arrived.

All the Audubons arrived in Charleston and spent the winter in the Bachman home. With the news of Chief Osceola's capture, meaning the war was essentially over, Audubon, his son Woodhouse, and Edward Harris, naturalist and Audubon benefactor, departed for Florida. They crossed the "Trail of Tears" and the sad sight was one Audubon hoped never to witness again.

Levi Woodbury, Secretary of the Navy, had written a letter of introduction for John James. The commander of the Pensacola Naval Station assured Audubon that a cutter would be available soon. Audubon described Pensacola to Bachman as a small place principally inhabited by low-class Creole Spaniards and some amiable Scotch and American families. He doubted the place would ever amount to much because the country was poor, sandy pine barrens for miles around, even though New York land speculators were selling town lots at high prices. Bartram's 1775 account of the area had been more forgiving. Two stout forts guarded the entrance to Pensacola Bay. Fort Pickens was completed in 1834 and Fort McRee in 1837.

John James failed to coax a boat from the Navy commander at Pensacola as quickly as he had hoped, for even if Osceola was no longer at large, holdout Seminole bands refused to surrender. Spare boats were in short supply. Ever impatient at being put off by the Naval commander, Audubon returned to New Orleans. In a few days, a government ship was ready and the party was whisked along the western Gulf coast. Before he left Pensacola, he might have probed Santa Rosa Island's dunes.

By the late 1960s, Pensacola had become a rough, sprawling town. Every day, cars destined for a parking space at one of the military bases or one of the many chemical plants surrounding Pensacola, clogged the roads. Those depauperate pinelands Audubon had deplored made excellent industrial sites. Military bases and chemical plants ran twenty-four hours a day. The Vietnam war was peaking and Pensacola Naval Station had become Pensacola Naval Air Station. At the edge of the swamps lining the Escambia River's entrance to Escambia Bay rose the new University of West Florida, where, along with other students, I slogged through torrid summers and sloshing winters. We changed classes to the tune of whipping helicopter blades, *whop, whop, whop*, for not five miles away Navy pilots trained to fly the aircraft before shipping out "across the pond."

Eglin Air Force Base, Whiting Field, Saufley Field, Santa Rosa Field, Ellyson Field, the university was surrounded by reminders of war. Yet, secluded in the forests well out of town, the campus was insulated from the sights. The sounds and *cognizance* of what was happening outside our secure little world hung over us like the due date for a term paper on a subject as foreign as the physics of calculus in everyday life. We knew about the war, but we sure as heck didn't want anything to do with it. The university population was not large enough at that time to have established college bars. Nights off campus in local bars brought hippies, navy pilots, and rednecks together in confrontational moods. Waterfront bars were visited only by the bravest for they made the country bars seem like tea parties.

With winter in retreat and sunlight lifting in the south, my thoughts turned not to classes, but to Pensacola Beach on Santa Rosa Island. I'd drive down twisty Scenic Highway, which hugged the bluffs along the west side of Escambia Bay, across the long Pensacola Bay Bridge to Gulf Breeze, and swoop over the high bridge above Santa Rosa Sound to the coast's leading edge and the magnificent white sugar sand beaches. Weekdays after classes were best when the beaches were near empty. A few hardy souls lived in weathered wood or concrete block bungalows, but most were weekend homes. The low-roofed structures hugged the sand, denying the wind a purchase. Beach decor ruled, nets hung with shells, crab floats, sponges.

Stormy days and sunny days attracted me and solitude was assured on grey days. Hungry waves pounded the littoral zone, frantically rebuilding, moving, reshaping the shoreline. Wind scraped dry grains from around my feet. Behind me, wisps of sand spun off the tops of looming dunes. Facing the wind, I sat hugging my knees and rocking to the rhythm of the sea. Some nights I slept on the beach without fear, waking to a quicksilver ocean gently caressing the shore awake. On sunny days in the early 1970s I scrunched over those hot sands and rode a dune buggy up their steep, slippery sides in sliding, exciting bursts of speed and noise.

It was great fun but left scars both visible and unseen. Sea oats, rhizomatous grasses, and other beach plants whose roots helped anchor the restless sand could survive saltwater inundation, heat, and hurricane winds—but not tires. Repeated trips over the same path packed the granules where, instead of oozing through lightly stacked sand, rainwater gathered and plowed down the compressed ruts.

The quartz sand of north Florida's beaches began forming far north thousands of years ago. As the Appalachian Mountains dissolved across the Piedmont, granite boulders wore down to rocks and pebbles that washed into streams and rivers. The ancient Ochlockonee and Apalachicola Rivers received bits of the mountains and carried them to the sea. During their long travel, the stones were pummeled and worn and spit out as the sparkly, white sands that form the panhandle beaches and barrier islands. The mountains are still eroding and rivers still carry quartz sand downstream.

Barrier islands are extremely dynamic habitats. Coastal forces act on the islands like a child continually making mud pies. Wind and water have reworked those prehistoric deposits into Santa Rosa and St. George islands and skinny peninsulas like Cape San Blas and Alligator Point. Like an artist never satisfied with a pot's shape, nature's forces remake the coastline every day. East of Cape San Blas the drift is east and west. West of the Cape, the drift moves primarily westward. Aerial photographs clearly show linear lines of accretion.

Salt and sand determine the vegetative makeup of coastal areas and the survivors have adapted to living in the harsh meeting ground between land and water. Salt air prunes coastal live oaks; winds and shifting sands keep them stunted and twisted. Sand pines point away from prevailing winds. Coastal slash pines add more bulk and less height than their inland cousins. Beach plants are stiff, leathery, and spiky, flexible but not supple.

Between 1969 and 1971, I made many trips between Pensacola and my family's home in Tampa, either along the coast on U.S. 98 or through the middle of the panhandle on U.S. 90, then followed a veined route of secondary roads home. Panama City Beach was crowded during the beach season, but other than military installations, only scattered dwellings habited the northwest Gulf coast. The action was in the central part of the state where Orlando was snuggled in bed with Disney. After the killing freezes of the late 1960s, orange grove owners were moving farther south, opening up thousands of acres for retirement villages. Not many people were willing to live on this coastal panhandle fringe so far from a major city. Sometime in the 1980s the forgotten coast was, sadly, rediscovered.

I had memories of Santa Rosa Island from my college years, a vision of what the island had been like in the 1830s, and stories of what the island had been like before that. I was afraid of what I would find when I headed west in late April 1999. It was a fitting time, just days before John James Audubon's two hundred and fourteenth birthday.

I drove from Tallahassee across State Road 20 through the Apalachicola National Forest and private timberlands. Over the Ochlockonee River, Big Creek, the Apalachicola River, the pretty Chipola River, Juniper Creek, Bear Creek, Little Bear Creek, the Econfina River, Pine Log Creek, the Choctawhatchee River, through scrubby sandhills and mesic pine flatwoods, past trailers, pastures, gas stations, garden patches. Civilization has increased in the central panhandle, but it is still underpopulated compared to other parts of Florida. I turned left on Route 83 and drove across a causeway and bridge spanning a thumb of Choctawhatchee Bay. Fish and Wildlife Conservation biologists had posted the roadside with signs warning of nesting terns and plovers, which favor grass-free shelly sand for depositing their eggs. The road intersected U.S.

98 in a section named the Miracle Strip Parkway. Two lanes soon became four, and pines, oaks, and rosemary gave way to manicured landscaping glistening under an intricate watering system spurting mists in the middle of the hot day. City officals must keep the Emerald Coast green even in early summer's drought. Golf course resorts, outlet malls, beach clothing stores, banks, interior decorating establishments, a real estate office on almost every corner, and enough seafood restaurants to empty the Gulf in a few years bordered the road. Traffic thickened on the high-way passing through Sandestin and Destin, over a short bridge above East Pass, across the eastern end of Santa Rosa Island, owned primarily by Eglin Air Force Base, another short bridge to the mainland and Fort Walton Beach, then past Mary Esther, where traffic began to thin a bit, to the junction with CR399 and the toll bridge from Navarre to Navarre Beach on Santa Rosa Island. It had been a stunning few miles. It seemed that every piece of forest sprouted a "For Sale" sign.

The bridge to Navarre Beach is still two lanes. When I was last there the beach was marred only by a Holiday Inn and a few beach cottages. The motel is now dwarfed by multistory condos. Expansive homes sur-rounded by brilliant green grass and ornate fences outnumber small cot-tages. It takes enormous effort, constant watering and fertilizers, to keep grass alive on a beach. The sun bore down but a strong wind blowing off the water cooled the temperature. It also obscured the air with fine sand and droplets of salty water that covered the windshield with a cloudy film in a few seconds. My progress was halted by a tank truck, followed by another truck carrying one of those blinking arrow signs warning motor-ists to pass cautiously. On the back of the water truck stood a man wield-ing a high pressure hose spraying the electrical boxes mounted on each power pole. Salt air quickly corrodes metal, and in the long run it must be more cost effective to employ three people and two large trucks to wash off salt deposits than to replace the boxes or risk power outages for those expensive homes.

Fortunately, the boundary of Gulf Islands National Seashore soon appeared, followed by a large parking lot (almost empty), several picnic structures, a bathhouse, and a wide beach backed by humps of sand. Boardwalks have been built over the mounds and signs direct beachgoers to use them and not walk on the dunes. One boardwalk disappears into a dune's side and beachgoers may now walk up the boardwalk and climb over the dune. Dunes migrate slowly, over the road and over structures

FIG. 11. Photograph of sand dunes on Santa Rosa Island taken in 1929. *Courtesy of Florida Archives.*

meant to protect them until a major force, like a hurricane, resculptures them quickly. Those large homes would suffer in a big blow. Their lawns would definitely be killed by salt water washing over them. Maybe the owners would then revert to natural landscaping adapted to the saline environment and save on lawn maintenance.

The thin paved ribbon ceases to be CR399 and becomes Via de Luna, swelling to four lanes plus a median and turning lanes. Most of the little beach shacks have been replaced by opulent homes, condos, other signs of civilization—and there are enough permanent residents to warrant shopping centers, a real grocery store, and an elementary school.

I turned away from the buildings to the park's main entrance on the island's western end. Bypassing the sign-in area I scouted the campground, chose a site, drove back to register, but the office had closed, so I returned to the campsite and settled in. The evening temperature was comfortable and the air humid. There were no mosquitoes—a blessing. Behind the dunes and under stunted coastal live oaks, wind was almost nonexistent. A one-legged male towhee and a tailless brown thrasher hunted the nearby palmettos while I ate dinner. This is one of the few national park campgrounds that has showers, and it is popular. Leaving a folding chair and camp stove out to show the site was occupied, I drove to Fort Pickens.

The park has preserved the fort and cleaned up the grounds. Several wooden houses and other buildings constructed at the turn of the last century have been refurbished and quarter staff, offices, a museum, and meeting rooms. Couples and anglers were situated along the concrete sea wall admiring the weak sunset or hoping for a nibble. I parked and walked around the massive brick walls, past the rooms where Geronimo and his defeated Apache warriors were displayed to triumphant white visitors in 1886. The Apaches were confined at the fort for two years before being removed to Alabama.

When Audubon was forming his dismal view of Pensacola's future, Fort Pickens was new, and smartly turned troops performed cadenced maneuvers for their commanders on the parade grounds. Perched on the stubby edge of the island, with Fort McRee guarding the opposite shore, it must have seemed that no enemy ship could enter Pensacola's harbor.

Fort Pickens was constructed over a period of five years. More than twenty-one and a half million bricks were manufactured on the mainland and barged across the sound. Maine sent twenty-six thousand casks of lime, granite came from Sing-Sing in New York, lead came from Illinois mines and copper from Switzerland, and a skilled slave workforce came from New Orleans. Shifting sands could not support the great weight of those bricks, so engineers used reverse arches to spread the weight and minimize settling. The simple design has worked remarkably well. Before and for some time after Fort Pickens appeared, native people rowed across the sound to fish and dry their catches in the strong salty winds and gather shells and grasses.

Union forces battered and captured the forts during the War Between the States. Storms and time have since completely erased Fort McRee. Fort Pickens still stands, though it has undergone a number of changes. In the 165 years since the fort was completed, the westward drift has placed about a half-mile of sand between the fort and the shore. Battery Pensacola was constructed on half of the seven-acre parade grounds in 1898–99. A fire in mid-1899 spread in spite of a bucket brigade and reached the rooms where eight thousand pounds of powder were stored. One man was killed by the explosion and the damage was never repaired. Outside the fort, a string of concrete batteries disguised as sand dunes were built during World War I. By World War II, advancements in ammunition and warfare had made those structures obsolete, but they were never removed and lend a sinister glint to the landscape. Fort Pickens was decommissioned and turned over to the Florida Park Service in 1949. By the early 1970s, when the property was in the process of being transferred to the National Park Service as part of the Gulf Islands National Seashore, Fort Pickens was in a state of decrepit decay. Apathy haunted the old walls.

In the evening twilight of 1999, Fort Pickens seemed a bit more at ease due to ministrations from park service personnel. After the fort ceased to be used as a fortification, cannons were removed, but a few have been replaced to give visitors a feel for what the armament had once been. Some areas are marked off-limits, but many crannies and stairways are open for exploration. Sand has been removed from the base of one of the arches to expose the intricate mirror image of a reverse arch; most of the fort's mass is underground. Overhead, nearly two centuries of rainwater filtering through many brick layers have leached Maine lime from the mortar and miniature stalactites hang from the ceiling. From atop the west wall, I watched the horizon swallow the sun. People leaned against the seawall but the beaches were empty except for the repetitive sound of water brushing the shore. A comforting, symmetrical sound echoing a heartbeat. Time to leave the fort to the night.

After a good night's sleep I felt a stroll on the beach under an overcast sky to be in order the next morning. Sanderlings investigated damp sand for delicacies. A great blue heron landed a few yards ahead. I stopped walking. It waited awhile and I walked forward. The bird flew ahead and landed again and once more I paused. It waited and then peered into the shallows in search of a snack. Obviously my presence disturbed its breakfast hour so I turned around. A couple behind me remarked on the bird and I told them why I'd turned back. They turned around too.

Unable to face the Miracle Strip morass again, I turned north on Route 87 through the western outskirts of Eglin Air Force Base. This is an unrestricted area and two-track roads lead off the highway to bump through young stands of longleaf pines. Eglin owns 463,448 acres in Santa Rosa, Walton, and Okaloosa Counties. Agreements with The Nature Conservancy and the U.S. Fish and Wildlife Service ensure sound management, restoration, and research on a large slice of longleaf habitat. Audubon, and others, were wrong to brush off the longleaf forests. They might appear barren at first glance but they are not.

Tall longleaf pines shade an understory of palmettos or a mixture of bunch grasses and turkey oaks. The composition of the understory depends on the underlying soil composition, water availability, and the frequency of fires. Such pinelands are home to an array of reptiles, birds, insects, mammals, and amphibians. Fall fills the woods with color—sunny goldenrod, magenta blazing star, white summer farewell—especially following a spring burn.

Periodic fires keep the forest open, curb competing species from over-colonizing, trigger a flowering response in certain plants, and return nutrients to the soil. Longleaf and associated species have adapted to fire over thousands of years. The pine's exceptionally thick bark protects against fire's heat. Longleaf seeds require open ground to germinate. Seedlings expend energy during the first few years establishing a deep root system and underground trunk. Young longleaf pines resemble clumps of green grass and remain in the "grass" stage for several years. Experts contend that the grass stage lasts from three to as many as ten years depending on a variety of factors. Even in the grass stage, dense needles burn and release moisture that insulates and protects the terminal bud. As long as the bud is unharmed, the tree will probably survive. Gopher tortoises, a keystone species of the longleaf ecosystem, also need open space. Their burrows provide homes for reptiles, insects, small mammals, and amphibians. There is a lot of life in a longleaf forest not readily visible to the casual observer.

I thought a lot about Audubon on the drive home and realized he could be compared to a longleaf forest. At first glance he had seemed a shallow egotist. Deeper evaluation was called for.

Audubon labeled his paintings "Drawn from nature by John J. Audubon," leading people to believe that he had caught the painted scene as it happened in real life. That was not the case. Fans and detractors must agree that Audubon killed thousands of birds and other animals and arranged their skins or their bodies in contrived poses. Birds quickly lose the depth of their colors after death and he needed a steady supply of fresh specimens; there was no way to preserve them. His subjects, portrayed alone or posed before a backdrop added by other artists, gained a passion not evident in Catesby, Bartram, or Wilson, even though the poses were sometimes impossible in real life. In a way his paintings were drawn from nature. He spent hours observing wildlife and recreated moments of tranquility or raw terror. Yet, from his trademark signature, "Drawn from nature," it seems that Audubon would have us believe he had whipped out his easel and paint box in the middle of a swamp or woodland to capture the grace of an egret's sumptuous breeding plumage or the desperation of a small creature about to be captured by a predator. It was not that easy. A lifetime went into perfecting his work.

His personal letters and writings reveal a man who often complained. The picture presented in his public works is indeed more rosy with rarely a hint of financial or family problems. The stories he wrote for the *Ornithological Biography* and other works are truly adventure tales. Audubon glossed over personal discouragements and polished details in prose not quite as flowery as William Bartram, but with an air of romanticism nonetheless. The reader may be dismayed by the numbers of birds he enjoyed shooting. His name now symbolizes the protection of birds and nature, but he took pride in his shooting skill. During his explorations in the Florida Keys "sixty-five Great Godwits lay at our feet" after a few minutes blasting. When herons and flamingos were driven off the mud-flats by incoming tides, "the shooting behind the bushes began, until we had a heap not unlike a small haycock."[5] Though he deplored the assaults of "eggers" who took eggs from nesting birds and sea turtles for food or for collectors, he did not hold his own depredations in the same regard. He needed fresh birds for staging poses, but it seems that two or three at a time should have been adequate. Perhaps he judged his prowess as a hunter, and as a man, by the size of the mound of corpses.

Though his fortunes rose after publishing *The Birds of America* in 1838, they were to fall again. In 1841, John James bought a large tract of land on the Hudson River and built a home for Lucy, calling it Minnie's Land, Minnie being her nickname. Gifford and Woodhouse had married and the house filled with grandchildren.

By 1846, Audubon's eyesight had begun failing. He seemed diminished when he could no longer draw and paint. He suffered a stroke in 1847 and though his health remained strong his mind was altered. He became childlike until the awful day when he gazed at his family without recognizing any of them. Gone forever was the gay, passionate hunter, artist, husband, father, friend. Lucy cared for Audubon until he died on January 27, 1851. He was sixty-five years old.

Gifford and Woodhouse constructed large homes on the property, an undertaking that consumed a good bit of the new Audubon wealth. In 1857, Lucy, at seventy, was again tutoring children to earn extra money. She cared for Gifford after an accident left him an invalid. He died in 1860. Woodhouse invested considerable money to bring out a single double-elephant volume of 106 plates from *The Birds of America*. Unfortunately, many of the subscribers were Southern and the money was lost when the Civil War broke out. Woodhouse died in 1862 and Lucy sold Minnie's Land in 1863 for her savings were depleted. She spent her last years living with a granddaughter and then her youngest brother. She sold her copies of Audubon's paintings and works for money to live on. Lucy Bakewell Audubon died in her eighty-seventh year on June 18, 1874.

Audubon loved the natural world. He was an artist who chose wildlife to represent his talent. It was what he knew best. Ornithological purists may find fault with his paintings woven in luminous, sumptuous, lavish colors, for his birds possess grace and perfection beyond nature's limits. His personality was not that of a suave André Michaux, a kind William Bartram, or a thoughtful Mark Catesby. Audubon was volatile, unpredictable, a ladies' man and a man's man.

His early biographers, for the most part, believed Audubon the finest ornithologist and naturalist ever to walk America. Peattie called André Michaux a "short shadow" next to Audubon, and dismissed Alexander Wilson's work in a few words. Audubon's bird studies were "without precedent in the history of ornithology. Without historic parallel, indeed, in the business of publishing. (Hadn't Wilson worked himself to death trying to sell his modest efforts?)"[6] Other biographers, whether Audubon admirers at the outset of their work or not, came to realize that he might be considered an icon standing on feet of clay. We must disremember his personal shortcomings. After all is written and said, though, he was only human and as flawed as any of us. People who viewed his art had the opportunity to absorb, understand, and appreciate birds for the magnificent creatures they are in a way they never had before. John James Audubon is forever associated with birds, and his name has been lent to many conservation and environmental causes. What better tribute than to remember him as the man who by painting nature's beauty awakened our instincts for its protection?

CHAPTER 8

The Garden of Eden

Hardy Bryan Croom
(October 8, 1797–October 9, 1837)

Magnolia macrophylla. Grows in Florida, on the outer margin of the swamp of the Apalachicola river. The petals of some of the flowers measured seven inches in length, while those of M. grandiflora measure six inches. I am informed that it grows in the upper parts of Georgia and Alabama. Its original region is probably sub-alpine, and the plants that grow in Florida may have sprung from seeds carried down by the freshets of the Chattohochie.

—Hardy Croom, "Floral Calendar of Middle Florida,"
American Journal of Science, Jan. 1834

E. E. CALLOWAY, raised in Alabama and then practicing law in Blount-stown, Florida, on the banks of the Apalachicola River, had studied biblical passages regarding the location of the Garden of Eden near a four-headed river. Just above the Florida-Georgia line, the Flint River and Spring Creek join the Chattahoochee River to form the Apalachicola. Noah was instructed to cut gopher wood from the Garden to build an ark. One of the trees growing in the ravines leading to the Apalachicola River is known by the common name of gopher wood. Gold had been abundant near Eden; Dahlonega, Georgia, the site of the East's Gold Rush, was situated not too far from the Chattahoochee. From these observations, Mr. Calloway ascertained that Eden had been in Georgia and that the Garden had been in North Florida on the eastern bank of the Apalachicola River, specifically just north of Bristol, Florida. This astounding theory contributed to the formation of "The Garden of Eden" tourist attraction in the 1950s. It survived for awhile, but North Florida was not quite ready for a theme park.

My father was an active man whose work took him on the road five days out of seven. This did not deter him from taking his family on weekend drives. He loved to travel and was always ready to stop at some scenic bend in the road. For this reason, one hot summer afternoon found us at the edge of Liberty County, just north of Bristol, Florida, at The Garden of Eden.

The day was hot and the trees that we had come to see seemed too puny to have composed something as grand as Noah's Ark. By the 1950s the torreyas, also known as savin, stinking cedar, and gopher wood, were heading toward extinction though no one would notice for another decade. Thirty years later, I returned to the area to work for The Nature Conservancy.

The Conservancy purchased the site from a private landowner in 1982 and began adding bits and blocks until the Apalachicola Bluffs and Ravines Preserve now totals 6,248 acres. The original intent was to protect Alum Bluff and rare plants and animals in the ravines from being obliterated by a proposed electrical plant. Alum Bluff soars 150 feet above the Apalachicola and reveals Miocene (twenty-three million to five million years ago) to Holocene (ten thousand years ago to the present time) strata. The bluffs face an outside curve in the river, where the current is strongest. Little by little, the river undermines the slope and chunks slough off periodically. Shark's teeth and blackened manatee bones are uncovered and spin away in the flow. Amateur fossil hunters and professional geologists are attracted to the area, but because the site is protected, not to mention unstable, the Conservancy has closed the bluff face to the public.

Torreya State Park is just north of the Conservancy's property. The park was established in the 1930s to protect the rare torreya trees and provide recreational opportunities. An old plantation house from Ocheesee Landing, across the river from the park, was dismantled, moved, and rebuilt in 1935 by the Civilian Conservation Corps. The former kitchen serves as the park's office, and the house is open to viewing by park vistors. At one time plans included a nearby motel, swimming pool, and stables. Fortunately they have not materialized. The park does have a peaceful campground and more than seven miles of hiking trails.

A broad floodplain forest flows west of the Apalachicola, but the higher eastern side contains a series of unique land forms known as steephead ravines between the towns of Bristol and Chattahoochee. The rounded head of the ravine resembles a narrow forested amphitheater with steep sides, hence the appellation, steephead. Tons of rain falling on the sandy uplands filter quickly through the porous soil. Eventually the water reaches a lower clay layer and inches along the lateral barrier seeking a path to freedom—in this case, the Apalachicola River. Streams spurting from the base of the steephead have carried away soil and decaying vegetable matter as the ravines have crept slowly back from the river over thousands of years. Those shallow, clear streams have a moderating effect on temperatures in the ravines, warming them in winter and cooling them in summer—though "cooling" is debatable in August.

In an area of Florida generally thought to be level, the casual hiker may ponder on these geological oddities: deep clefts in the earth with thin clear water moving intently through the bottom. The ravines are the extreme southern range of the beautiful copperhead snake whose skin perfectly mirrors the color pattern of dried fallen leaves. Beavers, true to their breed, have dammed some of the seepage streams to form private swimming holes. Several varieties of ferns grace damp stream margins in early summer. The ravines seem finished, complete, but they are ceaselessly and infinitesimally alive and changing.

Topographic maps of the region show that the ravines mimic splayed fingers edging to the east. From an airplane window, one sees dark green hardwood ribbons weaving through piney uplands. If they look idiosyn-

FIG. 12. A seepage stream rushes across the ravine floor at
The Nature Conservancy's Apalachicola Bluffs and Ravines Preserve
where Hardy Croom and Dr. Alvan W. Chapman botanized.
Photo by Steve Gatewood. Courtesy of The Nature Conservancy.

cratic on the map and from the air, the ravines are otherworldly to visit. Walking across a fairly flat land, one focuses on a verdant line of hard-woods where the land suddenly falls away. Longleaf pines, unable to thrive in the shade cast by a leafy parasol, fringe the lip of a sharply de-clining slope. The slope can be divided into miniature life zones—many species are confined to narrow bands defined by amounts of light and moisture. Lofty American beeches and glossy green southern magnolias reach for the sky along with tall, skinny spruce pines and hickories, while unassuming Ashe magnolias and pyramid magnolias nod in protective shade. Salamanders of several varieties, including the endemic Apalachi-cola dusky, live in the clear, cool stream. Ferns, lizard's tail, and Florida anise grow near stream edges and above them the rare, petite *Croomia pauciflora.* Endangered Florida yews and torreyas hang on in the slope's middle third.

During my tenure with the Conservancy, I spent many hours in the ravines, leading field trips and counting plants, warmed by the exertion of climbing up and down in winter and summer, often beset by voracious mosquitoes, and more than once unintentionally sliding down a slope on slippery leaves. I had often enlisted the aid of a fine botanist from Chat-tahoochee, Angus Gholson. Angus had walked this land all his life and was a font of lore about the plants and people who had passed through here before our lifetimes.

One who had been taken with this region in the 1830s and became intimately associated with the bluffs and ravines was a young attorney from North Carolina, Hardy Croom. Walking the land that Croom had trodden so many years before brought him to life again. His story in-trigued me and made me curious about others whose names are tacked to scientific epithets, the unique latinized names given to each species.

A WEALTHY PLANTER FROM NEW BERN, North Carolina, Croom received his education from the University of North Carolina. He repre-sented Lenoir County in the North Carolina state senate in 1828, eventu-ally resigning to look after his North Carolina and Florida holdings. He practiced law for a short time but presumably had no intention of mak-ing a career of it. Hardy's family owned vast lands in North Carolina, and his father had been purchasing land in Florida when the elder Croom died of an untimely illness. Following his father's lead, Hardy and his brother, Bryan, also traveled to Florida and purchased land around Tallahassee and farther west in Jackson County. The brothers planned to build plantations in the Florida Territory. Around 1832, Hardy leased a plantation opposite Aspalaga Landing on the west side of the Apalachicola River. For him the shaded lush ravines across the river, so different from the upland longleaf pine forests, were a garden for exploring. Hardy's passion was botany, and he was quite willing and able to indulge it.

The town of Aspalaga sprang up in the 1820s during Governor William P. Duval's term. The name is a corruption of that of a Spanish mission, San José de Ospalaga. Spain established a chain of missions across the territory in the early 1600s to reclaim the souls of Indians and strengthen Spain's rights to the land. Postal records show that Aspalaga actually had a post office from March 1828 to July 1837. The job of postmaster came with little remuneration and a wealth of record-keeping. Quite often there were breaks in operation when the post went unfilled either by death or resignation, and more than once a town simply faded away. Aspalaga's population gradually moved to more prosperous towns.

Aspalaga Landing is just north of the land owned by the Conservancy so it is fair to say that Hardy botanized extensively in the shaded ravines. He might have rented the plantation because of its proximity to the curious forests but that is impossible to know for sure. It seemed that Hardy had only to turn around to find plants unfamiliar to him and new to science. *Croomia pauciflora, Baptisia simplicifolia,* and *Taxus floridana,* the Florida yew, were among those he discovered. In 1833 Croom found a tree he had never seen before. The needles emitted a pungent odor when crushed. He could find no description of it and gathered some cuttings and seeds that he sent to Dr. John Torrey in New York with a letter describing the tree and its surroundings. At first, Torrey thought the tree might be similar to a yew found in China or another found in California. The more he studied the samples, the more certain he became that the tree was something never before described.

A fine taxonomist, well versed in assigning a plant to its proper niche, Torrey wanted corroboration of his decision. He forwarded the information to his counterpart in Scotland, Dr. Arnott, who determined the cuttings to be a separate, distinct species and awarded the name *Torreya taxifolia* in honor of Dr. Torrey.

On a cool April day in 1999, I drove fifty miles west from Tallahassee, partly on the wide bumpity concrete of Interstate 10, one of the nation's more boring roads, to the Greensboro exit where less traveled Route 12 moved southward. The asphalt coasted down the Cody Scarp, North Florida's ancient shoreline (give or take a millennium; this was waterfront property five million years ago), and ambled through a land of deep loose sands layered with clayey soils adorned with thickly sown rows of sand pines grown to fuel paper mills. Scattered pockets of young longleaf pines stood like bottle brushes. Their long, deep green needles would glisten in sunlight but not on this overcast day. A few were beginning to send out branches. If I squinted, they vaguely resembled hairy saguaro cactuses. The distance that took me an hour to cover probably took at least two days in Hardy's time.

I met Greg Seamon, the Conservancy's Northwest Florida land steward, at the preserve's headquarters. Teasing rain clouds overlaid the morning. Greg accompanied me into No Name Ravine on a trail narrow, steep, and glossy with fallen leaves. We soon warmed in spite of the cool day. Near the ravine's lip we passed an early blooming Indian pink, its scarlet upright tubular flowers topped with creamy yellow stigmas. Florida was beginning the third year of an exhausting drought and, luckily, just a few mosquitoes slowly bounced around. Ferns along the slope were not as lush as in the past, though the seepage stream steadily swirled through the bottom. Florida anise trees were blooming and we sniffed their spicy, licorice scented leaves. We passed by trilliums and violets. We crossed a log felled over the stream and clambered up the hillside. A slender pyramid magnolia leaned over the ravine's grade. Short planks lay over barely moist seeps that in wetter years would be tiny rills.

"There should be a torreya on a toe up here; we had to move the trail away from the tree to protect it," Greg explained as his eyes searched the slope. A toe is a hump of land that sticks out like a buttress against the ravine's flank. The stream dodged around it. Full sun rarely penetrates to the lower ravine, and on a day as dim as this, Greg had to conscientiously look to differentiate between plants. We strode on, I holding on to small trees for balance as we advanced up and down, Greg's longer legs making the trip easier for him.

We passed through a grove of Florida yews, which resemble torreyas, though the yew's needles are soft and pliant whereas the torreya's are stiff and sticky. Yews were once more rare than torreyas. The opposite is now true, though the yew is by no means a dominant tree.

We rounded another toe and Greg announced a patch of *Croomia pauciflora*. Several plants, rarely standing taller than six inches, grew in a small area. We carefully hunkered down with our faces close to the ground and lifted the tiny leaves. No flowers yet. As might be guessed from the scientific name, the small, greenish colored flowers hide underneath the stem. They are, as botanists say, inconspicuous, and not likely to be viewed at all unless one lays a cheek close to the ground and lifts a leaf.

"How many *Croomia* plots are on the preserve," I asked, "and how are they doing?"

Greg hunched over to take a photograph of the tiny plant and reeled off information like a fish striking a line. "There are ten known populations on the preserve. We look at the coverage area and count the number of stems in each. We look for sexual reproduction and damage which comes from feral hog rooting and flooding from the Apalachicola, though flooding hasn't been a problem for the last couple of years. Our data has only been gathered for a short time and is by no means conclusive but it gives us a baseline for the future."

"Where else is the plant found?" I quizzed as we continued along the trail.

"In the southern Appalachians and coastal plain of Alabama and along the drainages of Chattahoochee, Flint, and Apalachicola Rivers in Florida and Georgia. *Croomia* seems to be declining, but, again, we need a few more years of data before we can really answer that."[1]

The trail switched back as Greg muttered, "We must have missed that other torreya but there's another one farther along, though it's not easy to reach." This particular representative grew fairly tall on an especially steep slope. Most torreyas are stunted and look sickly. No one really knows why the trees started to wane, though several theories have been put forward and scientists as far away as California and Massachusetts are trying to save the species. Luckily, the Florida yew resists whatever is killing the torreyas. *Torreya taxifolia* is not found anyplace else in the world though it is related to other species found in California, Japan, and China. At its tallest, a torreya might achieve forty feet. Today we would be hard pressed to find in the wild a larger living tree than the spindly one standing fourteen feet tall in front of us. Residents once used the trees for fence posts since its white wood seemed impervious to the elements. Trunks of adult torreyas that toppled thirty or forty years ago still lie downslope, their hard wood intact.

FIG. 13. The endangered *Croomia pauciflora.*
Photo by Gil Nelson.

Robert Godfrey and Herman Kurz, botanists at Florida State University, first noticed the torreya's decline in 1962. A fungal disease affecting
the stems seemed to be the cause and the botanists worried that extinction lurked within the next decade. Had a drought in the 1950s stressed
the trees? Had the dam at Chattahoochee so altered the river's flow that it
affected the torreya? Why had the trees suddenly become so vulnerable to
the fungus?

Plant pathologists have isolated pathogens causing the fungus and
they are common natives, not some exotic little-known agent. Botanists
now feel a variety of factors combined to bring about torreya's downfall.
The tree has been around a long time. Fossils more than one hundred
million years old have been found in North Carolina, and the oldest remains from Europe checked in at 160 million years old.

Torreyas found in the ravines these days are juvenile trees, suckers, and
saplings germinating from the last seed crop generated decades ago or
straining to grow from old roots in the ground. About the time trees
reach sexual maturity, the fungal blight strikes. Few survivors are more
than twenty-five years old and only a handful have borne fruit. Sexual
reproduction is at a standstill. To add insult to injury, white-tailed bucks

favor the trees for rubbing velvet from their antlers. Many small trees have been enclosed in protective wire cages.

In all the years of research and with all the improvements in testing equipment, biologists still cannot answer how and why this tree is declining. From his boyhood, Angus Gholson knew the torreya as a tree valued for its durability and it saddens him now to watch it disappear. Mark Schwartz has been studying the trees since his doctoral student days and is not much closer to an answer now than he was a dozen years ago.

Cuttings taken from torreyas and grown in Harvard University's Arnold Arboretum have been growing disease-free for a number of years. The tree itself may never go entirely extinct but will probably never be found growing healthily, naturally, again. Like Bartram's *Franklinia,* the torreya may become a relict propagated only in nurseries for ornamental landscaping.

Why should we worry about the extinction of this tree of limited range and small commercial value? Many other plants and animals have gone extinct and the earth is still rolling around the sun. The loss of this seemingly insignificant tree should be a reminder to all of us that each species is allocated a certain time to flourish before it is replaced by another. Human beings, though many of us want to ignore it, are not exempt from the extinction process and we do not know and cannot tell whether we ride on the rising or falling side of the scale. If we do not pay attention to the state of the rest of the world's inhabitants—large and small—we may never recognize what tips us into an extinction mode until it is too late.

At this point the trail began an abrupt climb to the top of the ravine. We passed through a small copse of blooming Ashe magnolias, their great, creamy blossoms beginning to unfurl against their huge leaves. Some botanists maintain that the Ashe magnolia is a distinct species but others have come to accept it as a subspecies of Michaux's *Magnolia macrophylla,* the bigleaf magnolia. The rain that had been threatening began to fall as we walked the sandy track through young longleafs and then stopped after barely dampening the sand.

Greg had made plans for several prescribed burns the following week and had volunteer work crews lined up. But the summer wildfires of 1998 were still fresh in the state's memory and, since spring had not seen much rain, this little sprinkle might not be quite enough to convince the Division of Forestry to grant a burn permit for the preserve.

It is difficult to get a burn to accomplish much on this preserve even on a day with perfect conditions. Longleaf pines underscored with wiregrass, turkey oaks, and other sparsely spaced grasses and forbs once grew here. Former landowners, concerned only with immediate profits, cut the longleaf and bulldozed the groundcover and debris left from timbering into widely spaced linear piles, called windrows, leaving the ground in between level, bare, and ready to receive rows of slash pine seedlings. Silviculturists had not then bred a slash pine that could thrive in such poor soils and the pines that had been planted almost four decades earlier were rarely larger than a foot in diameter.

After the Conservancy purchased the land, people were hired to cut the slash. It didn't take long to remove the largest trees but, even in a county where timber jobs are difficult to come by, the others were hardly worth the effort. The abused uplands needed attention. Without fine fuels—dried grasses, small twigs and branches, and pine needles—to carry a fire, that tool could not be easily reintroduced to this ecosystem.

Within a few years of acquiring the preserve, land managers initiated a challenging restoration of the longleaf pine uplands. Teams of volunteers have been set loose on cool mornings in winter, one with a dibble tool and the other with boxes of longleaf seedlings. One dibbles a hole and the other inserts a tree and pats the sand around it, then they move off a few steps to repeat the process. It's back straining work for the planter. Over time more than 1.4 million longleaf seedlings have been planted in this random manner.

But planting longleaf pines is not enough. If the plant community is going to be restored, then all the components are needed. In the early 1990s, wiregrass and other understory plants were not commercially available, so the Conservancy had to grow its own and that proved tricky. Research has shown that while many plants produce thousands of viable seed each year, wiregrass—the main plant to carry fire—is stimulated to produce seed in the fall after a spring burn. The preserve harbors a small area from which to recover seeds and there is a small window of time in which to harvest them. A native plant nursery was built and volunteers gather seeds of wiregrass and other plants in the fall. Seeds are sown and tended until hardy enough to plant the next winter. Wiregrass seeds have a low viability, so each container is planted with a pinch of seeds. A few weeks after the initial planting, containers that have not produced any growth are resown. As the nursery can raise only about sixty-five thousand to ninety thousand plants a year, primarily wiregrass, this is a slow process. About 316,000 plugs have been planted on thirty-five to forty acres. Direct seeding experiments are proving successful and quicker. Thirty-five acres were planted in the winter of 1998 and ninety acres were planted in winter 1999.

Fire holds the longleaf/wiregrass ecosystem together, but along with timbering and bulldozing came fire suppression. Without fire to keep them in check, plentiful turkey oaks became large and prosperous. Their big leathery leaves do not readily burn and their shade denies sunlight to groundcover. Windrows add an impediment to an area already difficult to burn, and what little groundcover remains is often found on a windrow. Lazy flames spread across the flat area, desperately seeking something to burn, flare over large clumps of wiregrass growing on the side of a windrow, only to give out at the top where bare soil or a thick growth of shrubs caps the small hill. The windrows are rarely more than three feet tall so it is difficult to imagine that they can bring fire to a halt, but they do. Recently, the Conservancy secured funding to hire a contractor to spread the windrows and restore the land's smooth aspect.

In any event, restoring this area's landscape is a long and somewhat expensive process as well as a learning experience along the way. It cannot succeed without the help of hundreds of volunteers. Some are children from area schools, and, each spring, college students spend several weeks on the preserve in the Alternative Spring Break Program. On cool, sometimes rainy autumn Saturdays, families and couples show up to plant trees and collect seeds.

On warm spring and early summer days, trained volunteers don hot Nomex fire resistant suits and other protective gear and set fire to the woods. Conducting a fire at the Bluffs Preserve is often a matter of walking through the interior with a drip torch and leading fire to patches it would not normally reach because of spotty groundcover. Some volunteers are repeat performers while others may come only once a year. They come in all shapes, ages, and sizes and work in all sorts of weather. All gain hands-on knowledge of how an ecosystem works.

There were no volunteers out on this April day. Only the hint of rain on the young longleafs planted more than a decade ago and beginning to send out branches from their slender trunks. Greg and I walked toward the office and he doubted the scant rain would be enough to allow his burns. With luck, the rains would return soon and fire would crackle through the patchwork of plants while Mississippi and swallow-tailed kites glided overhead feasting on insects escaping the blaze.

I left the preserve and drove across the river, riding low between its banks, to Blountstown to meet a friend for lunch. Sybil Arbery was raised in Blountstown though she spent most of her working life in Atlanta. When she retired she returned to her favorite place and built a small home near the Apalachicola's floodplain. Sybil remembers big pine forests and torreya trees. She has seen changes in her homeland and not all of them for the better. To help preserve what she could, Sybil has donated hours to the Conservancy's native plant nursery.

This part of Florida's panhandle is a forgotten part of the state. There is no beach to attract visitors, though the forests attract hunters during the season. The sandy land is too poor for productive farming but it does grow timber and prisons. There is little opportunity that would hold a young person here. There are not enough timber jobs to go around and though each county clamors for a prison, those jobs, too, are limited. It is a scrape-by livelihood at best and those who can, leave to get an education and find a job someplace else. But for others, it is a home they cannot desert. The people who live in these counties are tough and hard-working and not always appreciative of outsiders who want to tell them how to run their lives.

Nearly two centuries ago Hardy Croom had envisioned a future here and made several treks to Florida from North Carolina between 1830 and 1837. The journey was onerous and took almost two weeks. Charles Joseph Latrobe traveled North America in 1832–33 and found little joy anywhere in the south. Of Florida he wrote, "The very name of Florida has carried a charm with it, . . . which has been perpetuated by lying romancers and mendacious travelers, with regard to its surpassing beauty, every one from whom we had obtained more direct intelligence had contrived, . . . to add to the false impression . . . when fatigued with the fir-forests and the half-exhausted fields of the Carolinas, and the swamps and rice plantations of Georgia, we still looked forward to Florida . . . But it was to us, as to [Ponce de León], 'the land of Disappointment.'" After arriving at St. Augustine, which Latrobe did find pleasing at first, he was again plagued with having to "labour for days and days before we could make any arrangements to cross the country to Tallahassee." At last transportation was secured, "a carry-all drawn by two wretched horses" for the 240-mile, ten-day journey to Tallahassee, across barren and uninteresting country.

That leg of the journey was likely in April, though Latrobe was not forthcoming with dates. Rain had swollen the rivers, so the travelers were forced to lay up at someone's house. Their host warned them of the "whip-snake, which would take hold of a tuft of grass with its mouth . . . and scutch you with its tail till you removed yourself out of the way!" Not to mention the horrible tornadoes and frequent conflagrations. Beware the traveler!

Latrobe called Tallahassee a pleasing town, home to about sixteen hundred people then. Since the once-weekly stage had just left, Latrobe hired a wagon for St. Marks, a day's travel across "a very fairish sort of a road,—one in which the stumps are cut pretty nigh level, that is, within two feet o' the ground!"[2]

Transportation difficulties aside, Hardy Croom was drawn to the Florida frontier. He found excitement and fulfillment in roaming the woods, but the time must have been bittersweet for his wife and family stayed behind in New Bern when not in Saratoga or New York City. Hardy was anxious to move his family to Florida, but his wife was reluctant to leave civilized society. No doubt her mother, Henrietta Smith, a strong-willed woman, had a voice in gainsaying her daughter's departure. Instead, Charleston was chosen as a worthy place to settle.

By the 1830s, the new United States was experiencing growing pains. The country had not yet adopted a standard currency. Because of the numerous types of paper money used as acceptable tender, inflation and land speculation skyrocketed. By the mid-1830s the country was in an economic depression.

In June of 1833, Hardy wrote to his brother Bryan, who had already built a home called Rocky Comfort in Gadsden County, Florida. The situation in North Carolina was depressed and not only because of a heat wave. Property values were falling. Hardy longed to return to Florida and he would do so in a few months.

A few years later times had not improved much. Bryan Croom wrote on August 15, 1836, that he had sent to Quincy, Tallahassee, and St. Marks and could not find a barrel of flour that had not gone sour, nor was there a decent ham or fruit of any kind, not even a bottle of lime juice. No amount of money could buy fresh food. The heat and damp, he declared, would rot a man as well as rust him.

Hardy had sold his Lenoir County lands in 1831 and removed his slaves to his Florida interests in Gadsden and Leon Counties. A rude cabin and quarters for his slaves had been built on his property surrounding Lake Lafayette but he had not established residency. One day soon, he planned to build a commodious handsome home on a rise surrounded by large live oaks on the land near Tallahassee. The home's shady porch would face the hard clay road to the south, one of several that ran like spokes from the hub of Tallahassee to outlying plantations and farms.

Tallahassee had been a substantial Indian town before it had been chosen as the site for the territory's capital in 1823. Roads that may have once led to outlying Indian villages now led to large plantations. A parade of wagons laden with produce and cotton bales, ladies coming into town to shop, men coming to keep an eye on the politicians, and travelers moving to and fro eroded tracks between steep red clay banks. Trees grew overhead until they joined branches across the road forming a shaded underpass. On bright days the canopy allowed dappled sunlight to shine through. On wet days, bright green, velvety resurrection ferns contrasted against limbs turned dark with dampness; in dry times the ferns shriveled and turned brown.

Despite its venerated position as Florida's capital, Tallahassee, until the latter years of the twentieth century, has been slow to grow. With that growth has come strain on an aged infrastructure. The city has a long-standing tradition of permitting development without improving roads. Historic canopied roads have brought people together in contentious debate on more than one occasion.

No one disputes their beauty: moss-scarfed oaks, leafy dogwoods, and red clay banks ushering the entrancing byways over Leon County's rolling hills. But the roads are narrow with barely a discernable shoulder. Cyclists love their dips and swells. Cars creep along waiting for a chance to dash around spandex-clad bodies hunched over a few pounds of metal frame. Dark nights, especially dark rainy nights, are like driving through a sideshow tunnel using a birthday candle for light while the road's periphery disappears and damp shadows absorb the headlights. If an oncoming car should happen to stray over the center line, there is no place to escape. Even in daylight, passing a large oncoming truck can be an adventure. There are factions who want to cut down the trees and widen the roads. There are more vociferous groups who advocate protecting and preserving the historic passages.

Automobiles, of course, were a long time in the future when the Croom family—Hardy, Frances, Henrietta Mary, fifteen, William

Henry, ten, little Justina Rosa, seven, and Frances's aunt, Mrs. Camack—boarded the steamship *Home* at the foot of Market Street on New York's East River harbor on the afternoon of October 7, 1837. With good weather, the ship would reach Charleston in less than three days. Hardy turned forty the next day, but if a celebratory dinner had been planned it had to be forgone; the ship soon encountered a storm and all available passengers were set to bailing with pots and buckets. This was in the days before hurricanes could be tracked, but by all accounts the gale, which came to be called Racer's Storm, had blown up south of Jamaica, run across the Yucatan, curved up the Texas coast, and slammed through Louisiana, Mississippi, Alabama, Georgia, and South Carolina before heading up North Carolina's coast.

The *Home* had been built in New York by James Allaire and then sold to the Southern Steam Packet Company, in which Allaire had a financial interest. Steam engines were still in their infancy and the mechanics not well understood. Bog ore, not a particularly high grade ore, mined in nearby New Jersey, was used to mold the *Home*'s engines. Though the ship was originally designed for river use, by October 1837, it had made two ocean passages from New York to Charleston, setting one record for completing the trip in slightly less than sixty-four hours. The same trip overland took nearly two weeks and was exceedingly uncomfortable. At 220 feet long with a twenty-two-foot beam, the *Home* cost $115,000 to build.

Surely humans who had been building ships for hundreds of years comprehended the different stresses applied to ships facing heavy winds and seas of the ocean as opposed to the relatively calm waters of a river. The *Home*'s narrow width made it unstable in rough seas and the ship had been fitted with structures called sponsons extending from the sides to add stability. In a later century the *Home* would never have been allowed on the open water. Because the boat was fast and in much demand, common sense was apparently superseded by the potential for profit. The *Home* carried ninety passengers, two of whom owned life preservers, forty crew members, and three lifeboats. Steamship companies were not required to provide passengers or crew with life preservers or to carry sufficient lifeboats.

At first the passengers might have viewed the bailing exercise as a sporting diversion. As seas worsened in the darkling tempest, it became obvious that bailing had become a losing battle. Stygian gloom came upon them. For hours they had been lifting heavy buckets and tossing water over the side only to have ten times more blown back onto the deck. They were soaking wet and tired and cold and the brutally slanting rain pasted their hair inside their collars and across their eyes. The ship bucked beneath their feet and they slid on the wet decks. The women's heavy sodden skirts impeded their movements. There was no safe place and the storm did not abate. Chances of their survival were being greatly outdistanced by the likelihood that they would perish.

Captain White, by reputation a good captain and not drunk during the storm as some later accused, reckoned he was past Cape Hatteras and attempted to beach the ship. The engines still churned the giant paddle wheels, but they were sometimes completely out of the water; the ship was impotent against the storm. A large wave hit the bow and washed several people overboard. Finally, water reached the boilers and the engines died. Using sail power, the vessel ran aground near North Carolina's Outer Banks about six miles northeast of Ocracoke.

The masts broke with terrifying crashes and the creaks and pops of timbers ripping away from the spars could be heard over the deafening roar of ravenous waves and rapacious winds. A mountain of polished onyx water exploded as it tore off the forward part of the ship and carried away screaming people dangling from the rails. Until the ship began to break apart, Andrew Lovegreen of Charleston had remained on the upper deck tolling the ship's bell in a vain attempt to summon help because he did not know what else to do. The hellish sound only increased the night's madness. A woman and child who had huddled under the protection of the smokestack were instantly killed when it and the wheelhouse fell on them.

One lifeboat had been launched and was immediately crushed. With the ship aground another boat was launched but was smashed to splinters before it hit the water. The third boat was loaded with fifteen or twenty people and had barely cleared the side when it overturned, spilling all into the sea. People tied themselves to pieces of the ship.

One portly seventy-year-old woman tied to a settee survived, and the men who owned the life vests both lived. All told, Captain White, nineteen crewmen, and twenty passengers survived the wreck. For days after the tragedy bodies and debris washed up on shore.

On October 5, 1837, Hardy Croom had sent a letter to Bryan Croom in Charleston letting him know that they had booked passage on the

Home, which would leave on the seventh, and that Bryan should send his carriage to meet them on the tenth of October. An earlier letter revealed that Mrs. Camack had not felt well and the Crooms had been waiting for her to recover her health before they left.

Bryan Croom probably did go to the Charleston docks along with others awaiting the ship's arrival. When the *Home* did not appear no one seemed too worried; sea travel was not always punctual in those days. It would be nearly a week before news of the wreck trickled into Charleston. William Croom's body washed ashore three weeks after the wreck and Frances's body was also recovered. They were buried near Ocracoke and later transferred to New Bern. The bodies of Hardy and Henrietta were never found and little Justina Rosa's body was either never found or never identified. Mrs. Camack also drowned.

The *Home,* of course, was not the first or the last ship to succumb to the Atlantic's storms. On June 14, 1838, the steamship *Pulaski* left Charleston harbor with 116 passengers. The boat was 206 feet long and twenty-five feet wide, with engines capable of almost two hundred horsepower. The voyagers soon met heavy waves. A boiler exploded and if seas had been calmer the vessel might have limped to port, but it rolled and shipped water and before long the masts snapped and then the boat broke apart. About one hundred passengers drowned. If it can be said that anything good came out of the losses it is that Congress passed the Steamboat Act effective October 1, 1838, requiring all boats to carry life preservers for all passengers and crew.

Hardy had mentioned his intention of leaving a will with a trusted New York merchant before sailing to Charleston, in a letter to Bryan written in September 1837, but no will was ever found. In addition to the grief that must have enveloped the families there arose the dreadful need to settle the estate; however, the absence of a will embroiled them in a legal battle that lasted twenty years. The Crooms and Henrietta Smith, Mrs. Croom's mother, could not agree on a fair settlement. Survivors of the wreck relived their horror in testimony time after time before the courts; the families' grief turned to thoughts of revenge.

Bryan Croom and his wife, Eveline, with no children of their own, had looked forward to having their nieces and nephew nearby. To assuage his anguish and establish a claim to his brother's estate, Bryan Croom set about building a home on the Tallahassee property. He planted a torreya in memory of Hardy in the surrounding gardens, but it did not flourish.

Under Bryan's stewardship Goodwood Plantation produced cash crops of cotton and corn as well as enough food for the family and employed as many as 240 slaves. By the 1850s the enterprise covered some eight thousand acres of Leon County.

Bryan Croom lost the plantation in a court decision in 1857 and moved to Montgomery, Alabama. He and Eveline kept in touch with Tallahassee friends but probably never returned to Florida. Henrietta Smith held the property for only a few weeks before selling it. She must have become a bitter woman by that time; no amount of money could restore her daughter or grandchildren. Arvah Hopkins bought the property in 1858; his widow sold it in 1885. Goodwood Mansion is now being meticulously restored by the Margaret E. Wilson Foundation.

William Warren Rogers and Erica Clark have compiled a detailed study titled *The Croom Family and Goodwood Plantation,* published in 1999. Their research covers the family's early history through the Reconstruction era and explains the complicated legal battle over Hardy's estate.

Hardy Croom, a slight man prone to coughs, loved the woods and avidly studied botany. He loved literature, geology, and paleontology. Though an amateur botanist, he was regarded by many in the scientific field as a promising talent. His descriptions and observations were as carefully made as a trained botanist and he wrote several papers that were published in the *American Journal of Science.*

When Hardy Croom had rolled into Quincy, Florida, on a long-ago October afternoon to visit Dr. Alvan Chapman, it was Chapman who was a beginner. Croom was far ahead of him in botanical knowledge. The two men became friends and had planned to search all of Florida for new plants. After Hardy's death, Dr. Chapman continued exploring the land around the Apalachicola River and became a premier botanist.

In the southwest corner of St. John's Episcopal Church on Monroe Street in Tallahassee stands a marble obelisk dedicated to the memory of Hardy Bryan Croom and his family. Bryan Croom paid for the monument on behalf of the Croom family. In the other corner is a similar memorial to Rev. J. L. Woart and his wife, who drowned in the wreck of the *Pulaski.*

Though he died young, and is chiefly remembered because of the notoriety surrounding his death, Hardy Croom stamped his mark on the period's botanical annuals as well as the area surrounding the then small town of Tallahassee. The city has grown around Goodwood Plantation, located behind Tallahassee Memorial Medical Center on Miccosukee Road. Thirteen miles north of Bristol, Florida, on CR 1641, Torreya State Park beckons campers and hikers. A few miles south of the park on State Road 12, just off the Garden of Eden Road, a hiking trail on the Apalachicola Bluffs and Ravines Preserve ascends and descends the forested ravines to the high bluff overlooking the Apalachicola River. Those who choose to do so can still walk the lands where Hardy Croom wandered so many years ago.

CHAPTER 9

Medicine Man

Alvan Wentworth Chapman
(September 28, 1809–April 6, 1899)

If I could in safety explore the uninhabited region towards the coast many rare and choice things could be brought to light. Your city botanists with polished boots rolled to your favorite haunts in steam boats and cars have but a faint idea of the figure a Florida botanist cuts in these wild woods—I take a thick bundle of newspapers which I tie behind my saddle. When I fill these I pack into my saddle bags as long as there is room—then my *hat*! is brought into play as long as it will stay on my head. Lastly I strap a bundle as large as a sheaf of wheat on my back and then start for home on a large white horse. (My horse is nearly as good a botanist as I am.)

—Dr. Alvan W. Chapman, from an unpublished letter to
Dr. John Torrey, January 1, 1842

DR. ALVAN CHAPMAN rose from his desk as a slight noise floated through the study window. To anyone else, it would have sounded like the breeze soughing through live oaks and moss, but to him it meant a clandestine hunt in the salt marshes. He pulled a tasseled cord and a dark-skinned servant appeared. The doctor requested a glass of cool buttermilk and when the man returned and bent to serve the beverage he laid a folded message near the glass. Dr. Chapman picked up his papers again and shuffled the note amongst them. It was dangerous business he was about. His house was watched and he could not be too careful. Once he had been a schoolteacher and had turned to medicine as a career. His true avocation, however, was botany. Dr. Chapman had been studying some specimens collected earlier in the spring and preparing notes. Few things distracted him from his plants but the evening's mission was of utmost importance.

The doctor donned his hat and coat. Sea breezes hardly cooled the sultry summer evenings but the coat gave him protection from mosquitoes. As a gentleman, he could hardly be publicly seen in his shirtsleeves at any time. He snuffed the one feeble candle in the room and left by the front door. To any observer he would be going on an evening stroll and no one could see the small packet he carried beneath his coat. He was a lean man, well over six feet tall. His stance was attention-straight, but he bent over when walking, a habit grown out of scanning the ground for new plants. The town was quiet that evening. Here and there couples and children hurried between houses, visiting in the dusk. Slits of light winked from gaps in drawn drapes. This was wartime. Candles and oil were hard to come by and lights made convenient targets for bored cannoneers on enemy ships offshore. Fortunately the town had not yet received a shell.

The doctor stopped at a neighbor's house and spent a polite time inquiring after everyone's health. Then he asked if their young son might go walking with him. They had become fast friends, the doctor and the boy on the cusp of his teenage years. Surely, the parents said. They felt Dr. Chapman a worthy companion for their youngest son, even if the older man was a Northerner. Truth be told, the family was tired of the war, the deprivation, the uncertainty.

The country was divided now, and even though Florida had hardly felt the bullets and bayonets of clashing armies, the coastal town lived constantly under the eyes of blockade ships. Because Dr. Chapman was

Apalachicola's only surgeon, most of the townspeople tended to forget that he was not a Southerner but a Union sympathizer.

The two made their way to the edge of town unnoticed. The boy, infused with the indestructibleness of youth, forgot his fear of the marshes and pushed aside the palmetto fronds and stiff grasses hiding a small boat. Something plopped into the water—a frog, a small gator, a cottonmouth? No time to look, and if the creature were leaving it was hardly worth the trouble. Nudging the boat into the water, the two poled their way through the trackless tidal creeks. Soon they reached the rendezvous. A man, dirty, unkempt, barely recognizable as anything but a scarecrow, shivered in the darkness. He stank. Used to sickroom smells, Dr. Chapman ignored the stench, but the boy would forever remember.

The man attempted to introduce himself, speaking in a voice suffering from disuse, low and rattling as if a plug of phlegm prevented it from rising. He gratefully accepted a crust of bread from Dr. Chapman, who cautioned him to chew it well and slowly. From under his coat the doctor pulled a rough-spun shirt and draped it over the man's shoulders. Still the man shook, from relief, from hunger, from the night chill. Best not speak nor tarry, warned the boy as he guided the listless man toward the small boat.

Ironically, being too young to join Apalachicola's Home Guard, the adolescent thrilled to these rescue adventures. Someone's eye was usually on the doctor, so the boy had made the crossing on his own more than once. He felt even more important and virtuous on those nights. Dimly he understood that the slovenly strangers were the enemy, but to a man their eyes were old and haunted. They drew into themselves until they seemed no bigger than whipped dogs, and he could not fear or hate them. When the silhouetted Union vessels were reached some men huddled in the bottom of the skiff and had to be lifted up, blubbering like children. They could not believe they were free and were afraid they were being handed over to the Confederates to be returned to that drear Georgia prison. The blue-garbed soldiers lavished kind words and sweet treats on the youngster. They would have given him more, but how could he explain a bolt of calico or pearl buttons? What might they have for him tonight, he wondered.

A thousand croaks, rustlings, and creaks of the fecund wetlands spread the news of their journey. The marsh's breath, a fermented bouquet of life and death, overcame the stranger's rankness. Ravenous mosquitoes, delighted at the presence of three warm-blooded mammals, relentlessly lanced unprotected skin. Droves of insects canvassed the men's ears and noses while moths and hard-shelled flying insects blundered against their shoulders. Night lives at a frenzied pace in the marsh. Decaying animals and vegetation combined with silt carried down by the powerful river formed a thick mass of rich ebony earth. Tough rubbery roots of tenacious serrated grasses held the soil together. Upon this oozing deposition the lives of animals who dwelled at land's edge depended. Incessant insect hums and wind-whispers through the black needlerush and spartina grasses filled the night. In their self-imposed silence accompanied by fear of discovery, each cracking branch sounded like a rifle shot that jolted their hearts.

The creek widened as it slipped into the Apalachicola River. The blunt-nosed boat's bow rose slightly as it caught the outflowing tide. A light breeze stippled the water's surface. Tonight they had hit it right. By the time they turned over their passenger, the tide would be slack and they would not have to fight the current back to the shore.

They neared the broad bay and shipped the cloth-wrapped oars. Hunched down in the boat as much as possible they hugged the eastern shoreline. Their chances of being seen or heard greatly increased as they floated past the town's docks. Each held his breath. Once out in the open they left the insect fusillade behind. Now they had only to reach the ship and hope an eagle-eyed Yankee gunner did not use them for target practice before they delivered their human cargo.

Their passenger had escaped from Georgia's Andersonville Prison, the south's largest prisoner-of-war camp and despicable shame. Officially known as Camp Sumter, Andersonville had begun accepting the first prisoners in late February 1864 and by August of that year held more than thirty-three thousand Union prisoners in a twenty-six and a half acre stockade. As the Northern army began closing in on Richmond, prisoners were funneled farther south, behind the lines to Camp Sumter. Before Sherman captured Atlanta in September most of the prisoners were shipped to other camps. Andersonville received many of them. A sudden influx of captured enemy soldiers into an overburdened area was a recipe for disaster. The few trees had gone immediately for firewood. Cover was nonexistent and industrious men scooped warrens into the red earth for shelter. Otherwise they endured the heat, the cold, the rain. Their only source of drinking water was also their latrine. Food, when available, was rotted and contained vermin. Men prayed for death rather than spend another day in that hellhole. Almost thirteen thousand had their prayers answered.

There were a lucky few who escaped. Joan Stibitz, Park Ranger at the Andersonville National Historic Site, related that approximately 329 men did escape from the stockade and lived to tell about it. Conditions were so bad inside those thick wooden walls that when prisoners weren't thinking of food, for they were starving, escape was on their minds. To actually attempt escape required extreme bravery and extensive planning, for as horrible as the inside was, the outside was worse.

Once the men managed to get out, few were certain of their exact location in Georgia so they struck off in various directions, hoping for the best. Of the many who tried to escape, some were captured and returned or killed by gunshots or other hazards of the area. The Flint River was only three miles away from the camp, not a great distance, but reaching the Flint was just the beginning. Following the river, a fugitive had to traverse unknown country for almost two hundred miles before freedom was within sight. Along that watery route he faced snakes, alligators, exposure, drowning, and—since his Northern accent gave him away if he chanced to speak to anyone—recapture was a constant specter at his side. If an escapee reached the salt marshes around Apalachicola, he stood a good chance of rescue.

Charles M. Smith published an account of his escape from Andersonville along with two other men. The three used turpentine on their shoes to foil tracking dogs and crept overland to the Chattahoochee, then followed it to the Choctawhatchee River. They stole boats along the river and were almost captured on at least two occasions. It took twenty-five days to reach Choctawhatchee Bay, a journey for which they had allowed sixteen days at the most, and when they arrived there were no Northern ships about. Using the bravado that had led them to escape, they implored a man to help them reach the gunboats at East Pass near Santa Rosa Island.

The scenario that opened this chapter is fabricated, though the horrors of Andersonville are well documented. Dr. Chapman's alleged exploits of rescuing escaped prisoners-of-war were written in the recollections of Winifred Kimball, who had met the doctor in 1887 when he was an old man and she was a young girl. She recalled learning botany from him on walks through nearby pine woods and titi swamps. Being a gentleman, he always carried the specimen box. Ms. Kimball wrote that the unnamed boy who helped Dr. Chapman spirit away escaped prisoners was never so royally treated as on board the Yankee cruisers, and he then had to go home and hold his tongue when his parents said he was too young to join the home guard. Whoever that young man was, if there was such a person, no one knows his name today.

John Kunkel Small knocked on Winifred Kimball's door one morning in December 1917, and inquired about a plant growing in her front yard. It was a coontie and not known to occur naturally so far north. She related her acquaintance with Dr. Chapman, which pricked Small's interest. He requested that she write down her memories of the doctor; the article was published in the *Journal of the New York Botanical Garden* in 1921.

Dr. Small had used Chapman's *Flora of the Southern United States,* published in 1860, while studying botany at Columbia University. Small's own work on southeastern plants was based heavily on Chapman's text. Because of his interest in Chapman, Small later transcribed some letters from Dr. Chapman to John Torrey and copies are among the John Kunkel Small Collection at the Florida Archives. Those letters afford a glimpse into the life of a rural doctor and botanist in panhandle Florida of the middle 1800s.

Alvan Wentworth Chapman was born on September 28, 1809, in Southampton, Massachusetts. He graduated with honors from Amherst College in 1830 and went south to teach school in Georgia. Arriving in Savannah in 1831, Chapman meandered beyond the city's limits, found a pitcher plant and identified it with the help of Amos Eaton's *Manual of Botany for the Northern and Middle States.* A brief biography written by John Ruge states that Chapman had a fondness for plants and nature since a young age. The teacher's casual acquaintance with botany grew into a full-time career. Chapman taught for a family on Whitemarsh Island near Savannah until he was elected principal of the academy of Washington, Georgia, where he apprenticed under Dr. Albert Reese. In those days, obtaining a medical degree was much abbreviated from what a student must go through today. Alvan Chapman, in an alumni sketch written for Amherst College, indicated that he received his medical degree on March 9, 1836, from the University of Louisville; a later university medical catalog stated that it was an honorary degree. Other sources state the degree was received in 1835 or 1846. In any event, the doctor

FIG. 14. This photograph of Dr. Alvan W. Chapman was taken in 1896, a few years before his death. Dr. Chapman is seated at the left rear; others are unidentified. *Courtesy of Florida Archives.*

moved to Quincy around 1835, set up his practice, and began collecting plants for and corresponding with Dr. John Torrey.

When the torreyas were healthy and vistas of longleaf pines dominated the upland landscape of Florida's panhandle, the paths of Hardy Croom and Dr. Alvan Wentworth Chapman crossed for a brief time. Their friendship lasted until Croom's death. Neither was formally trained in the art of botanical science. Both were correspondents of Dr. John Torrey, one of the era's preeminent botanical taxonomists. Croom died tragically in midlife as his star was rising. Chapman died in his ninetieth year and contributed one of the best compilations of southeastern flora. Both live on in the plants they discovered and described, but outside the botanical world, both men are largely unremembered.

It was in Quincy in 1835 that Chapman first met Hardy Croom, on "one of those calm, hazy October evenings, peculiar to the climate of Florida, [when] the quiet of the pleasant town of Quincy was interrupted by the rapid approach of a carriage with attendant outriders, which, having made part of the circuit of the public square, drew up before my office, and a gentleman of middle age, spare habit, light hair, and blue eyes, came forth and introduced himself as Mr. Croom, of North Carolina."[2]

Personal details about Chapman's life are spotty at best. Other than publications of his botanical articles, Chapman left few personal writings behind and they are scattered. In between patients Chapman roamed the countryside as his interest in botany grew, collecting specimens for himself and for Dr. Torrey, Asa Gray, and other correspondents. Aspalaga Landing, where Hardy Croom had rented a plantation, was not too far from Quincy and Chapman occasionally stopped there in his rambles.

Florida's panhandle was wild in those days. In fact, the low and swampy land south of Quincy and Marianna was one of the last strongholds of several Indian bands and a hideout for outlaws. Chapman was still learning the botanical arts and his specimens were sometimes ruined by ill treatment. Separated by distance from skilled botanists, Chapman learned by trial and error. In his excursions around the Apalachicola River, he probably came upon the torreya tree about the same time as Hardy Croom, but Croom was the one who collected it and saw that it was different.

Eighteen thirty-seven found the doctor practicing in Marianna, though intermittent fever laid him low for three months. Chapman never passed an opportunity to botanize. In May of 1837, he was summoned to perform an amputation at a place called Tennessee Bluff, which was eighty to one hundred miles away. "Crossing the river at Aspalaga, I was conducted along an old Indian 'trail' through 'bogs & fens & moors' to the place of destination." On the way, a new plant drew his attention: *Spigelia gentianoides,* commonly called gentian pinkroot. Sadly, it is now a listed endangered species, staying only a few steps ahead of extinction in scattered sites in Florida and Alabama.

Imagine the life of a country doctor on Florida's frontier. "I have a very good opportunity to find new things as my professional calls are frequently from twenty to fifty miles distant. But I can do but little about the fields, the season is so intensely hot. Our thermometer has been lingering around 100° in the shade for nearly three weeks." Florida's summers are still intensely hot—but try to get a doctor to make a house call. Even when the weather cooled, Chapman faced other problems: "I trust & I intend to scour this region effectually & gather in large quantities—the Indians in this neighborhood are quiet at this time & I can extend my tours."

In early September of 1837, Chapman had ranged up and down the bluffs around Aspalaga searching for seeds of *Croomia.* A few months passed before he wrote Dr. Torrey of the search. His hunt had been in vain for, disappointingly, none were found. He guessed it was too late, that the fruit must mature in late June. Another year would have to pass. Chapman did, however, find many torreya fruits and dried them in the shade. During this time, Chapman voiced his reservations about a list of Gadsden County plants in letters to Dr. Torrey. Hardy Croom had agreed to see to its publication; his untimely death had made that impossible and Chapman was unsure of how to accomplish the task. Nonetheless he was "reminded by the melancholy fate of my excellent friend, [Croom] that what is to be accomplished in this way must be done speedily."

The doctor returned to Quincy in 1838, and lived at a small settlement about eight miles south of the town named Rocky Comfort, probably near Rocky Comfort Creek. In a letter written to Dr. Torrey in October 1840, Chapman related that rain had fallen steadily from June to September and the crops were almost ruined, and "then came the Cattirpillar and swept them entirely"; on March 15, 1841, the doctor mentioned that the Apalachicola River was high and the boxes awaiting a northbound ship were stored in a warehouse now almost underwater; again he reminded Torrey that he was "on the frontier and the Indians hold undisturbed possession of the county between me and the Gulf. . . . it is as much as my neck is worth to venture down. Although parts of this Co. have been settled since 1825 yet no white person to my knowledge has ever traversed that unknown region and you can imagine my anxiety."

A near encounter in 1841 reinforced his decision to avoid the wilderness between himself and the coast:

Last summer I went down into the lower part of this country to get some of the Rhododendron punct. The whole country is a perfect wilderness where deep swamps and dry sand ridges alternate. I rode to one of the larger creeks and then took it on foot through a swamp nearly a mile wide. In this swamp I found a *moccasin track* but as it did not appear recent I ventured on some five miles farther and to my great mortification I could not find the spot where I had seen it before. The next day some hunters on the frontier fell upon thirteen Indians three of whom they killed. It seems they had found *my trail* and were following it up towards the frontier!! I need not say to you that it was my last visit to that region.[3]

The Apalachicola National Forest now protects most of that patchwork of rivers, creeks, cypress bays, hammocks, and swamps defined by two main roads passing east-west, Route 20 to the north and Highway 98 on the south. Only a few accessible roads cross from north to south, Highways 65, 67, and 375. Though the interior is crisscrossed by a number of sandy timber roads and drainage ditches, it is still unwise for a person unfamiliar with the area to wander far from a road because the chances of becoming lost are great. The place names are picturesque: Thousand Yard Bay, Barbeque Branch, Bradwell Bay, Black Cat Islands, Indian Creek Islands, Sopchoppy River, New River, and Tate's Hell Swamp. Tate's Hell did not gain that name because it is a pleasant place to stroll. Red-cockaded woodpeckers fussed in the pines when Dr. Chapman nosed around the edges of that tangled wildland; they are still there today though in smaller numbers. The woodpeckers excavate a cavity in mature longleaf pines to raise their young. Biologists have neatly encircled the cavity trees with colorful flagging tape or bands of paint so they know at a glance which pines are for the birds.

Dr. Chapman married Mrs. Mary Ann Hancock, of New Bern, North Carolina, a widow with one daughter, in 1839. Mrs. Chapman bore a second daughter, Ruth, but the child died in infancy. Dr. and Mrs. Chapman had no other children, as least none that survived childhood. When Mrs. Chapman's first daughter married and had children, Dr. Chapman looked upon them as his own grandchildren.

Between 1839 and 1847, Chapman dabbled in medicine and surgery, botanized around Quincy, and finally published his extensive Gadsden County plant list in the June 1845 issue of *The Western Journal of Medicine and Surgery*. In 1847, the couple moved to Apalachicola, which would be their permanent residence.

Apalachicola had grown up around the customs office established at the mouth of the Apalachicola River in 1823. Initially known as Cottonton, it was incorporated as West Point in 1829. No one really liked that name and it was changed to Apalachicola in 1831. By the mid-1830s Apalachicola was Florida's most prosperous town. Only New Orleans and Mobile boasted more commerce or population and the town also acquired a reputation for vice and sin. Doomsayers predicted little success for Apalachicola because of its low swampy location. Port St. Joe on St. Andrews Bay, nestled inside the protective arm of St. Joseph Peninsula a few miles west, was lauded as a better port.

FIG. 15. Apalachicola's harbor and waterfront drawn in 1837,
about ten years before Chapman moved there.
Courtesy of Florida Archives.

Work on the Chipola Canal connecting St. Andrews Bay with Lake
Wimico was restarted so that steamships could turn from the Apalachicola River into the Jackson River, cross Lake Wimico, and exit at Port St.
Joe, thus avoiding the shallow Apalachicola Bay and unhealthy Apalachicola. Malaria, "bad air," and yellow fever were uninvited summer guests
along the coast. A series of hurricanes struck Port St. Joe in the late 1830s
but the worst blow came from an 1841 yellow fever epidemic that
decimated the town's population. Economic depression combined with
devastating disease and weather brought Apalachicola's prosperous period to an end in the mid-1840s, but the town pulled through while Port
St. Joe declined.

We cannot imagine the fright once attached to news of yellow fever.
Illness began with fever and chills, unquenchable thirst, excruciating
headaches, extreme back and leg pain, internal bleeding, jaundice, spells
of vomiting black blood, coma, and, all too often, death. Malaria victims
normally survived, though the illness recurred, but few survived yellow
jack, another name for yellow fever. No one was quite sure what caused
either disease, but both nearly always occurred in warm months in places

near salt water and a cure was unknown. Wealthier people abandoned the lowlands in summer with good reason.

Yellow fever killed thousands of people in large cities and small towns. In 1900 a team led by Dr. Walter Reed substantiated Cuban physician C. J. Finlay's theory that it was a mosquito-borne disease, carried by the *Aedes aegypti* mosquito. Based on Finlay's work, in 1897 British physician Ronald Ross determined that malaria was spread by the *Anopheles* mosquito. Quinine was already known to ease malaria's chills and fever, but medicine to fight yellow fever was not developed until the 1930s. Wetlands were attacked with an arsenal of poisons, which, in the long run, have proved more harmful to birds, fish, and mammals—including humans. Dredges set to draining marshes for flood and mosquito control along with projects to bring more land under cultivation and raise it high enough for building. Now, millions of dollars are being spent to undo drainage projects. Those mistakes will be evident in our environment for years to come—and mosquitoes are still with us. As annoying as mosquitoes are to humans, they are delicate threads that bind the global food web; small fish and crustaceans feed on the larvae and birds and bats prey on the adults.

Apalachicola was fortunate that another physician practiced medicine in addition to Dr. Chapman in the 1840s. Dr. John Gorrie attended many fever victims. A breeze blowing across a block of ice cooled a room and Dr. Gorrie noticed that patients benefited from the lowered temperatures. Ice, however, was not always readily available in Apalachicola during the middle 1800s, even though ships regularly brought ice from the north. Dr. Gorrie fiddled and tinkered with a device that would freeze water.

Dr. Chapman recalled the day when John Gorrie fairly floated into the pharmacy, his eyes alight. Come see, he entreated Chapman. The men hurried across the street and there in Dr. Gorrie's workroom was a piece of manufactured ice. Coincidentally, that day the ice boat was late for its regular run. Gorrie and Chapman made a wager with the "Yankee cotton-brokers" that they would produce ice for dinner that night and they won the bet. Experimental ice had been made before, but Gorrie was the first to invent and patent the machinery. By May 1844, he had built a working machine and refined it; in February 1848 he submitted a patent petition. The doctor received a London Patent in August 1850 and a U.S. Patent in May 1851.

Although the machine worked, it did not always work well, and Dr. Gorrie could not raise the capital to bring the machine into large scale manufacture. Unfortunately, John Gorrie died in 1855, at only fifty-two years of age, and never realized any profit from his machine. Of course, he did not invent his machine so that we could enjoy air conditioning on a hot day. He sought to alleviate the distress of fever victims. There is a small museum devoted to Dr. Gorrie in Apalachicola. Entering the town from the east, visitors must first cross the long John Gorrie Bridge spanning the Apalachicola's broad mouth. If no one else remembers who Dr. Gorrie was, the people of Apalachicola do.

In 1856, North Carolina botanist and minister Moses Ashley Curtis had suggested to Dr. Chapman the need for a complete flora of the Southeast. Years earlier, the novice Chapman and the experienced Croom had talked of exploring Florida and the Southeast together, with the intent of publishing a work on the flora. Sadly, Croom's death in 1837 precluded a joint project, but in the intervening years, Chapman had become an authority in his own right. He enthusiastically pursued Curtis's suggestion for three years, at times laboring late into the night.

Chapman dedicated the *Flora of the Southern United States: Containing an Abridged Description of the Flowering Plants and Ferns of Tennessee, North and South Carolina, Georgia, Alabama, Mississippi, and Florida,* first published in 1860, to Reverend Curtis. Dr. Chapman would not see a copy until after the war. At the outset, he intended to confine the work to the Carolinas, Georgia, and Florida, but friends' entreaties, and the need for an expanded coverage, compelled him to include all of the Southern states. As more sections of the country were minutely explored, revised editions were published in 1883 and in 1897. His book remained the standard for Southern flowering plants until Small's *Flora of the Southeastern United States* was released in 1903.

Florida's population in 1860 totaled 144,024, about half of whom were considered white. Apalachicola had survived hurricanes and disease and by 1860 slightly more than nineteen hundred people lived there. When war broke out in 1861, Mrs. Chapman, being a Confederate, and her Union husband did not see eye to eye. She moved to Marianna and Chapman remained in Apalachicola. They did not meet during that time, though she did send him four shirts. He thanked her for them as they were good shirts. After the surrender, Mrs. Chapman returned to Apalachicola and life continued much as before. That is the scenario from Kimball's recollections. A more likely explanation is that the doctor sent his wife to Marianna for safety.

Kenneth Wurdack has been gathering background on Croom, Chapman, and other naturalists since 1985 when not working on his Ph.D. in botany at the University of North Carolina. He graciously shared bits of information about the doctor. An unpublished anonymous biography reveals that Chapman prevented Union forces from destroying Apalachicola and saved two men from a long imprisonment under Federal authorities by speaking on their behalf. Another source remembered that Chapman mentioned in a letter to prominent Missouri botanist George Engelmann in October 1873 that he had been a prisoner of the U.S. Marines in 1863. Another story that circulated in an Amherst College alumni publication indicated that Chapman was urged to enter the Confederate Army three times and always refused, but he was never bothered by Confederate officers because of his refusal.

Whether Chapman voluntarily remained in the town or was prevented from leaving is just another in a list of unanswered questions about this botanist. Whatever the reason, he was in Apalachicola during the war and if he was unable to travel far from the city on plant searches he continued doctoring and selling medications from his pharmacy.

President Lincoln ordered a blockade of all Confederate ports. The plan to seal Apalachicola was implemented in 1862 with one Union ship patrolling the bay's four entrances. Service on a blockade ship could be tedious at times, but the boat was more than a visual threat. It intercepted inbound and outbound vessels, accepted runaway slaves and escaping Union sympathizers, and fired upon the numerous salt works set up along the coast. The South needed salt to preserve meat and any man who operated a salt works was exempted from service. Age and health were not considered in granting exemption, and complaints were lodged that many men were able-bodied and should have gone to the front. Some might have found salt-works duty more onerous than going to war.

Salt works varied in design and size, and location was important. Some families set up a few kettles while other enterprises were elaborate affairs of brick and mortar. Most installations were kept to a size that could be easily moved, and they used materials such as ships' boilers cut in half. Except for the hand-dug canal, there were no freshwater drainages into St. Andrews Bay and that meant the water had a high salt content. In 1864, the official government price for salt was $12.50 for a bushel at the site. As salt traveled farther from the shore the price rose until a bushel demanded $40–45. Most vats operated twenty-four hours a day and were vulnerable to Union attack because of telltale smoke plumes during the day and cooking fires visible at night. It was hot work even in winter and always dangerous. Workers could be killed when a site was shelled. Afterwards, materials had to be salvaged and set up elsewhere. One hundred and thirty-five years later, scattered piles of weathered bricks and bits of rusted metal, slowly disintegrating, can still be found in panhandle marshes—disappearing reminders of that chancy wartime enterprise.

The town of Apalachicola was poorly defended but more ships joined the blockade. Federal troops came ashore in 1862. No one volunteered to surrender the town and the Union Commander declared Apalachicola captured without a battle. He told people they could continue fishing and he allowed them to keep small boats, but any aid to the Confederacy would bring the soldiers back. The soldiers fired a few shots and returned to their ships. Here was a town in an odd position—captured, but unoccupied. Apalachicola, isolated on the coast, straddled the fence. Scattered units from both sides appeared from time to time. Residents warned Confederate soldiers hiding in the swamps when Union soldiers were passing through, and they warned Dr. Chapman when Southern troops came hunting Union sympathizers and supplies.

Then Dr. Chapman would hastily grab some victuals on his way to Trinity Episcopal Church across the street. A pillow and blanket were permanently folded in his pew, for he spent the night where he was safe. He did not talk much of the war, remembered Kimball, but his life must have been anything but boring during those four years. As a staunch Unionist, Chapman never turned against his neighbors though he might have disagreed with them.

Apalachicola was still governed by Reconstruction laws when Harvard botanist Asa Gray and his wife visited the Chapmans in 1875. Since Chapman was color-blind he depended upon others to describe reds and pinks. He thought he had found a new plant but he could not be sure until Dr. Gray saw it. The renowned botanist gave the plant a short look, congratulated Chapman on his discovery, and named it *Rhododendron chapmanii* in honor of his old friend. Chapman's rhododendron has become another name on the federal list of endangered species.

Photographs of an older Alvan Wentworth Chapman show a person

FIG. 16. Chapman's rhododendron, *Rhododendron chapmanii.*
Photo by John K. Small. Courtesy of Florida Archives.

of stern visage, but he was a kindly man, especially toward children. A civic-minded individual, the doctor served as Apalachicola's internal revenue collector from 1865–66, as customs collector from 1866–69, and as probate judge for Franklin County in the late 1800s. During his life he received a string of honors: membership in the New Orleans Academy of Sciences in 1854; membership in the Philadelphia Academy of Natural Sciences in 1861; member of the Buffalo Society of Natural Sciences and Associate Fellow of the American Academy of Arts and Sciences in 1866; an honorary LL.D. from the University of North Carolina in 1886; honorary membership in the Trinity Historical Society of Dallas, Texas in 1887; and honorary membership in the Botanical Society of America in 1895. As his botanical reputation spread, he received correspondence from around the world. He read French, Latin, Greek, and, after he turned seventy, began studying German. Ironically, outside of his civic duties most of Dr. Chapman's neighbors knew nothing of his prestige. He was just their doctor, though he had pretty much withdrawn from practicing medicine by 1880. Botany commanded his time and, besides, increasing deafness made it hard to treat patients; he remarked that they called on him less and less as he could not hear their moans and groans.

Mrs. Chapman died in Rome, Georgia, in 1879, and her body was brought to Apalachicola for burial. While out searching for plants in early 1898, Dr. Chapman suffered an attack of vertigo. He curtailed extensive travel after that, but even a few weeks before his death he had walked several miles to collect a flower for a small collection he was compiling for Charles Sprague Sargent of the Arnold Arboretum. Chapman died peacefully in his home on April 6, 1899, a few months short of his ninetieth birthday. His funeral on April 7 was one of the largest ever seen in the town. The mills and stores closed to show their respect. Alvan Chapman was buried next to his wife and daughter in the Chestnut Street Cemetery just behind his home. Coonties planted on his grave may be descendants of the plants he originally brought from South Florida.

Chapman's old federal style home has passed through different hands, each owner renovating some aspect until it little favors the original house. A move was launched a few years ago to purchase the home for a reasonable sum and convert it into a botanical center, but sufficient funds could not be raised. In recent years it has been a private home, a medical office, and, in 1999, a real estate office. In 1925, the town had honored Dr. Chapman by naming the new high school after him. Since then another high school has been built and named Apalachicola High. The old Chapman High is now Chapman Elementary.

I HAD NOT VISITED APALACH, as the town is fondly called, in five or six years. A friend from California wanted to see the Gulf coast so I put off going to Apalachicola until he arrived. It was a grey day and the clouds ameliorated late June's heat. Finally, much needed rain had returned to the parched state. As we drove through the Apalachicola National Forest, I saw Florida through his eyes. Dan remarked on the monotony of green and endless pines. But they aren't endless. Each habitat is a whole composed of puzzle parts; there are creeks and swamps and sweet bays and cypress—not just pines. I leaned back in the seat and stared out the window, tried to see it as a visitor new to North Florida might. The scene blended into a green wall with pines predominant. There were no rock outcrops and rarely a single tree stood out as a reference point. Dan was used to seeing a mountain backdrop.

The topography in this part of Florida varies only a few feet up and down; not enough to give an impression of hilliness. Landmarks are more subtle here: a bird's nest, lichens, or scars on a tree. Of course, all of that can change in a few years—or in one hour of pelting rain. Time brings familiarity to a place so that a neighborhood becomes recognizable, and the same is true for a forest. Seeing it only as a whole without knowing the parts, without poking into the details, is not enough.

Once we reached Apalachicola, Dan wandered the streets while I met with George Chapel of the local historical society and Sandy Madsen, park ranger at the Gorrie Museum. We talked about the Apalachicola of long ago and the town today. Apalachicola has remained small, and at the threshold of the twenty-first century has changed only a little since Dr. Chapman's day. The streets are paved and outsiders have moved in, bought old homes, and gentrified them. George has lived there for fifteen years or so, but at a local theatrical production the previous evening he had known fewer than a dozen out of about a hundred people in the audience. The rest were apparently part of the vacation crowd.

From the time of its inception, Apalachicola has been a town in transition. It sprang up as a commercial town, and as a result the population was largely transient. The traders who oversaw their shipping concerns returned north in the warm months of sickness. When cotton was diverted to Georgia ports via railroads built during the war to haul troops and materiel, Apalachicola shipped timber. During World War II the town experienced a boom of sorts; hundreds of servicemen were stationed at Camp Gordon Johnson and trained in warfare. Later, when the forests were shorn of the best lumber, interests turned to seafood.

Though once profitable, fewer people are now engaged in commercial fishing because of increasing expenses and laws protecting marine life and the aquatic environment. It appears that Apalachicola is testing tourism as a viable industry. Tourists come for a short time and leave money behind. It sounds like a winning combination, but tourists place a strain on roads and utilities. Businesses may be flush when the tourist season is in full swing, but they can find it difficult to survive during slack times.

U.S. 98 passes through town, but most traffic speeds across Interstate 10 farther north so Apalachicola remains rather isolated. Property values fluctuate, but the days of drifting into town and purchasing an elegant but dilapidated old home at a low price are over. Speculators have remodeled several homes into charming Bed and Breakfasts. Other homes are on the market—and have been for a while—listed at high prices. They are waiting for the day when Apalachicola trades in its rundown shoes for designer fashions and becomes another Sandestin resort area. It could happen and though it will bring a measure of prosperity to some, many are not likely to profit.

A map for a walking tour shows the locations of points of historical interest. We tried to find the Chapman School, but the map confused us because of what was left off. As one moves back from the respectable waterfront neighborhoods, streets, not wide to begin with, become even more narrow. Mowed lawns become overgrown jungles. Genteel painted walls become scarred plywood and windows are lucky to have screens. Instead of trimmed hedges, derelict cars and mounds of junk line the property. This is where Apalachicola's impoverished residents live. Some are white, but most are black. The blacks are leaving when they can; there is a blank future for them in this town.

Apalachicola's downtown may be getting a facelift and may seem on the fringe of becoming trendy, but the visual slide from wealth to poverty is not gradual, it is sudden. If a visitor should stray into the back streets a feeling of hopelessness is likely to follow when leaving. Where does one start to overcome the situation? The rough back streets house the majority of the town's young people. Apalachicola High, with fewer than four hundred students in grades seven through twelve, has a mission to prepare its students for the twenty-first century. Of those students, 30 percent came from families living below the poverty level; both parents work outside the home in 64 percent of the families, leaving a number of children unsupervised in the afternoon; 41 percent of the students partake of the free lunch program. The seafood industry is dwindling and jobs are hard to come by. There are community colleges in Marianna, Niceville, Panama City, Tallahassee, and Fort Walton Beach. Young people, and now their parents, must commute a great distance or relocate if they want to gain more education.

Alfred and Jessie Ball duPont and Mrs. duPont's brother, Ed Ball, moved to Jacksonville in 1926 and built an estate called Epping Forest on the St. Johns River. At that time Jacksonville was the state's financial center, but all the starch had just leached out of the land boom. From their Jacksonville base, the duPonts planned to revive Florida's economy and, to this end, Alfred bailed out the ailing Florida National Bank by putting $15 million of his own money into it. He felt they already had enough money and that it was time to give some back.

With Florida's land selling so cheaply, Alfred sent Ed to west Florida with instructions to buy land, thereby acquiring seventy thousand acres in Frankin, Bay, and Walton Counties. In the 1930s duPont instructed Ed to convince the Tallahassee legislature not only to build roads to the west Florida timberland, but to improve the entire state's highway system. Ed further exerted his influence to make sure that the Eastern Time Zone, which followed the Apalachicola River, hitched west near the coast to include Port St. Joe. This ensured that he would not lose a minute in making deals with people in large eastern cities while he was in the town.

He was a canny guy, that Ed Ball. His tenacity and business acumen became legendary in Florida; he built St. Joe Paper Company into Florida's largest landowner and a huge business operation. He was short, but what he lacked in stature he more than made up in drive. The man had a presence. Few said no to Ed Ball, and it was not because his brother-in-law was really rich.

Alfred died in 1935 and Jessie continued their philanthropic work: funding hundreds of college scholarships, augmenting faculty salaries, and building libraries until her death in 1970. Churches, museums, historic buildings, and children's homes received gifts during her lifetime, and the Jessie Ball duPont Fund continues her tradition. After Alfred's death, Ed proceeded to fulfill one of duPont's wishes by setting up the St. Joe Paper mill in Port St. Joe to create jobs for people. Though he carried out Alfred's plans, Ed was more concerned with profit. The business world has been revamped since Ed died in 1981, and St. Joe's managers have lost sight of duPont's vision. They closed the paper mill in 1998, thereby shutting down the major employer of people in Port St. Joe and Apalachicola. Some longtime workers are still in denial. St. Joe Paper was their life for years, and they cannot believe that the company would treat them that way. One day a paycheck, the next day, the mill is shut. No benefits, no severance, no hope.

After pausing in front of Dr. Chapman's old home, strolling through the headstones of the Chestnut Street Cemetery, cruising neighborhoods, and stopping for lunch at the restaurant featured in a scene from the recent movie "Ulee's Gold," we diverged temporarily, Dan to cast an eye on fishing boats, and I to walk through the Chapman Botanical Garden, enclosed by a wooden fence.

Apalachicola has remembered Dr. Chapman, but unfortunately has misspelled his name ("Alvin") on a monument in the garden and on the historical marker at the Chestnut Street Cemetery. A concrete path winds past benches to a short boardwalk through a low spot—still dry in spite of the rain. Grapevines were about to take over the boardwalk, and though the grass needed mowing, the enclosure gave the air of being maintained but not used. Plenty of trees have been planted, but not the diversity of plants expected in a botanical garden. It felt incomplete.

Passing through downtown on the way out of town, we saw groups of people looking in shops that cater to customers with steady, above-average incomes. Visitors are drawn to the area's semidetached position on the coast. Apalach is a great place to escape big city living. Franklin County, of which Apalachicola is the county seat, stretches across the northern Gulf coast from the Ochlockonee River to west of the Apalachicola River. Marshes edge the coastline around the river, but just offshore are miles of pearly barrier island beaches.

Dog Island guards Apalachicola Bay's easternmost entrance and provides critical nesting habitat for shorebirds and sea turtles. Houses congregate primarily on the western end; most are vacation homes, but a handful of people live on the island full-time. There is a small landing strip, a ferry runs a regular schedule from Carrabelle, and residents use their own boats to make the island-to-mainland run. The isolation appeals to a rare personality and residents oppose any plans to build a bridge, which would bring inevitable crowds. Of prime concern are fresh water sources, trash and derelict car removal, and fire fighting difficulties. The island's sand pines will burn one day.

The eastern end of St. George Island, 1,962 acres, was set aside as a state park in 1963. A causeway completed in 1965 made the beach easily accessible and led to development of privately owned land. The island's pine forests were turpentined in the early 1900s; scars on the trees endure. St. George Island State Park includes nine miles of beaches and dunes, a 2.5-mile trail, and a campground. Birds are the chief wildlife found on the island, but raccoons beg from campers, diamondback terrapins bask in the marshes, and loggerhead sea turtles nest along the Gulf beaches. On the island's western end there are about twelve hundred rental units and three hundred permanent homes. A few are quaint, but most rise on spindly stilts straining for a view and as a precaution against high storm tides.

Cape St. George, sometimes known as Little St. George Island, appears as a separate island on maps but was actually once a part of St. George Island proper. In the past, storms regularly blew out a pass at a narrow point, allowing fishing vessels a nearby exit to the Gulf. Without the pass, boats had to travel a longer distance around St. George. Sikes Cut was authorized in 1954 and has been kept open ever since. While it provides easy ingress and egress to the Gulf, it has also slightly increased the bay's salinity. Cape St. George, twenty-eight miles long, is reachable only by boat. The island's pines were turpentined during 1910 to 1916 and again from 1950 to 1956. Remains of a turpentine camp persist near the Government dock. Heavy equipment gouged roads through marshes and dunes for military training in the mid-1960s and left behind rusted skeletons of equipment. Those kinds of scars take longer to heal.

Cape St. George is shaped like a boomerang, and a lighthouse was built on the elbow jutting into the Gulf in 1833, but it didn't last. A new lighthouse was constructed in 1848 with salvaged materials from other abandoned lighthouses. A hurricane in August of 1851 toppled that lighthouse along with lights at Dog Island and Cape San Blas. A third tower, also constructed from salvaged materials, was completed 250 yards farther inland in 1852. Like other lighthouses, the lens was removed during the Civil War so that it would not be destroyed if the lighthouse was captured. After the war, the lenses were reinstalled.

The men who worked as lighthouse keepers, and their families, too, were strong independent people. During the heyday of the Cape St. George lighthouse, there were several dwellings for the keeper and assistants. There were no pension plans for the keepers and when their days of service ended, they were discharged with only their savings to live on. Cape St. George light was decommissioned in 1949, and since then, weather has taken its toll. Most of the buildings have been burned or destroyed by storms. The beach has moved considerably. The lighthouse had begun to lean by the late 1980s, but portions of the keeper's house and some of the other buildings were still there. By 1998 the tower had been completely lifted off its foundation. The high tide mark is above the tower's base. Funds are being raised to save the structure, but the Coast Guard has decided not to expend any efforts toward preserving it. Meanwhile, the lighthouse continues to deteriorate. It is, after all, built on a beach and a beach is determined to travel.

Unlike long and stringy St. George Island, St. Vincent Island is shaped like a bird's wing. An aerial photograph clearly shows linear dunes running northeast–southwest; these are visible records of old shorelines. The island's 12,358 acres support ten distinct habitats: tidal marshes, freshwater lakes and streams, scrub oaks and live oak/scrub oak mix in the dunes, cabbage palm stands, and four separate slash pine communities.

Pottery shards dating from A.D. 240 indicate that Indians occupied the site or at least used it at various times. Franciscan Friars named the island in 1633 while harvesting souls among the Apalachee Indians. Creeks and Seminoles inhabited the area in the middle 1700s but had to move on as Europeans moved in. George Hatch bought the island in 1868 for $3,000, and his is the only marked grave on St. Vincent.

Dr. Ray V. Pierce, a patent medicine manufacturer from Buffalo, New York, purchased the island in 1907 and stocked it with Old World game animals. Island-grown beef was sold to Apalachicola markets in the 1920s, and the first oyster lease was granted in 1840. Dr. Pierce's estate sold the first timber lease, and St. Joe Lumber Company built a temporary bridge to facilitate timber removal. The Loomis brothers bought the island in 1948 for $140,000 and imported more exotic wildlife. In 1968, The Nature Conservancy paid $2.2 million for the island. The U.S. Fish and Wildlife Service then purchased the land with revenue from Duck

Stamp sales. Sambar deer are still there, along with white-tailed deer, bald eagles, peregrine falcons, piping plovers, wood storks, alligators, indigo snakes, loggerhead sea turtles, and gopher tortoises. The refuge became a red wolf captive breeding station in 1990. St. Vincent's visitor center is located in Apalachicola, and the island, accessible only by boat, offers superb opportunities for fishing, hunting, hiking, and wildlife observation; primitive camping is allowed only during hunting periods.

The Apalachicola National Estuarine Research Reserve cares for 246,766 acres of land and water, including the lower fifty-two miles and adjacent floodplain of the Apalachicola River. Located at the bottom of the Apalachicola-Chattahoochee-Flint River system, the reserve is responsible for providing facilities for visiting researchers as well as for its own programs.

The Chattahoochee River rises northeast of Atlanta and flows southwest, draining about 8,650 square miles, until it butts against Alabama and begins a southerly flow that defines the delineation between Georgia and Alabama. There are thirteen dams on the Chattahoochee; the last one is Jim Woodruff, just below the Georgia/Florida line. Each one extracts an allotment of the water supply for agriculture and drinking water along the way.

The Apalachicola drains 2,400 square miles in Florida, and the Flint drains 8,494 square miles of Georgia. The Apalachicola is Florida's largest river and the only one carrying snowmelt down its length to the Gulf. Although the overall health of Apalachicola Bay's estuary is good, a flow and availability of fresh water dictated by dams rather than nature, coupled with the additional salt water allowed by Sikes Cut, has at times proved deadly for marine life. High salinity weakens oysters, making them susceptible to disease and parasites.

Around the corner from Apalachicola is the town of Port St. Joe, hanging on since the paper mill's abdication. A turn onto County Road 30A, then another onto 30E, leads to St. Joseph Peninsula, the long barrier arm wrapped around St. Andrews Bay and the site of St. Joseph Peninsula State Park. A broad beach backed by dunes faces the Gulf and the interior is heavily forested. On the way to the park, the road passes through developed areas that make visitors all the more appreciative of the park's relatively unscathed lands.

Like St. George and St. Vincent islands, the peninsula was first used by Native Americans. The pinelands were turpentined and later used for military training. This is a good time to mention that, because these coastal areas were used for target practice, shell casings lie beneath the surface and often come to light as the sands shift. Blanks as well as live ammunition were used, and both small bullets and large artillery shells can be found. Because some of them can be live and possibly unstable it's best not to pick them up and haul them home as souvenirs.

Apalachicola at the beginning of the twenty-first century is a city of parts. On the whole it is a quiet backwater town where time passes at a slow pace. There are, however, painful problems to overcome in a community lacking the financial wherewithal to do so. Some residents hope that another coastal resort does not spring up here; others see development as the way to prosperity. Would the wealth extend to everyone or only a few? How will a larger population affect both fresh and salt water supplies, not to mention the wildlife? These are hard questions to answer. In the meantime, the town adapts.

Coastal pinelands around Apalachicola have been timbered and re-planted with slash and sand pine. Jim Woodruff Dam holds back the Apalachicola just south of the confluence of the Flint and Chattahoochee Rivers, and the Army Corps of Engineers dredges a channel to keep the big river navigable for barges up to Bainbridge and Columbus in Georgia. Changes in the river's flow regime have had an impact on the marshes and bay. Additional pollution from runoff, residue from motorized boat traffic, and the levels of invasive hydrilla and water hyacinth are closely monitored.

Returning to Tallahassee along the coast, U.S. 98 runs tight along the shore in some places, across spots that are demolished in hurricanes and then faithfully rebuilt. The coastal forest on the north side of the road has begun to sprout For Sale signs with alarming regularity. For now the woodlands have thrown up a thick tangled defense of vegetation against the wind and salt. When the land is sold new owners are likely to hire bulldozers to raze the formidable and forbidding barrier, except for a few tastefully spaced clumps. Another part of Florida will be lost.

Alvan Chapman explored North Florida fairly well on his travels as a doctor and when searching for plants. He also visited Key West in 1843 and botanized along Florida's west coast from Anclote Key to Cape Sable. He traveled the Caloosahatchee River collecting tree specimens for the

Centennial Exhibition in 1875. The legend of ferrying Union escapees to freedom may only be the product of Winifred Kimball's fanciful imagination, but Chapman's life was far from mundane. He was highly regarded in his field and made a singular contribution to the study of southern flora that stood at the top for decades. Chapman's life begs a biographer with time and resources to uncover more.

CHAPTER 10

Walking in Heaven's Light

John Muir
(April 21, 1838–December 24, 1914)

But in Florida came the greatest change of all, for here grows the palmetto, and here blow the winds so strangely toned by them. These palms and these winds severed the last strands of the cord that united me with home. Now I was a stranger, indeed. I was delighted, astonished, confounded, and gazed in wonderment blank and overwhelming as if I had fallen upon another star.

—John Muir, *A Thousand-Mile Walk to the Gulf,* 1916

BORN APRIL 21, 1838, in Dunbar, Scotland, John was the third child and first son of Daniel and Anne Gilrye Muir; the surname means a moor or wild wasteland in the Scottish tongue. There could have been no better match between a name and a personality. John Muir was destined to become the most eloquent voice for wilderness protection around the world.

Situated near the North Sea, a stormy untamed ocean, Dunbar provided an apt training ground for young John. Like his friends, the boy craved adventure. Slipping away from home, against their parents' warnings, carefree boys tested each other's abilities. Who could run the fastest. Who could find the most birds and how many nests did they ken. Who would dare clamber down the rocky coast to capture strange denizens left in quiet pools by the turning tide. Who would be the first to scale Dunbar Castle's craggy ruins. All good practice for future explorations. Daniel Muir did not spare the rod, but no measure of punishment quelled his oldest son's inquisitive spirit. By his own account, John's childhood was a series of physical battles. He learned Bible verses at home by "sore flesh" as the father tried to beat the "deevil" out of the boy, and there were schoolyard scrapes galore. Later, John rationalized this treatment by saying it was the Scots way, but he never quite forgave the father he loved.

John entered primary school before his third birthday and started Dunbar Grammar School at age seven. Beginning education at an early age stimulated his nimble mind. His grammar school studies included Latin, French, English, mathematics, geography, history, and enticing tidbits about America. The country across the sea exuded a mythical attraction for young Muir. One textbook contained illustrations by the famous Scots-born American ornithologist, Alexander Wilson. Muir studied the description of a graceful osprey—stooping to catch a fish, dogged by an eagle until the hunter dropped the prize that the eagle then stole for itself—until the encounter was etched against his eyelids. John envied Wilson's luck in being able to wander wild America. Audubon's account of passenger pigeons seeped into his young mind, and he longed to feel the resonance of their wingbeats.

As John and his brother, David, sat studying by the fire one evening, Daniel Muir unexpectedly announced that they would leave for America in the morning. The boys were wild with anticipation. The land they had studied in their books was about to become real. Muir took the two boys

FIG. 17. A young John Muir taken ca. 1870 in San Francisco after his
thousand-mile walk through the South.
Courtesy of Florida Archives.

and a daughter, leaving the rest of the family to follow when their new home was found. Hard work lay before the immigrants. They would have to fight nature for the right to live on the land.

Daniel had expressed a vague plan to settle in Canada, but conferences with others during the six-week Atlantic voyage persuaded him to look to the western states of Wisconsin and Michigan. In Buffalo, New York, a grain dealer allowed that most of the wheat he handled came from Wisconsin, convincing Daniel to settle on the western frontier. After an arduous overland journey to the new homesite, John and David jumped from the groaning wagon and shimmied up a tree for their first find—a blue jay's nest sheltering unhatched pale green eggs.

Over the ensuing weeks they searched meadows and trees and found more nests. The lake and the stream held all manner of frogs, turtles, and snakes. Ah, but we are rich, rich, thought the boys. The natural world became John's classroom without whippings or walls, and he came to learn its colors and textures and disguises. Freedom to roam the wild land without the gamekeeper's heavy hand chasing them away was what the boys had longed for, but there would be endless hours of farmwork, with never time enough to wander during their growing years. Running the farm consumed the family, especially since the elder Muir equated work and suffering with a straighter path to heaven.

Daniel Muir was stern and unyielding in his thinking. He had been orphaned at an early age into brutal poverty and he and an older sister were taken in by relatives to provide cheap labor. As orphans, they hardly expected more than scraps in exchange for a roof over their heads. Daniel's childhood had been a constant struggle for bare survival, and he had been inoculated with a particularly fervent fundamentalist Presbyterianism. In later life, he leaped from one sect to another, as long as it was more extreme and self-denying than the previous one.

The Muirs immigrated to America in 1849, when John was just eleven years old. That same year, hundreds rushed to California's gold fields as the Muirs wrestled their Wisconsin prairie into a productive farm. Nearly two decades would pass before John traveled to California and lost his heart to the regal Sierra Nevada Mountains.

There were few neighbors in Wisconsin when the Muirs began putting down their American roots. Flights of passenger pigeons still shadowed the sky. Conquered people from the Winnebago and Menominee tribes passed the Muir home now and then. An Indian trail along the Fox

River between Portage and Packwauckee Lake was the neighborhood's only man-made road. But the paucity of neighbors would not last; before long, roads, fields, and towns were carved from the prairie as new immigrants pushed the frontier westward. John played his part in taming Wisconsin's wilderness: driving a plow and breaking up prairie clods with a hoe, cutting and girdling trees, building fences, planting and harvesting crops. Only later did he realize that his actions, and those of his neighbors, irrevocably changed the landscape.

Spending nearly every day outside, he became aware of how alterations in plants and animals indicated the changing seasons. More of the land came under cultivation and the farm child noticed fewer birds; certainly wildflowers were harder to find in fields of corn and wheat. John watched the displacement of animals and the shifts in plant populations and gradually realized that America might not be large enough for all who wanted to claim a piece of the country.

Except for one short term, John had received no formal education in America. None of the family could be spared from the grueling farmwork. A desire for knowledge came over John in his midteens. He had studied mathematics in Scotland, but had understood very little. After five years of no school, John began to teach himself. A neighbor loaned him books, since only religious books were found in the Muir household, and John found snatches of time to read—a few minutes at midday, and at night after chores, before the stern order "to bed" was spoken. Daniel groused that his growing son should not have to be told to go to bed each night. He did not approve of the books his son read; the Bible was the only worthwhile book in his eyes. John could rise early if he wanted to read, the father grumbled, never dreaming that the boy actually would. Rise early John did, waking from sleep by 1:00 A.M., bending to his books in the quiet house for five wonderful hours before tramping to the fields in frozen stiff boots at dawn's first light.

The house was frosty during winter evenings; Daniel allowed no fires to be banked at night. Literature and poetry exercised his mind, but when he could sit still no longer in the glacial atmosphere John began whittling and carving to keep his blood flowing. Clocks and all manner of implements came out of his head. In spite of, or maybe because of, his father's rigid and somewhat narrow mind, John's spirit longed to soar and his hands were always busy. He enjoyed experimenting and tinkering with machinery, searching for imaginative ways to save time. John designed an early rising bed that tilted and dumped the occupant out at a set time, a self-setting sawmill, hygrometers, barometers. Neither the father nor the son believed in wasting time, but they had differing views on how it should be spent.

As soon as his sons were of an age and strength to run the farm, Daniel left the fields and devoted himself to Bible study and preaching. He was home, therefore, when John had completed one of his clocks and set its mechanism before going out to work the crops. When Daniel heard the clock strike he went in to examine it, one of John's sisters later reported. He seemed proud of his son's talents, but offered no encouragement.

John's brothers left the farm and their father's strict rule as soon as they were able, but John stayed a bit longer. His mother hoped he would be a minister; his sisters encouraged him to travel. Medicine appealed to him, but neighbors suggested he take his inventions to the state fair.

In 1860, John left the family's Hickory Hill farm for the state fair at Madison. This was Muir's first parting from his family, a difficult time for all. When John asked for a bit of money from his father, Daniel replied that John would have to depend entirely upon himself. Leaving home with about fifteen dollars and his unique contraptions, the shy young man headed to Madison. John's inventions attracted attention and praise, especially from Jeanne Carr, wife of University of Wisconsin professor Ezra Carr, and one of the exhibit judges. Mrs. Carr had a far-reaching influence on Muir's life and introduced him to the writings of Thoreau and Emerson. Later the Carrs moved to California where Jeanne orchestrated Muir's marriage to Louie Wanda Strentzel when he was forty-two years old. After the exposition, John determined to stay in the city. His thirst for knowledge was not yet quenched, and the University of Wisconsin waited for him to enter.

The hopeful student had no money, but was willing to work any job. He sold a few of his early-rising beds, ran errands, addressed circulars, and worked in a stable. He spoke with a university student who recalled John's display from the fair. Muir told the young man that he was saving money for tuition; the student replied that it did not take much money and John should start as soon as he could. Soon the nervous but earnest young man explained his situation and lack of education to the Dean who, impressed with Muir's manner, willingly welcomed him to the university. Upon entering the freshman Latin class, John recognized a text he had used in Scotland and soon caught up with the others.

John's university years began as the North and South went to war. Even though the conflict was far away, hundreds of soldiers from both sides were shipped to Camp Randall on the university's grounds. The Union's wounded, sick, and dying and Confederate prisoners of war were a graphic reminder of the horrible toll war took on able-bodied men, who went into battle whole and came out bloodied and missing arms or legs because they could not agree. Muir, the pacifist, opposed war and lamented friends who entered the fray. Yet he volunteered to help the wounded soldiers. It was the war he protested, not the boys who went to fight.

To fund his education, John worked as a fieldhand in the summer and taught school during the winter. As teacher, John had to arrive well before the students to get the potbellied stove going. He quickly employed one of his clocks in that endeavor, which left more time for his own studies. After school was out, John cleaned the stove, laid the morning's fire, and set the clock. Every morning at eight, the clock's mechanism dripped a bit of sulphuric acid onto a teaspoon of powdered chlorate of potash and sugar set near the kindling. The acid ignited the mixture which lit the kindling and by the time teacher and students arrived, the room was warm.

The most distasteful part of teaching was meting out whippings as the standard form of punishment. He remembered his own childhood beatings, often for some trifling act, and shook for hours after he was forced to whip a student.

He made good use of his time at the university, but left in 1863, at age twenty-five, without a degree and far from satisfied with what he had learned. This was not the university's fault, but it was time for the inventor to move on. As Muir later said, he was only trading the university in Madison for the university of the wilderness.

At this juncture, John was presented with several life choices. He had been accepted to the medical school at Ann Arbor. At the same time, friends urged him to marry, settle down, set up a business, continue inventing. John did want to settle down and raise a family, but he knew the time was not right. He lacked enough money for medical school, and he was afraid he would be called to fight in the war he abhorred.

Muir returned to his family's home and waited for his number to be chosen in the newly instituted draft system. In a letter to his brother, Dan, who was already in Canada, John wrote that he was saving his money to return to Scotland where a man could live in peace. It seemed there would be no end to conflict. Although the theater of war was mainly in the southern regions, the pall of it hung over the north as sons, husbands, and fathers joined the fight. Fortunately, his number did not come up, and John took his first botanical journey to the Mississippi River. Then he returned home, still indecisive.

In the midst of agonizing over sending thousands of young men to their deaths, Abraham Lincoln signed over Yosemite Valley and Mariposa Big Tree Grove to California as state park lands in the country's first wilderness preservation act in 1864. When President Lincoln issued a call for five hundred thousand fighters, Muir made a decision to join his brother in Canada. He stayed there for two years.

Muir returned to the United States in 1866 and found employment as foreman and engineer at a carriage factory in Indianapolis. On March 5, 1867, while he was working late to complete a project, a sharp file slipped and pierced the edge of the cornea of his eye. He spent weeks in a darkened room, eyes bandaged, in pain and again uncertain of his future. This was a tumultuous period. He was twenty-nine years old; twenty-two of them had been spent under his father's repressive influence, and Muir was still searching for his own sense of self and not ready to settle down. Pondering his future, he knew he might not regain vision in his right eye, the one he said he had assiduously trained to observe a plant's minute components. His extraordinary flair for inventing, improving, and repairing machinery would provide an honest living for him even with diminished sight; nonetheless, if his sight returned, John decided to devote his life to the natural world. "Heaven's light," he called it, a world not yet complete, but one that a higher entity was still building. His religion lay not in machines, but in nature.

Long before the accident he had begun planning an extended journey through the South, the West Indies, South America, and Europe. The day came to test his eyes. Gingerly he opened them to unaccustomed light. His vision seemed no better or worse than before. He took it as a sign to follow his dream and revived his plans for the southern excursion.

John returned home in midsummer at his father's request. As Daniel Muir aged, his thinking became even more constricted, and he met his son's decision to study nature with strong disapproval. But if John could not please his father, he would please himself. As John was bidding his mother and sisters farewell, Daniel asked if he had forgotten something.

John asked what it could be, and Daniel replied that he had not paid for his board and lodging.

His son handed over a gold piece, saying, "Father, you asked me to come home for a visit. I thought I was welcome. You may be very sure it will be a long time before I come again."[1]

By the end of August 1867, John was making farewell visits to friends in Madison and Indianapolis. He would be gone for several months. Two days before leaving John wrote to another friend, wishing he could be "more moderate in my desires, but I cannot, and so there is no rest."[2] Apparently, little short of death would stay his overpowering wanderlust.

On April 8, 1865, General Robert E. Lee had met General Ulysses S. Grant at Virginia's Appomattox Courthouse and signed the papers ending our young country's most brutal period. For four years, friends and strangers driven by savage zeal had fought furiously over the South's right to enslave other human beings. Bloody battles left thousands dead and dying on the fields of conflict. The great war was over, yet peace did not come easily. To say the years following the war were hard on the vanquished South would be an understatement. The region vacillated between agitation and bewilderment as people attempted to bring together a land torn and families rent apart by their beliefs. Nearly every battle had been on Southern soil. Ravaged fields and burned homes, woodlands, and towns lingered as grim reminders for decades. Military rule prevailed in many areas. All facets of society, rich and poor, once bound by proscribed rules of class and race, jostled for position in their shattered world. Tempers teetered on edge into the 1870s. Small outlaw groups, acclimatized to theft and intimidation, roamed civilization's outskirts, preying upon travelers and rural dwellers.

It was through such an unsettled country and time that John Muir walked, little more than two years after the surrender. Whether Muir thought about political and social tumult or not, he knew that it was the right time for his personal journey. Years of heavy work combined with immense curiosity had hardened John's body and disciplined his mind. The walk to the Mississippi River and the years spent in Canada had been mere warm-up exercises. He was physically and spiritually prepared for the trip.

Steeped in religion his whole life, John's study of nature led him to question his father's fanaticism. On his long walk, Muir reflected on man's place in the universe and on his own place in the world. John found his religion not in written words or a musty church, but in every insect, bird, and flower. John became as adamant about his God in nature as his father had been about the biblical Lord.

Whatever conflicting emotions he might have felt before he left, once his feet turned southward and he stepped into the shaded vales of Kentucky oaks, he was at ease. He traveled light, carrying only a few toiletries, a change of underclothing, a New Testament, a book of Robert Burns's poems, a copy of *Paradise Lost,* and Alphonso Wood's *Class-book of Botany, with a Flora of the United States and Canada* in his knapsack. He carried no weapon or cooking utensils and neither hunted nor fished. Though he carried a rough map, he planned to follow the least worn track.

John Muir set off from Indianapolis on September 1, 1867, for his longest excursion to date. The first leg, from Indianapolis to Jeffersonville, Indiana, was by rail. After crossing the broad Ohio River to Louisville, he walked through the emerald hills of Kentucky and the Cumberland Mountains of Tennessee. Few towns were mentioned in his journals, probably because he avoided them except when necessary. He stopped at Mammoth Cave near Glasgow Junction in Kentucky and was pleasantly surprised to find the cave in a relatively undisturbed setting. Noble oaks, Muir proclaimed, were Kentucky's grandest plants and the ferns were magnificent.

Soon after entering the Cumberland Mountains, the first mountains he had ever seen, John encountered a young man on horseback. The man insisted on carrying John's knapsack and John finally relinquished it. Since the man was mounted, he had no trouble trotting ahead—but not too far because Muir was an excellent runner and kept the rider in sight. The horseman rounded a bend and John came upon him going through the sack, but having found nothing of value the rascal tossed it down and quickly rode away.

Somewhere south of Jamestown, Tennessee, as the afternoon bore toward night, John stopped at a house looking for a place to sleep. The woman had no change for the five-dollar greenback he offered and, apologizing, sent him on his way. She called him back as he started off and proffered a glass of milk. Are there any other houses down the road he asked her. Two miles to the next house she answered. Muir passed several empty houses, their owners killed or driven out by battles, before finding hospitality at the next occupied house that night.

The next day, September 11, he walked through wide-spaced oaks and tall pines sheltering a varied display of wildflowers, goldenrods, asters, and milkworts. Still the dwellings were empty, their orchards and fences ruined. Suddenly the path disappeared into thickets of briers that tore his skin and clothing as he fought his way through to a larger road. There, a row of tattered, mounted men faced him, a guerilla band. He continued toward them, said howdy and skirted the group. They watched him pass but did not give chase; he thought his plant press packed with greenery showed that he was nothing more than an herb doctor and not worth bothering.

He crossed rivers and streams bordered by lush vegetation and had no use for Philadelphia, Tennessee, though Madisonville, he wrote, was brisk. The mountain regions of Tennessee and North Carolina were more primitive than the remotest parts of Wisconsin. He forded the shapely Hiwassee River and strode into Murphy in western North Carolina, where the sheriff questioned him because he was a stranger and then invited him home to dinner.

By late September John had descended the mountains and entered Georgia's Piedmont region. He passed quickly through Blairsville on his way to the comfortable hamlet of Gainesville on the banks of the Chattahoochee River. John had worked with a man named Prater in Indiana and paused to visit his former co-worker at the Prater home in Gainesville, Georgia. Lake Sidney Lanier, formed by damming the Chattahoochee, sprawls beside Gainesville now.

Athens was the next town reached, on September 26. It was a place he might revisit one day, the most beautiful town he had seen on his journey. John followed the flattening ground southeast to Thomson through forests of leafy water oaks. The first longleaf pines appeared, strong and straight. Purple liatris and yellow-topped goldenrod bloomed among graceful grasses and he saw fewer familiar faces among the plants. He was as smitten with Georgia's grasses as he had been with ferns in Kentucky's verdant hills.

He walked forty miles on September 30, found no family who would receive him, and went to bed hungry at an Augusta hotel. After a good meal the next morning, he set off along the Savannah River through a land covered in splendid grasses and rich, dense, vine-clad forests filled with bounteous leguminous plants, muscadine grapes, and moss-hung cypress swamps, but goldenrod and asters were few.

Muir stopped at the home of an evidently wealthy planter on October 3. Gangs of freedmen worked the cotton fields, and the planter allowed that his labor costs were actually lower than before the war. The planter himself was engaged in removing rust from some gin saws recently retrieved from a pond bottom where they had been hidden from the Union army.

New plants accosted him on the way to Savannah, which he reached on October 8. He had been traveling for thirty-eight days, covering about twenty miles each day. Muir was weary and expected to find money expressed by his brother to Savannah, but it was not there. Days of solitary wanderings interspersed with rambling conversations with new people had tired him; he longed for contact with home. Down to hardly more than a dollar, and feeling lonely and poor, John spent the night at a mean-looking boarding house.

There was not much else to do on the following day except wander. He found himself on a smooth, white shell road leading to Bonaventure graveyard. Even in his lonely state, John found his spirits uplifted by Bonaventure's splendid live oaks draped in skeins of grey moss. Bald eagles roosted in the trees edging the Wilmington River. Colorful butterflies dipped and bobbed, sipping from each wildflower. Though it was a graveyard, Muir believed the peaceful place teemed with life.

He returned to town and bought some bread. It was all he could afford. Too poor to purchase another night's lodging, John went to the shore hoping to find a quiet spot in the low dunes. The beach, however, was skulking with others whom he did not trust. Pastoral Bonaventure came to mind.

The prospect of sleeping amongst the tombs delighted him, and he was certain no one would bother him in the burying ground. A great oak served as his ceiling, just as oaks had served as William Bartram's shelter nearly one hundred years earlier. John rested his head on a small mound. When he rose with the scolding of birds, he saw that his pillow had been a grave. William Bartram saw that he, too, had slept upon a grave after a night spent on a shell midden along the St. Johns River. Though John did not read Bartram's *Travels* until several years after his own southern walk, the two men shared a common quest, a search for self-identity in the natural world.

A few crackers served as breakfast. John watched the birds and squirrels, then trekked to Savannah's express office. No package. Returning to

Bonaventure, he selected a sparkleberry thicket for his camp. He returned there to sleep for almost a week, walking to town each day and growing hungrier and weaker until the package finally arrived.

The clerk was unwilling to hand it over at first as he did not trust Muir's identification, but finally relented. Nearly fainting from lack of nourishment, John received his money and bought the first food he saw, a large slice of gingerbread, from a street vendor. How sweet that must have been to a hungry man. Muir made no attempt to conceal his eating enjoyment.

I SPENT SEVERAL HOURS wandering Bonaventure's paths on a pleasant March day. Savannah's suburbs have grown around the cemetery and the white shell road leading to it is now paved.

Bonaventure had not always been a cemetery. In 1753, John Mullryne of Beaufort, South Carolina, requested five hundred acres south of the Midway River as he desired to become a Georgia planter. He was awarded the land and by 1771 Mullryne and his son-in-law, Josiah Tattnall, had increased their holdings to more than nine thousand acres stretching from Ebenezer to Sunbury. Bonaventure, "Good Fortune," comprised some six hundred acres about three miles from Savannah. The first home burned in 1771; another burned in 1800. Tattnall and Mullryne had been pillars of the growing community but after declaring their fealty to King George in 1775, they were arrested and banished from Georgia forever as traitors.

The plantation house became a hospital for French troops wounded in their battles to wrench Savannah from British control. Surely French soldiers had been buried on Bonaventure's grounds. When the British were finally rousted from the city in 1782, John Mullryne left America and later died in Nassau. Josiah Tattnall, Sr., established residency in London.

Josiah Tattnall, Jr., returned to Georgia in 1786 and purchased Bonaventure from John Habersham. Tattnall married, introduced cotton from the Bahamas, was elected state senator, and became Georgia's governor in 1801. Mrs. Tattnall died in 1802, and officially became the first adult to be buried in the family plot. Four of her children had already been interred there. In 1803, Josiah died while in Nassau. His body was returned to Bonaventure for burial, and the surviving Tatnall children were sent to their grandparents in England.

Edward Tattnall returned to the plantation in 1817 and lived there until his death in 1832, at which time his son, Josiah Tattnall III, became the owner. He sold the land, less the family burial plot, to Peter Wiltberger in 1846. Seventy acres in the northeastern corner were designated for use as a public burial ground. Peter died around 1853 and his son, William, formed the Evergreen Cemetery Company in 1868. Congregation Mickve Israel, Savannah's oldest synagogue, requested that a Jewish section be added. Evergreen Cemetery was purchased by the city of Savannah in 1907 and renamed Bonaventure.

Thus, Bonaventure was called Evergreen when Muir slept amongst the grave markers and was much smaller than its present 160 acres. The ruined mansion is completely gone now, as are the sparkleberry bushes. Though Bonaventure is larger, the peace that Muir found can still be felt under moss-bearded oaks standing as sentinels over the graves. I ambled the rows, reading epitaphs, admiring statuary, especially drawn to a group plot, the Order of Railroad Conductors. Plenty of oaks, palmettos, and magnolias shaded the tombs but not one sparkleberry branch. Birds chittered in hushed tones, and the Wilmington River appeared unconcerned.

An active historical society amasses information about those buried under the shady oaks. But do not expect to find the "Bird Girl" statue depicted on the cover of *Midnight in the Garden of Good and Evil*. The owners have placed it in a museum for protection.

It is not inconceivable that John and William Bartram, John Abbot, Alexander Wilson, André and François Michaux, and John James Audubon all passed near Bonaventure Plantation in their peregrinations. Each passed through Savannah, pausing to rest and restock and to ship or receive packages, and the surrounding area was rich in wildlife.

With money in his pocket and a full belly, Muir left Bonaventure behind and booked passage on the steamship *Sylvan Shore*. The vessel cut through the safe waters between Georgia's coast and the barrier islands toward Florida. They docked at Fernandina on Amelia Island on October 15. Muir was discouraged, for his first sight of the state showed a reclining coast lined with marshes behind which clumps of squat trees marched inland. Muir had expected a tropical forest redolent with the color and fragrance of heady blossoms. Instead he found a land barely

FIG. 18. Downtown Fernandina in the 1870s with wharves on the
Amelia River in the background, about ten years after John Muir
paused to purchase bread before walking to Cedar Key.
Courtesy of Florida Archives.

above water, a tawny embroidery of salt marshes and braided creeks, "a
flat, watery, reedy coast, with clumps of mangrove and forests of moss-
dressed, strange trees appearing low in the distance."[3] He stepped onto a
rickety dock, bought bread in Fernandina, and set off for the woods. The
low country seemed to belong more to the sea than the land, he thought.
Feeling lonely, still weak from his days of near-starvation, he paused, nib-
bling at his meal. A noise sounded behind him. He could almost feel the
hot breath of the snapping alligator. Luckily, it was only a tall wading
bird but it jarred him to reality.

Fort Clinch State Park, 1,121 acres and named for the fort built in the mid-1840s, now caps the northern tip of Amelia Island. The garrison was greatly reduced after 1865. The St. Marys River, which rises from the Okefenokee Swamp, empties its tannin-stained waters into Cumberland Sound before sweeping a cut between Florida's Amelia Island and Georgia's Cumberland Island. Florida's parks strive to preserve Florida as it appeared at the time of European contact while providing amenities for visitors. A narrow trail for bicyclists and walkers winds through the coastal hammock on either side of a paved road bisecting the park. Coastal hardwood hammocks fringed with grassy marshes line Amelia's western side. The Atlantic beach allows for strolling, fishing, birding, and sunbathing on the eastern side.

I visited the park on a warm October day, about the same time of year that Muir had been there. An inner tier of coastal live oaks and palmetto has grown over large, relict dunes. Between the older dunes and the ocean, limber sea oats nodded, compact blossoms of gilded goldenrod dipped, and feathery, raspberry-colored seed heads of "mulhy" grass shimmered in the steady wind blowing from the Atlantic. Knobs of ripening fruit topped flat cactus pads, and butterflies—bright orange viceroys, creamy yellow sulphurs, muted long-tailed skippers—bobbled from flower to flower. Warblers wheedled berries and insects from bushy wax myrtle branches. Masses of tangled green smilax vines blanketed the low dunes. To the south, an indistinct skyline of motels and condos sullied the coastline.

Standing on the beach I blanked out the modern structures with my thumbs and ignored both the pier edging into the sea and the boardwalk built over the dunes to protect their fragile integrity from tramping feet. I drew the sea's salty breath into my lungs. Sandpipers fervently needled the sand between waves and gulls wheeled overhead.

This scene, not quite the tropical paradise he had hoped for, might have been similar to Muir's first glimpse of Florida, and it dampened his expectations. The land of his dreams had been trellised with a rainbow of flowers, but Florida's tropical heart beats farther south. North Florida would have been exchanging its worn summer dress for winter's somber austerity in October. Even the greens would be dulled, as if summer's enervating heat had drawn the color into the stratosphere.

John had not stayed long on Amelia, and neither did I. On the way out, a frazzled-looking couple, necks slung with binoculars, waved their arms and asked for a ride to the gate.

"We had no idea it was such a long walk!" they said. In town for a meeting, they took advantage of an afternoon break to do some birding. This was a pleasant change from their Pacific Northwest home and offered several new species for their list. If they could just get to the gate, a bus from their hotel would pick them up.

Fernandina claims to be the second-oldest city in America, having been settled by the Spanish in 1567. It may have been named after Spain's King Ferdinand or it may have been named after Don Domingo Fernandez, who received a large land grant in 1785. Regardless, "Beach" was later tagged onto the end, lending the small town a resort air.

Muir had followed the rail line from Fernandina to Gainesville, then on to Cedar Key. Men had started laying rails before the war, but the entire line was not truly operational until after 1865. Portions of the damaged tracks were probably still being repaired when Muir made his passage.

"Florida is so watery and vine-tied that pathless wanderings are not easily possible in any direction. I started to cross the State by a gap hewn for the locomotive, walking sometimes between the rails, stepping from tie to tie, or walking on the strip of sand at the sides, gazing into the mysterious forest. . . . It is impossible to write the dimmest picture of a plant grandeur so redundant, unfathomable," Muir recounted.[4]

Reversing my route on A1A over a tall bridge lunging over the Amelia River—not a true river, but a mingling of fresh water, tidal creeks, and sloughs that sever Amelia Island from the mainland—I glimpsed a low railroad bridge paralleling the bridge. Once on the mainland, A1A shadows the tracks to Yulee, where they veer away and return near Callahan, newly settled in 1860. From there U.S. 301 follows the tracks. Coffee-colored water fills ditches lining the roadside between small towns. Similar borrow ditches, left from scooping soil to build up the railbeds, had escorted the tracks that Muir followed. The low land is pocked with cypress bays and moist flatwoods. For the most part, the soil is porous sand and water is not too far from the surface. The next town, Bryceville, was not settled until 1886, but Baldwin, intersected by Interstate 10, had been a small collection of buildings when John passed this way. Beyond Baldwin, there is little else for several miles until Starke, another fresh settlement when John walked there. Muir might have paused at one of these small outposts, though he did not mention them by name.

Florida was sparsely settled until after the Civil War. Railroads built to move troops and supplies made travel easier and once the war was over, people were on the move. Northerners came south to escape harsh winters and many Southerners removed to Florida to avoid what they perceived as unfair Reconstruction practices. The state's population blossomed from 144,000 in 1860 to 270,000 in 1880.

At last John found beauty in North Florida's mysterious forest. The glossy green Southern magnolias and tall, flat-topped cypresses he had met in Georgia were here also. Then he reached the pinelands. They were mesic flatwoods, that is to say, they were often wet in places. In the closing daylight, Muir searched for a small dry place to sleep and ate his last crust of bread. Owls and other night noises sounded around him. He trusted nature and expected no harm.

In the morning he woke to beautiful surroundings but had no food. He supposed if he could learn to forgo eating, civilization might never see him again. New to him was the sabal palm, which he found "indescribably impressive." Long, pointed leaves of the sabal palm, and the shorter palmetto, form a circular fan so symmetrical in shape as to be almost mesmerizing if gazed upon for long. In the evening breeze the fronds rustle and gently tap against each other, a low hollow sound that can lull most anyone to sleep. Muir found it plain but possessing an expressive power not found in any other tree he had met so far.

An autumn walk in North Florida's pinelands hails a changing season. Tall stems of fuchsia liatris, yellow-topped goldenrod, and ginger bracken fern clothe the ground. Clumps of slender wheat-colored grasses sprout stalks of filmy seed heads. Muir thought that not another plant in the forest surpassed Florida's tall grasses in wind-waving grace. Light breezes dance through flowers and play tag in the treetops. Wind soughing through a pine forest is one of the most peaceful sounds on earth. It is as if the currents carry secrets between plants.

Today, Highway 301 passes through a few more towns than were there in the late 1860s. Beyond the towns, a few homes are scattered along the roadside, but for the most part the road traverses heavily shaded hardwood hammocks and flatwoods thickly sown with pines, vines, and palmettos. Rows of young slash pines stand in line where naturally occurring flatwoods have been cut. A mixture of slash pines, longleaf pines, and sabal palms screen pine plantations from the view of passersby. The railroad is within sight, flashing through breaks in the woods, most of the way. The highway widens to four lanes in Baldwin, traffic picks up, towns

FIG. 19. Saw palmetto, *Serenoa repens,* admired by John Muir.
Photo by Gil Nelson.

become closer together, and soon the town of Waldo, a little north of Gainesville, appears.

All along, clearcuts and recently burned pinelands lined the road. The spring and summer of 1998 had been almost desert dry in Florida; tens of thousands of acres had burned as fires flickered across the state. In the summer of 1998, fuel loads—dry grasses and fallen timber—were high after a wet winter. A dry spring cured the grasses to tinder. When thunderstorms laden with abundant lightning and not much moisture moved in, fire began to reclaim its rightful position in the landscape. Coupled with natural fires were those started by arsonists, who hoped their illegal fires would be masked.

Florida's fires made the front pages of newspapers across the west as hotshot crews and firefighters traveled east to lend a hand. Usually, eastern firefighters go west to help, but western fires were relatively quiet while fires flared in every county of the Sunshine State that summer.

While most of Florida's residents had viewed the fires as devastating, they are part and parcel of the state's natural heritage. Almost every Florida habitat depends on fire in some way. Situated between two large water bodies, the Gulf of Mexico and the Atlantic Ocean, and strewn with plants adapted to burning, Florida draws thunderstorms like a magnet. A recently burned forest may seem devoid of life, but residual ash adds nitrogen to the soil, new growth bursts forth in a few days, and before long the forest thrums with life.

As the 1998 fires came under control, timber crews moved in to salvage the wood before it was invaded by an algae that leaves behind a blue stain. The dye lessens the value, so the rush to cut was justified. A timber man had once related that when the large pines were about gone and it became more difficult to cut wide lumber without knots, companies marketed "knotty pine" as something unique and valuable. Maybe they should market the algae-shaded wood as "naturally stained."

The rails from Waldo to Gainesville have been pulled and a landscaped bike/walk trail stretches into Gainesville. Several people were exercising on the former railbed when I drove into town. Gainesville was much smaller when Muir walked through on October 18, 1867. He bought food and lodging at a tavern and described Gainesville as "rather attractive—an oasis in the desert, compared with other villages. It gets its life from the few plantations located about it on dry ground that rises island-like a few feet above the swamps."[5] He would not recognize it today, but he would appreciate the large university's fine botany department. Not one to tarry long in town, he headed for the Gulf coast the next day.

It had taken me less than three hours to drive from Fernandina to Gainesville. It took Muir four days, stopping often to botanize, to reach the village. During that time he had regained an appreciation of Florida's unapparent beauty. The inland forests and swamps presented an astonishing variety of greenery. Again and again something would attract him and he would wade into the moat between the roadbed and the forest until it became too deep and he would turn back to try crossing at another place. If it wasn't water, then it was the matted forest itself that conspired to keep Muir from entering. "I endeavored repeatedly to force a way through the tough vine-tangles, but seldom succeeded in getting farther than a few hundred yards."[6]

From Gainesville, Muir likely continued following the rail path to Cedar Key. Though he does not mention the railroad again in his narration, he might have zigged into the forest and zagged back to the tracks now and then. He met people along the way: a gang of loggers he described as worse than any guerrillas he'd met in the Tennessee mountains; a trio of men and their dogs—the men fed him and the dogs tried to maul him; another solitary man he expected might rob him—John bluffed that he possessed a gun and the other man backed down.

As Muir headed toward the coast, the land became lower and wetter; swamps abounded. He met one alligator, which hastened away from him. Muir did not mention alligators in the large numbers described by Bartram, but then John spent more time on land. He heard plenty of stories about them and, though others regarded them as evil creatures, John found them to be beautiful in God's eyes. Florida's waters were different from other rivers and streams he had crossed. While other streams appeared "to travel through a country with thoughts and plans for something beyond . . . those of Florida are at home, do not appear to be traveling at all, and seem to know nothing of the sea."[7]

Muir must have been weary from his travels. Though he was a hardy man, days of going without proper nourishment had weakened him. On October 23, he reached the Gulf of Mexico. Catching the sea scent a few miles before he caught sight of it, John was taken back to his Dunbar childhood. He saw craggy coasts and the village of his long-ago home vividly in his mind, but nothing could have been farther from the reality of the flat marsh-tasseled Gulf coast. Perhaps he was more deeply affected because his journey in this region was so near to an end and he was so far from home. His plan was to sail for Cuba and thence to South America, but he was not quite ready to leave. There was still the Gulf coast to explore.

Route 24 wanders out of Gainesville and shoots a pretty straight road to the town of Cedar Key. West of Archer, traffic thins and pine flatwoods and higher sandhills replace the suburbs that house people who work in Gainesville. The road crosses busy Highway 19/98 at Otter Creek and tiptoes through Rosewood. In January 1923, a black man's alleged assault of a white woman caused a race riot in the pleasantly named community. When black residents tried to defend themselves a white mob burned most of the town's buildings. At least six people were killed and the blacks abandoned their homes.

The region is lightly populated, but the pinelands began changing even before Muir ambled through. In 1855, timbering had begun in the thick coastal forests around Cedar Key. The Faber Pencil Company and the Eagle Pencil Company built mills on Cedar Key. A million cubic feet of cedar, trimmed and ready to be made into pencils, were shipped in 1872. The *Cedar Key Telegraph* on April 7, 1860, proclaimed that timber resources of the Suwannee River were inexhaustible, were easily reached, and could be brought to the mills with very little trouble.

After the railbed had been restored, all mail bound for Havana, Cuba, exited through Cedar Key. Fish, fruit, timber, cotton, and other merchandise crossed the peninsula by rail and was then loaded on ships bound for other ports. That pair of iron rails brought commercial prosperity to both Fernandina and Cedar Key for awhile. The route was much shorter and less dangerous than sailing through the Florida Straits. By 1885, Cedar Key, then known as the Venice of Florida, was Levy County's principal town with a future. But by 1900, the "inexhaustible" supply of timber had run out. Larger ships and the need for deepwater ports brought Cedar Key's boom times to an end.

Cedar Key relies more on tourists these days than on any other industry, but the tourist season had not quite geared up and downtown streets were quiet. Activity at the docks centered on the never-ending tasks of boat maintenance. The highest point is about fifty feet above the Gulf's waters and the town is often beset by storms. Just about every scrap of land has been built upon, and I had to admire the tenacity of the people and the old buildings. Beside the walkway to the state museum, the Sierra Club has added a monument to John Muir.

Since he planned to stay for awhile John sought work and a place to stay at a sawmill near Cedar Key. The next day he began feeling ill. Thinking a swim in the sea might do him good, he plunged in. This only made him feel worse. He longed for something sour and trudged into the village to buy lemons. By the third day his fever was higher and his strength lower. Again he craved lemons, plodded to town, and collapsed on his return. He awoke and staggered toward the mill-house. Lying in a heap he asked the night watchman for help, but that fellow thought him drunk and would not help. John literally dragged himself to bed.

The next day, Mr. Hodgson, the mill owner, had John moved to the Hodgson residence. The family nursed him back to health, though it was a long road. Muir convalesced from late October until January.

As soon as he was able, he sat in the shade and watched shore birds feeding at low tide and clouds changing shape. He sailed a light skiff across shallow water to explore small offshore keys. December's temperature hovered around 65°, but one day a little damp snow fell.

He had not given up his dream to see South America. On a January day, when he'd climbed to the rooftop to view a fine sunset, he noticed the white sails of the schooner *Island Belle,* about to sail with a load of lumber to Cuba. Muir booked passage, hurried back to the Hodgsons, and bade them farewell, promising to return one day.

The voyage was rough at times, but Muir was glad to be on his way again and happy to reach Cuba. He longed to climb the high mountains, but tired easily and could not go far, so each night he returned to the ship. After a month, his health had not improved much and he gave up his plan to continue to the Orinoco basin.

California's mountains and forests would restore his strength, he decided. None of the California-bound ships stopped at Havana, so Muir sailed to New York on a ship carrying oranges. While he waited to sail to California, Muir did not stray far from his berth in New York's harbor. Crowds, noise, and big buildings were more than he could handle. He landed in San Francisco around the first of April, stayed one day, and headed for Yosemite Valley.

Along his walk to the Gulf of Mexico, John noted the unhealed scars of war: burnt fences and mills, ruined fields, ravaged forests, and the beaten faces of the people. Fences and mills could be rebuilt, fields could be tilled, forests would regrow, but the people were slower to mend. They had lost loved ones killed or maimed, homes, businesses. He met all sorts of people on this journey, former slaves and former slave owners. Most were generous and friendly. Muir was grateful for their food, conversations, and advice, but he was always anxious to return to the woods. He could not be deterred for long. Though he was somewhat threatened on occasion, the greatest enemy Muir encountered was thick tangles of vines and brambles: "Vegetable cats of many species will rob him of his clothes and claw his flesh, while dwarf palmettos will saw his bones, and the bayonets will glide to his joints and marrow without the smallest consideration for Lord Man."[8] He loved every step.

It was this tour that proved Muir had chosen correctly to follow his path into heaven's powerful light. Here he found God's cathedrals and chapels where he was free to worship in his own way. In all his life, John never met a snake, a tree, a rock, a stream, or an insect that he did not realize and admire its position, however humble, in the larger scheme of life. His long walk represented a true break from his father's will. John Muir could walk his own path now.

It was the land, always the land, and all the creatures sharing it that held Muir in the greatest thrall. He had rejected his father's religious fervor, but was intensely religious himself, finding the creations of the Creator to be his church. When in Canada, John had been asked to teach a Sunday school class. He had offered the children a lesson in botany rather than scripture.

John Muir was a free individual, dressing in comfortable clothes, not always according to convention, but always clean. Though he stood under six feet tall, he bore a commanding presence. His piercing eyes were deep blue and his auburn hair turned silver as he aged. He never shaved. He lived by an honorable creed and disliked politics. During John's childhood, only Scots was spoken at home and only English in school. A slight Scots burr clung to his pleasantly modulated voice and he enjoyed conversations and, even better, a good debate. His father had once called him "a contumacious quibbler too fond of disputation."[9]

He wrote and published several articles, but few books during his lifetime. He left an abundance of unpublished notes about his travels, ruminations, and observations, though he maintained that he did not want to be a writer. He was too busy learning, and helping others learn, to stop and write. When he wrote of his youth and relationship to his father, his tone was often ambivalent; it seemed as though he might have been testing his view of nature and how he should live his life against a lifetime of admonitions from his father. After Muir died in 1914, the notebooks and thoughts he had written about his first long journey were compiled and edited into a book titled *A Thousand-Mile Walk to the Gulf,* first published in 1916. Several editions have been released since. A good accompaniment to the narrative is a pictorial essay by John Earl, *John Muir's Longest Walk: John Earl, a Photographer, Traces His Journey to Florida,* published in 1975. Several other writings were compiled, edited, and published after his death. Many are still in print.

When he discovered living glaciers in the Sierras, he postulated that they had formed the beautiful gorges and scarred cliffs of Yosemite Valley. Dr. Josiah Dwight Whitney, then California's state geologist, dismissed the "uneducated sheepherder." Whitney believed that earthquakes had formed the valley. Over three summers, Muir explored, measured, sketched, and described the course of the ice sheets and, in the end, was proven correct. In his wanderings, Muir discovered new species of plants and insects, but more than that, John Muir is remembered as a conservationist.

The conservation movement did not begin with the first Earth Day on April 22, 1970. Ever since the first boulders were rolled into water to divert a stream, after the first acre was cut and the trees left to rot, from the first time waste was poured into a river to wash downstream, someone has cautioned care. Almost anyone who has studied natural history in depth, or watched a forest fall to make way for a hundred homes, or noticed that fireflies are fewer on summer nights knows that all life on this earth is an ethereal and precious thing.

Muir spent three days camping in Yosemite with Theodore Roosevelt; out of that meeting came a plan to preserve some of America's most spectacular areas, the Grand Canyon and the Petrified Forest. His last fight to save the beautiful Hetch Hetchy Valley from being flooded by a dam to provide water for San Francisco failed in 1913. John Muir died of pneumonia on December 24, 1914. Some say losing the Hetch Hetchy finally defeated him, and maybe that is so.

His spirit did not die but lives on in the Sierra Club and in all whose hearts race in the presence of vast mountain ranges and valleys or feel a small flutter when recognizing a familiar bird or flower. The thrill of discovery never dulled for Muir. He might see the same leaf a thousand times or watch the sun rise every morning but each time he was as awed as the first. During walks alone or with others, he would stop to watch a bird or a tree until he had given it its due—that might be an hour or more. Learning was a mountain Muir eagerly climbed until his death. To learn and to teach others was one summit he could not conquer for there was always more to learn, always more to teach. John Muir's compelling voice and his commitment to natural beauty stand above others. He desired to convert us all to his religion.

CHAPTER 11

A Voice for Florida Conservation

John Kunkel Small
(January 31, 1869–January 21, 1938)

The wholesale devastation of the plant covering, through carelessness, thoughtlessness, and vandalism in the Peninsular State, prehistoric and historic, was everywhere apparent. Frequent references to it are made in the narrative and special examples are mentioned in detail. A series of pictures is inserted through the text with which they are directly or indirectly connected. They show, in each case, localities as adorned by nature and as "improved" by man. It may be said, however, that the plant covering has had to contend with destruction and changes for ages, and would reassert itself in one form or another in time. For example, local hammocks and pinelands might restore themselves in comparatively short periods, but the Lake Okeechobee region might take a million years.

—From John K. Small's preface to *From Eden to Sahara: Florida's Tragedy*

THE RATTLING CAR jolts along sandy roads, mires in bogs, and crunches over crushed shells that once formed burial mounds for extinct native tribes. Unforgiving springs lift me off the seat, about every hundred yards it seems, causing me to bang my head against the unpadded steel struts supporting the canvas roof. Wind whistles through the open windows as we clip along at ten or fifteen miles an hour, sometimes sideways as the car squirms through gritty ruts. Sand glare burns my eyes. Every now and then we sink to a stop and everyone jumps out, laughing and joking, to horse the car through a mucky place, then all jump back in and jounce along as before until the next sudden halt. All the while our leader excitedly flings his arms this way and that, points to plants and calls out their names, spouts a rhapsodic running commentary on the land and natural history, rarely slowing except to take a breath. His dark coat is rumpled and the pockets bulge with notebook, pens, wilting leaves, mosses, and rocks, but the jacket is neatly buttoned and he wears a tie. He has been along this road a dozen times; the first time in a horse-drawn wagon.

A bony brindled cow jumps away through the underbrush, frightened by the car's noise and billowing dust cloud. A rabbit bolts across the well-worn track. There are no fences, no power lines, no mailboxes, no traffic lights, no road signs, no trash along the shoulders. This is Florida in the early 1900s, the province of John K. Small.

John Kunkel Small was born in Harrisburg, Pennsylvania, on January 31, 1869. His mother was forty-four years old when her only child was born. In 1888 John entered Franklin and Marshall College at Lancaster, Pennsylvania, and found his career in botany. Small, during his sophomore year, published his first article in a college magazine, "Classification of Plants Endowed with the Habit of Sleep." He became good friends with Arthur Heller, equally enthusiastic about botany, and the two took a botanical journey to the western North Carolina mountains over the summer of 1891. Heller also became a professional botanist and later moved to California. He and Small traded plants and letters for years.

After graduating, Small received a botany fellowship in 1892 to Columbia College, now Columbia University. He remained at Columbia for three more years as herbarium curator. During his service in that capacity, Dr. Small began work on his own *Flora of the Southeastern United States,* an expanded study based on Dr. Alvan Chapman's work, including many new species and tropical plants Chapman had not seen. Though he knew the area around Quincy and Apalachicola well, and had

FIG. 20. Dr. John Kunkel Small, John DeWinkler, and Charles A. Mosier pose
with a weed wagon on a South Florida plant prowl in the early 1900s.
Courtesy of Florida Archives.

explored parts of the Gulf coast and the Florida Keys, Chapman had not
ventured far into the peninsula's interior, nor had he touched on the
unique Everglades ecosystem. There were more plants to be found, but
by the time Chapman had given up his medical practice he was past devoting energy to the endeavor.

Small married Elizabeth Wheeler in 1896 and they produced two sons
and two daughters over the next ten years. The New York Botanical Garden, conceived in 1891, opened its doors in 1900. Dr. Nathaniel L. Britton
was named director and he chose Dr. Small to organize the museums and
build the herbarium collections. It is recognized today as one of the
world's finest botanical gardens, and John Kunkel Small was largely responsible for building its foundation: identifying and classifying thousands of plants from around the globe. Dr. Small's discerning eye split a
number of plants into subspecies or even separate species. He separated
Magnolia ashei from Michaux's *M. macrophylla*. Others were not always
pleased with Dr. Small's propensity to break species into subspecies on
the basis of minute differences. After his death a number of his divisions
were rejoined; *M. ashei* is now considered a subspecies of *M. macrophylla*.

During his tenure at Columbia's herbarium and later at the garden, Dr. Small formed a lasting friendship with Roland Harper, who recognized Small's talents and respected him, although that is not always apparent from some of Harper's letters. From about 1902 until Small's death, Roland maintained a peevish correspondence, writing long chatty letters sharing news and asking questions, constantly niggling Small about mistakes and misprints, arguing where, when, and if plants had been found, taking him to task for not writing ("Write Soon." "Do it now."), wondering when the next flora was coming out, or the next "bedtime story," Small's popular travelogues published in the garden's journal.

Harper harangued for three, four, or five pages, and Small answered with one page. The two did botanize on occasion and Roland was always pestering Small to give up Florida and come to Alabama or Georgia or Tennessee—wherever Roland was then employed.

In addition to Roland, Small corresponded with a cadre of professional and amateur botanists who sent specimens familiar, rare, and unknown, and not always well preserved. Small's responses were short and to the point; he had not the time to ramble in reply. Sometimes he wrote with instructions for obtaining a better specimen, sometimes he asked for clarification of where it had been found. Refusing to play favorites, he was not overly forthcoming with praise nor was he harsh with those who sent less than satisfactory representatives.

The St. John brothers of central Florida were fellow fern enthusiasts. Harper connected with them and Small warned his friends about Roland's prickly side, "When you meet Roland Harper do not let his off-hand outspoken attitude toward theory, a proposition, or a person surprise you. Harper is very able, but he has the unfortunate habit of generally 'rubbing the fur the wrong way' thus irritating people generally and making many enemies."[1]

Aside from his gifts as a taxonomist, Small was an excellent and dedicated field botanist. With the New York Botanical Garden's backing, Dr. Small launched repetitive, exhaustive examinations of the Southeastern region, beginning in 1901 and continuing for almost three decades. He found South Florida a rich area for new tropical discoveries and home to many of his special interests—cacti, ferns, and irises.

He published lively chronicles of his journeys with hopes of making readers aware of the beauty and the dangers facing natural lands. Underlying his written words was the surety that those magnificent places were being destroyed and would soon be forever lost. A great many of them have since felt the not-so-gentle touch of dredges, rock bulldozers, and dynamite. Whenever I read one of his accounts, I feel as if I am rocking along in the weed wagon, as he called the vehicles, through a Florida not too far past.

Think of Florida's southern tip as a hand with the hammock region as fingers. Held in the palm is Lake Okeechobee and leaking between the fingers are the Everglades. Three distinct types of limestone formations support hammock vegetation.

Miami limestone forms the Miami rock ridge, broadly spreading from Miami to Homestead and narrowing as it reaches Long Pine Key in Everglades National Park, the lower Keys from Big Pine Key to Key West, and an outcrop in the southeastern third of the Big Cypress Swamp. Miami limestone is composed of small roundish pellets of calcium carbonate deposited during the Pleistocene. When sea level fell, the pellets dried and cemented together. The rock is hard at the surface, but a few feet lower it is soft and can be cut with hand tools. Exposure to air hardens the stone, and the early settlers found it an ideal building material.

Tamiami limestone underlies Big Cypress Swamp and is considered older than Miami limestone. It is much more fossiliferous than the Miami formation, but like that rock, it hardens upon exposure to air.

Key Largo limestone, comprising the upper Keys, is formed from consolidated reef corals and other rubble. The unique designs and impressions left by the skeletons of different corals are the hallmark of this formation. It is highly valued as a building material.

Limestone is the natural sponge that holds Florida's groundwater. It is porous rock, filled with holes and gaps and crevices where water pools as it makes its way toward ever larger caverns of the aquifer, the Floridan for North and Central Florida and the Biscayne in South Florida. Streams, lakes, ponds, and most areas covered with loose sand are surficial catch basins that slowly recharge the aquifers. Think of all the wells, shallow and deep, tapping into the underground storage cavities. Think of the millions of septic tanks, slowly releasing partially treated waste high in nitrogens and phosphorus. Everything that seeps into the ground eventually reaches our hidden water supply. Think about it.

A hammock of the vegetative variety, not to be confused with a wedge of cloth strung between two shade trees on a lazy summer afternoon, is a great tangle of trees, vines, and epiphytic plants. The ancient limestones lie exposed or covered with a layer of humus and soil containing high amounts of organic material that can be consumed by infrequent fires. Solution holes, left where the rock has dissolved, dot the interior. The holes are anywhere from one to thirty feet across at the surface and generally widen toward the bottom. Some are quite deep with ferns clinging to the craggy walls. Though the rest of the hammock seems relatively dry, water held in the holes increases the hammock's overall humidity and moderates temperatures, allowing delicate orchids and bromeliads to thrive along the limbs of hospitable trees. Inside these shrouded, rocky forests a perfect mixture of light, moisture, and nutrients supports plants more common to the West Indies, tropical beauties unlike anything found elsewhere in the state.

Originally about five hundred distinct hammocks ranging in size from less than an acre to around ninety acres covered the rock ridge area. They were set apart by bands of pinelands and glades, and each was prevented from encroaching on the other by periodic fires. Because hammocks were discrete and slightly different from each other, settlers named each one for a person or an outstanding feature, such as Castellow, Addison, Brickell, Matheson, and Royal Palm.

Broad-leaved evergreen and semi-evergreen tropical hardwoods such as gumbo limbo, pigeon plum, and white stopper make up tropical hardwood hammocks. Thick underbrush usually defends the hammock's perimeter, leading to the mistaken belief that it is an impenetrable jungle. The leafy canopy obstructs sunlight so that the open interior lacks significant understory and groundcover plants. The composition of each hammock is determined by rainfall, temperature, saltwater influence, surrounding vegetation, and disturbance such as fire or hurricanes.

It was Standard Oil magnate Henry Flagler's Florida East Coast Railway, built to carry the wealthy to South Florida's winter playgrounds, that opened up the state's Atlantic coast for development. Julia Tuttle, and to some extent Mary Brickell, swapped land with Henry so he could extend his railroad from Palm Beach to Miami, a quiet fishing village of around a thousand residents when the last spike was driven through the steel rail in 1896.

Most Miamians drew their existence from the sea and liked, even desired, their isolated living conditions. But the rich came to enjoy the mild winters, and for two months every year—"the season"—locals tolerated the influx of people who spent money and then went home. It was not long before those not so rich, but hoping to be, invaded the small town, packing dreams of buildings and businesses. They did not leave. And that was the beginning of the end for the majestic rocklands. Miami has remembered the women who indirectly connected the town to the outside world by naming roads after them: Brickell Avenue and the Julia Tuttle Causeway, which connects Miami Beach to the mainland.

It is difficult enough to build on top of rock, but South Florida's limestone—brittle or soft, pitted with holes that were often filled with sand or water, lying near the surface or hidden under layers of sand with the water table not far below—made for tricky construction. As more people moved to the area, more buildable land was required. The hammocks were almost eradicated as a result.

Even before bulldozers crushed the hammocks, they had faced another, clandestine threat. Collectors stripped the groves of rare orchids, bromeliads, and ferns, tree snails (there are sixty named color variations), and insects. Such people are still about and are willing to pay a hefty price for a protected specimen. The thieves are usually never caught, and cases are difficult to prosecute. Those proven guilty are given hardly more than a slap on the wrist, certainly not enough to deter them from doing it again.

And there are other forces working against the hammocks. South Florida's water table has been significantly lowered ever since the stupid—the incredibly stupid—plan to drain the Everglades was initiated in the late 1800s. As land south of Lake Okeechobee was ditched, diked, drained, and converted to farmland the water table was lowered. Rain does not fall every day in Florida, so farmers must take an allocation of water when needed. With an ever increasing population comes the need for more fresh water and down goes the underground level, low enough to allow salt water to seep in. Several public and private wells have been tainted and closed over the years and deeper wells dug. How long those deep water sources can be drawn on and how long it takes to recharge the Biscayne aquifer are difficult if not impossible questions to answer.

Historically, water drained south, west, and slightly east from the big lake (730 square miles), moving about one hundred feet a day. At that rate, the liquid nourished a variety of wildlife from mosquito larvae to Florida panthers, from tiny orchids to royal palms, from warblers to eagles. In spring and summer migratory birds pause in the Glades to refuel on their way to or from South America. In summer the vast wet sheet fed clashing thunderstorms, sending thousands of gallons of water sky-ward through evapotranspiration to fall back to earth to replenish lakes and rivers and provide drinking water for people. In 1950, South Florida's residents used a half billion gallons of water each day. In 1990, they confiscated 14.1 billion gallons a day, far outstripping agriculture, which extracted a mere 3.8 billion gallons a day.

If the demand for water is not enough to lower the water level, the drainage canals are still flowing. On one hand water is helped to leave the ecosystem much faster than it should, especially in times of abundant rainfall. On the other hand, water is held against the months when little or no rain falls. And there is the poisonous soup dumped daily into the ecosystem—nitrogen, phosphorous, pesticides, herbicides, fungicides. One dairy cow produces as much waste as twenty people in one day. It all goes into the Glades and into the shallow waters of Florida Bay and the Gulf of Mexico. The habitats are skewed. Wildlife, especially birds, have flown to better neighborhoods—but these are also in increasingly shorter supply.

As the water table has been drawn down so have water levels in solu-tion holes in the existing hammocks. The delicate tuning of humidity levels has been altered, meaning that some plants are no longer able to survive. It is not clear how land managers can combat that problem.

Perhaps most insidious are an army of exotic plants set loose in the hospitable climate. Many human residents, new and long-time, some-times fail to recognize the interlopers, judging them to be native because they appear to be everywhere. Australian pine, melaleuca, gold coast jas-mine, Brazilian jasmine, chinese fever vine, wood rose, air potato, red sandalwood, Brazilian pepper, woman's tongue, and scholar tree are just a few of the non-native plants taking over natural habitats.

By the time John Kunkel Small arrived, the hammocks were begin-ning to fall and he soon realized that only a handful of people appreciated their beauty. He witnessed Florida's first boom, when developers rode a crest of unparalleled growth, though they have since surpassed them-selves. It was all the more evident because he walked in almost virgin territory only to return in a year or two to find that the hammock or pine rockland had been erased and some manmade structure erected in its place. No wonder he was appalled.

Among those moving to the land of never-winter were the Deering brothers, James and Charles. Their father, William Deering, had made a fortune in farm equipment, International Harvester. Both brothers bought property in Dade County and built large estates, and both sought to protect the hammocks surrounding their homes. Early in the construction of James's palatial home in Brickell Hammock he sent this directive to all workmen: "To me the charm of this part of the world is the jungle effect, and anything done to interfere with this must be against my wishes and without my knowledge."[2]

Deering agonized over every tree or shrub that had to be removed to accommodate the Mediterranean-style villa he called Vizcaya. James was quite a playboy and Vizcaya was the ultimate party home, with sensual furnishings and small hidden rooms. A wall disguised with shrubbery separated the home from the view of passersby. Unfortunately, James Deering died of pernicious anemia in 1925 and enjoyed his home for only nine years. He had never married and left the opulent property to his nieces. Over time they sold parts of the property; in 1952 Dade County purchased the home and gardens for one million dollars. I remember riding past the property as a child while my mother and grandmother speculated about what lay behind the vine-draped barrier. Vizcaya is now open to the public as a priceless repository of European decorative arts.

Charles Deering's home is restrained compared to Vizcaya, though the living quarters are commodious and Charles, who loved fine wines, kept a hidden cellar stocked during prohibition. In fact, James was chagrined at Charles's plain tastes. To please his brother, Charles ordered blue and white Italian marble tiles to pave the large room where he displayed his collection of art and tapestries. Charles Deering died in 1927. Mrs. Deering lived there until her death in 1942, and his descendants used the grounds off and on until 1980. Miami-Dade Parks and state and federal funds purchased the estate in 1985. Just as private as Charles, his offspring removed all traces of family records, but left the priceless wine collection, so staff must often guess as to the history. No one even knows what caused Charles's death. His 420-acre estate at Cutler on Biscayne Bay operates as a center for education and recreation and is a fantastic ecological and archaeological site.

Mammoths, prehistoric horses, tapirs, jaguars, and bison once roamed the area and their bones and teeth have been recovered from a dig on the property. Ten thousand-year-old human remains indicate that Paleo-Indians, the earliest known inhabitants, lived there as well as the more recent Tequesta Indians. The estate protects more than 115 acres of tropical hardwood hammocks and 150 acres of endangered pine rockland forest.

Small knew both Deerings and lent his expertise to preserving their hammocks and advised them on native plantings. As can be learned from his writings, the botanist often collected seeds and plants to enhance the natural areas. Since Charles had an interest in botany and preserving native vegetation, he financed several of Small's Florida excursions. It was a dream come true for the zealous botanist. The *Barbee,* Charles's unpretentious yacht, about thirty-two feet long and twelve feet abeam with an open roofed area in the center, was made available to Small and other scientists for their searches into the Keys and other watery habitats. Even though the boat was motorized with a shallow draft, many photographs show it being pushed along by wading scientists.

The hammocks that Small so loved to explore were like a flawless diamond necklace that today has been shattered. Managers hover over the surviving hammocks preserved by the Miami-Dade Parks system, guarding the few precious remaining stones. But even if all the gems could be recovered they could not be put back together because they have forever lost their integrity. Removal of native plants and animals, invasion by exotics, and water deprivation threaten their existence.

Luckily, in 1991 the department incorporated a Natural Areas Management section to assess and prioritize problems facing the lands they oversaw. It was just in the nick of time. They had barely begun gathering data when Hurricane Andrew dropped in, in August 1992. Exotics took an olympic jump forward.

Andrew's winds swirled away the tops of canopy trees and sunlight flooded the vulnerable hammocks. Saltwater inundation stressed and killed some plants. In addition, winds and flood waters spread legions of seeds across South Florida. Andrew was not the deadliest or the strongest hurricane to hit the area but it was the costliest—more than $26 billion in damages. Initial clean-up was inhibited by lingering rain showers following the storm's wake. Rain that, no doubt, helped seeds take root and grow.

After extensive training, restoration teams moved into four hammocks, R. Hardy Matheson Preserve, and Castellow, Matheson, and Addison hammocks. Dividing the area into square plots, crews cut fallen debris with chainsaws and hand pruners into manageable sizes and stacked them to decompose and be recycled back into the hammock soils.

Leaning native saplings were propped up to help them grow straight. Helping hands collected seeds from South Florida slash pines and propagated seedlings to be planted in the hurricane-devastated pinelands. Exotic stems and stumps were treated with herbicides, then crews moved on to the next plot. Removing exotic plants is a constant, never-ending battle: job security for anyone willing to tackle the muscle-building labor.

South Florida's big three invasive trees are Australian pine, melaleuca or paperbark tree, and Brazilian pepper. Australian pines were planted for windbreaks and they colonize rapidly, creating dense shade. Their leaf litter contains chemicals that hold native groundcovers at bay. Melaleuca, another Australian import, has infested 1.5 million acres and continues to take over another fifty acres every day. Brazilian pepper, erroneously called Florida holly, was once sold as an ornamental and now invades more than seven hundred thousand acres in Central and South Florida. Many of the shrubs lining the verge along Florida's Turnpike and other South Florida highways are Brazilian peppers. John Small was not nearly so concerned about exotic plants as he was with bulldozers, dredges, and dynamite. No one guessed the havoc those alien plants would cause decades later.

Some exotic plants and animals were inadvertently brought in, but humans have a long history of deliberately transporting plants—for a familiar food supply or comforting reminders of home. In most cases the plants fulfill their roles without fanfare, but there are those that take over at an alarming rate. There are two ways to view them: as noxious, invasive, destructive exotics or, if we are to acknowledge our human actions (misguided as they often are), as simply part of our evolution. Each view is valid. Each living creature, to some extent, exerts influence on our environment; humans have been messing with the environment with spectacular results for thousands of years. We have come to realize that our actions sometimes backfire on us. We must all, from seller to consumer to natural lands administrators, accept the responsibility of learning which plants can become too well established at the expense of native plants and take measures to remove them or not plant them. Our landscape, whether a wild one or the one that grows outside our livingroom window, is a feast of color and form. Who among us really wants to see only one kind of plant—a monoculture, scientists call it—growing in our yards? The Florida Department of Environmental Protection's Bureau of Invasive Plant Management identifies and implements eradication programs across the state. Florida is not the only state battling botanical aliens. Federal officials estimate $123 billion is spent annually in the nationwide fight.[3]

When John Small reached Florida he was like a hound striking a fresh scent, and little stopped him. There is an urgency to his writing, as if there was not a moment to lose. By far, most of his trips were to southern Florida, the Miami vicinity, and the Florida Keys, but he did occasionally stray into the Carolinas and Florida's interior, making quick forays into the area around Apalachicola explored by Alvan Chapman, and across the peninsular regions. As his children grew older, he brought his family with him—partly as a vacation for them as his trips would last several weeks. His family was important and Dr. Small involved them in his work to the extent they wanted to go.

Dr. Small was quite vocal in his abhorrence of burning. I first read his fine little book *From Eden to Sahara: Florida's Tragedy* about fifteen years ago. I recently reread it and his protestations about fire are glaring in light of what has been learned about fire in Florida's ecosystems. Land managers have come to realize that fire is necessary to the health of many ecosystems, but the fires, or the damages left by fires, that Small witnessed were indiscriminately set by humans and meant to destroy rather than rebuild. Fire sometimes rampages through a hammock, but it is not a common occurrence and most plants are not adapted to it. The hammock's natural moistness usually repels fire, but the lowered water table has constricted dampness, leaving hammocks susceptible to fire.

Since the hammocks were situated on higher land—a few feet makes a difference in this region—Indians used them for camps and settlements. Shell middens and burial mounds rose within, and Small was fascinated by the number of shell middens and the mixture of plant species associated with them. Though Small did not document his first work with photographs, he later wielded a camera with exuberance and ease. George K. Small, one of the doctor's sons, thoughtfully donated his collection of papers and photographs to the Florida Archives in Tallahassee. The Small online photographic collection, thirty-five hundred images, contains shots of repairs to the weed wagon in the middle of nowhere, trips on the *Barbee,* fern grottoes, Small's children with pinelands or a hammock as a backdrop, and Mrs. Small and Elizabeth Britton (Mrs. Nathaniel Britton) sifting through shell middens. A virtual tour of early Florida awaits anyone with Internet access and time to browse.

By the turn of the last century, modes of travel were infinitely improved. Ironically, it was Flagler's railroad that allowed Small, along with thousands of tourists, to reach Florida with ease. He sought the least expensive travel fare, usually a $30 excursion ticket. Most any town could be reached by rail, even if it was only a spur line. He sometimes stopped in South Carolina for a few days' botanizing and then boarded the coaches for his next destination. After detraining, there was no Avis counter, but livery stables rented horses and buggies; later, friends and benefactors provided more modern modes of transportation.

On a trip to coastal North Carolina in February 1919, Small landed at Snowden, not too far south of the Virginia border. Several hours passed before friends secured a horse and buggy and began hunting for plants on a mild day. The search was successful, but temperatures fell and puddles began to ice over as the winter evening closed in. By moving steadily, they and the horse kept warm and reached the station in time to catch the night express for New Bern. That town brought to mind Hardy Croom, whom Small called "evidently the most wide-awake native botanist in the southern states during the earlier decades of the last century."

Small's cohorts provided a car in Charleston. The weather had been wet, so roads were muddy; though Small had experienced some exciting car trips in Florida, "this one eclipsed them all." Long stretches of mud could be traversed only by getting up a head of speed and holding on as waves of mud splattered the car. They had no way of knowing what might lie under the muck. Sometimes the car became airborne but it always landed right side up. Only once did the vehicle become too mired to move, and luckily a nearby chain gang was enlisted to dig them out. Aside from bruises and smashed watch crystals it was a great trip.[4]

Small's circuits around Florida were a far cry from those of the Bartrams, André and François Michaux, Audubon, or Muir. There were more roads, and villages had grown into towns. Inns were not quite the atrocities experienced by earlier travelers. Electricity and telephones provided almost instant communication. Still, most roads were not paved (only 144 miles of the nation's roads were paved by 1900) and modern amenities were available only near larger cities and towns. On one trip in December 1918, Small and his companions found themselves on the western shore of Lake George, perhaps "on the very spot where the Bartrams camped during their travels in that region about a century and a half ago." After pausing for a while, the party went on, zigzagging around the state until they reached sleepy Orlando, where they received directions to Inverness.

They had good roads for several miles but "they began to fail us about sundown, and it was dark when we reached Bushnell." They ate their first regular meal in many days and inquired of several individuals about the right way to Istachatta from whence they would turn north for Inverness. The same directions were obtained from all, but clouds intensified the night's darkness and there were no reflective markers or painted lines on the road. All went well until they passed near the site where the Seminoles had massacred Major Francis L. Dade's troops during the Seminole Wars almost a century earlier. There they met a stream and bridge and a fork in the road, which no one had included in their instructions. All the other turns had been left so they took the left fork. They should have taken the right fork. After traveling deeper into the sandhills they realized the mistake but kept going rather than turn back. The country became more hilly and sandy and quite uninhabited, but they finally reached the Withlacoochee River, crossed it, and ended up in Croom (probably named after one of Hardy Croom's distant relatives), about halfway to Inverness. Luckily the local constabulary did not notice them or accost them as bootleggers on that trip.

By next morning they were in the area of Pineola Grotto, a haven for twelve fern species. It was truly a captivating place, but even then a limestone crushing mill worked nearby, grinding the soft rock into powder for liming fields.[5] Since then, the lovely grottoes have, like the tropical hammocks, mostly disappeared. Pineola Grotto's owners cut the shielding pines in the 1970s and glaring sunlight scorched the tender ferns. Surviving ferns have since gone to collectors or died, vital water supplies have been drawn away, and exotic skunk vine blankets what remains.

On a collecting trip in late November 1921, backed by Charles Deering, Dr. Small, with his son, George, began with a cactus hunt in South Carolina. Florida was his objective and after arriving in Jacksonville, the pair made a side trip to Saint Marys, Georgia, to find two prickly pears, the large-jointed and the crowfoot. Both cacti were associated with cedar trees, the latter especially close to the trunks where it received a measure of protection. Winter's frosts had not touched those woods yet and asters, ladies'-tresses, lobelias, and tickseed still bloomed. They passed thick stands of loblolly bays festooned with strands of greenbrier (a smilax) interspersed with "high-as-one's-head" cinnamon ferns.

They reached Amelia Island and could not drive across the beach to Fort Clinch—there was no road then—because the tide was too high and the car would not make it over the dunes. A recent storm had stripped leaves away from live oaks, but abundant rains had brought forth a large number of fungi. Crowfoot prickly pear grew amongst the dunes and the botanist noted two kinds of lantana, one a native of South America that had naturalized. Dr. Small surveyed Fernandina's cultivated gardens, for he was always interested in what wild weeds he might find: sago-palm, oleander, lilies, begonias, coleus, jimsonweed.

John and his son headed across the peninsula toward Cedar Key, loosely following Muir's route, with a brief stop near Lake George, where they remarked on copious growths of water hyacinth and waterlettuce. West of the St. Johns River they drove over blackjack oak ridges, sandy scrub, savannahs, and high pinelands. The floristics, Small noticed, were quite different on either side of the river. Onward through the Ocala National Forest, Gainesville, Archer, and Cedar Key. Red cedars were still being cut for pencils and then, as now, the serried forest harbored many game animals. Small mentioned a number of shell middens and lamented their destruction. "The Mounds have been partly leveled and much disturbed, so that some of the native vegetation has doubtless been lost to us. Still much of interest remains." The pair planned to locate shell middens at the mouth of the Withlacoochee River, but suspicious locals took them for federal revenue agents; Prohibition laws were in force and illegal stills were secreted in the woods. Strangers were not encouraged to linger.

On to Crystal River, then the site of a pencil factory instead of a nuclear power plant, where they passed through inland hammocks, which lack the tropical flavor of coastal hammocks. From there they branched over to Homosassa, passing through the primeval forest of a low hardwood hammock comprising oaks, sweet-gums, hickories and beeches. They returned to Crystal River and turned for Inverness, stopping at Pineola Grotto to collect fern spores, which Small would use to begin colonies for the Deering Estate in Cutler.

Brooksville was the next stop, to find the only known locality for the West Indian bracken fern, a patch about fifty feet square. Next was the Gulf coast along Pinellas County into the Tampa Bay region for a night at the home of a local botanist, Mrs. Katherine B. Tippetts. They then undertook a futile search for a peculiar palm said to be growing on the dunes of Long Key.

The following day they crossed the peninsula. Nighttime showers had scrubbed the sky a deep blue and green palms and pines posed a picture "of unforgettable beauty as we drove up the Pinellas Peninsula. There we recrossed, evidently near the present site of Clearwater, the trail of Panfilo de Narvaez, who, in 1528, went inland there."

Passing through Kissimmee, they soon met the east coast and turned southward. Following the Indian River and past St. Lucie Sound, they drove amidst the great ancient sand dunes of Hobe Sound, where they noted the growth of Australian pines. They passed cypress heads on the old sand dunes south of Jupiter, then through Palm Beach, stopping to investigate at every turn. Finally they reached Miami to establish headquarters at the U.S. Department of Agriculture's Plant Introduction Garden of the United States.

Time to rest was never mentioned, for John and George soon headed to Cape Sable and Royal Palm Hammock, now part of Everglades National Park. Returning again to Miami, father and son embarked on Deering's *Barbee,* to explore the Keys. At night with a full moon the sea bottom was clearly visible through the crystal clear water and in daylight the plants, tracks of crabs, and various corals provided an ever changing array of color and design. Also visible were "empty cans and bottles nestling discordantly among the corals, sea-feathers and sponges!"[6] The rest of the trip to Key West reads like a trip to paradise, compared to conditions in the Keys today, but Small himself was listing the loss of plants as he went.

In describing Snapper Creek Hammock in 1919, Small stated that before "drainage fever became epidemic and rampant" a subterranean stream merged with one above-ground, forming a boiling spring that was destroyed by an engineer who mistakenly dug a ditch through the spring.[7] Fortunately, Charles Deering had just acquired the property and the site would be protected. Snapper Creek Hammock has been renamed R. Hardy Matheson Hammock and is owned by Miami-Dade County Parks.

Small viewed roads with a jaundiced eye. They enabled him to reach remote areas, usually just before they were converted to agricultural land or subdivisions by saws, fires, or dredges. Dr. Small deplored what was happening in the 1920s and 1930s, but if he returned in 1999, I believe he would be as devastated emotionally as Florida has been environmentally. The state's total population on April 1, 1950, was 2,771,305, with 495,084, or 17 percent, living in Dade County. In 1990, the state's population totaled 12,937,936 and in 1999 topped 15,000,000.

I was born in Miami. When we left the city on trips northward, in the days before interstate highways, even before Florida's Turnpike, it seemed we were setting out on an adventure. The day before leaving, my father checked the oil, tires, and radiator, and filled our car with gas. Before we had an air-conditioned vehicle, my father always rousted us in the cool predawn, anxious to roll miles onto the odometer before the day's heat took over—and before heavy traffic. Usually, I was tumbled into the back seat where I slept the dark hours away, awaking with the inevitable, "are we there yet?" I wonder if children traveling in wagon trains ever voiced that question. Of course, we were not there yet; we had a long way to go. Our route was U.S. 27 through the heart of the peninsula. The section between Okeechobee and Miami, as I remember, was called "Bloody 27" because its two lanes were bordered by drainage and irrigation canals used for sugar cane fields and truck farms. Traffic stacked up behind slow movers and too many impatient drivers tried to pass where there was not quite enough room—meaning one car either went into a canal or the vehicles hit head on. The road earned its bloody reputation.

Route 27 coiled around the bottom of Lake Okeechobee and up the southwestern shore through the unpleasant odor of Moore Haven's sugar mills. It was the smell of money, just as the sour smell of paper mills was North Florida's scent of wealth, though not much trickled down to the workers in either industry. My father was always looking for another route because he liked a change of scenery and because he wanted off the dangerous highway. There were not a lot of options then and we often wandered skinny farm roads through miles of fenced rangeland where lean cattle of mixed heritage and pale, lop-eared, hump-backed Brahma cattle endured the heat and scrubby feed. Burma Shave signs entertained us and we knew where all the gas stations were located. Back then they were few and far between and rarely open past 6:00 P.M. My mother packed food and cold Cokes in little six-ounce bottles because Ray Kroc had not yet opened McDonald's. The Old South Bar-B-Que was about the only trusted place to eat.

Acres of dark green citrus trees commanded the land above the lake and were replaced with rows of tall pines farther north. To my young eyes, Florida seemed a vast wilderness in the middle 1950s, and in many locales it was, but huge blocks had been brought to order under an agricultural rule.

Small's voice had vigorously protested unchecked development, but his protestations fell mostly on deaf ears. He was disturbed about losing natural places and his enthusiasm crept to near hysteria as he allowed himself sometimes to exceed the truth. It was not because he disregarded validity, but because he hoped to stop the madness of destruction. Of course, he could not. He was a scientist and his work, his love, was field botany; he rushed to document what he could find before it disappeared.

I cannot honestly think of another region that has been so transformed and obliterated as South Florida. The places John Small loved were long gone before I arrived and even the Miami I loved as a child will never be seen again. These days, traveling much farther south than Gainesville in my home state leaves me drained, disappointed, frustrated, saddened, distraught—any emotion but happy. When it came to writing about Small, I knew I had to face that tropical journey one more time.

STALLING THE INEVITABLE, I headed for South Florida on February 19, 2000. I first stopped in Sanford to visit Pat and Fred Harden and spent the next night in Cooper City with friends I had not seen in more than a decade. Then, I could avoid it no longer and wrapped myself in a mantle of detachment. So far the trip had been every bit as bad as I had feared. A bewildering number of cars, roads, exits, shopping areas, and people.

I arrived in Homestead to meet Roger Hammer, naturalist with Dade County Parks, whose home is a bit of heaven amidst the urban sprawl. He and his wife live in a small building that was once a jelly factory for a long-defunct lodge that used to be on the edge of the Glades. It is surrounded by tropical and semitropical plants. Ferns and bromeliads cling to limestone rocks lining a freshwater pool where carp keep unwanted plants in check. The sky was blue and as the temperature climbed to near 80° a refreshing breeze shuffled the leaves.

When asked if he would leave Miami, Roger replied, "No. My wife and I don't like the cold. Miami's highest recorded temperature is 98°, we're just a few miles from the Everglades and not far from work. We love the Caribbean and we're a short plane ride away. We're near a fabulous variety of ethnic food and music. Miami's out there, but I don't have to go if I don't want to."

I'll remember that in Tallahassee's sweltering summer when the humidity strives to keep abreast of plus-100°-days.

Roger offers popular wildflower walks in the remaining hammocks and in Everglades National Park. Along with natural history he spices his talks with folklore and the stories of scientists who explored the area. He is a fan of Dr. Small and has a great library of other writings describing the difficulties of moving in a land that was hot, soggy, and sometimes studded with rocks so sharp they sliced the soles of men's boots and made it impossible for a horse to walk.

After leaving Roger's comfortable patio, I headed for the Everglades just a few miles away. It was a holiday and numerous people had been attracted to the visitor's center to begin a pleasant outdoor excursion. This section of the park offers two campgrounds; one on Long Pine Key is situated in a pineland fairly close to the entrance. The other is at Flamingo, some thirty-eight miles distant and on the edge of Florida Bay. I opted for the longer drive. Besides, Small had written about the area in a 1919 self-published article titled "The Cape Sable Region of Florida."

In the preface, Small explained that he had first come to Florida in 1901 on a mission for the New York Botanical Garden. He had been studying plant life of the region for a decade, and that first trip had convinced him to return as often as he could. Beginning in 1903, whenever his vacation time allowed, he broke for the southern latitudes. The garden did provide some assistance at first, but Charles Deering became his patron, probably around 1912 or 1913.

The trip described in his article began on March 28, 1916; Small was accompanied by Charles Torrey Simpson, John Soar, Victor Soar, and Paul Matthaus, captain of the *Barbee*. Their objectives were to study the distributions of plants as well as tree snails, collect living palms and orchids, and take pictures. Winds were strong the first day and Matthaus sought shielding islands and calm water. They stopped at Lignum Vitae Key where they discovered a new prickly-pear cactus. After exploring Lower Matacombe Key and Upper Matacombe Key, smooth water induced them to head for Cape Sable and the settlement of Flamingo.

They anchored offshore and spent the afternoon collecting in the hammocks. The next day they transferred their gear to smaller hired motorboats on a course for Cuthbert Lake. Very soon the tide receded and the boats mushed along on a thin layer of water overlying slick mud. The lead boat's engine backfired steadily and Small commented, "by day, we were led by 'a pillar of cloud' and by night we could follow 'a pillar of fire.'" This was a strange world, wrote Small, where little terrestrial vegetation was displayed but a beautiful variety of orchids, bromeliads, and large cactus plants grew everywhere on the trunks of dead and living trees.

Finally, after about six miles of tortuous passage through seven snag-pricked creeks and seven clear saltwater lakes, the party reached Cuthbert Lake, where they found saw-cabbage palms. They filled the boats with orchids and palms and started back. Darkness descended and then, one by one, the engines gave out. They resorted to rowing. About midnight they came upon an anchored boat and—tired, wet, and cold—clambered aboard only to find out in a hurry that it was not the *Barbee*. As Small drily said, "On discovering our mistake we disembarked with unanimous spontaneity." Within an hour they located another anchored boat and made sure it was the *Barbee* before attempting to board.

The next morning, they set out by horse and buggy for Coot Bay, a place as different from Cuthbert Lake as could be imagined and had the greatest orchid hunt any of them could have hoped for. In Snake Hammock, they found one butterfly orchid with thirty-one flower stalks bearing scores of blossoms. It was difficult to leave such a rich place, but finally they did, reaching Flamingo after sundown and stowing the orchids in a shed.

The next day they explored Cape Sable, a land where the flora of the Everglades Keys and the lower Florida Keys mingled. This was very nearly virgin country, traversed only by settlers, hunters, and anglers, little scarred by the mechanical ravages that were assailing Miami and eating away at the edge of the Glades. The group anchored at Shark Point for the night and set out for Chokoloskee Bay the next day.

They were lucky to find Chokoloskee Pass right away as it was an obscure narrow channel. The boat sailed into the bay and surprised the native villagers who came aboard and directed the men to a safe anchorage. The Small collection contains many photographs of Seminole villages and people of the early 1900s.

The day they departed from Chokoloskee Island bound for home, they first ran onto an oyster-bar and "deferred our departure, therefore, until we should have more water." Once in the Gulf of Mexico, they met heavy weather, "a sea so rough that we were compelled to eat our dinner off the floor of the boat instead of off the table." In all, the men spent thirteen days in the Cape Sable region and a week later returned for another three days. Small ended the article with an ominous warning:

> The results of this reconnaissance revealed the need of more thorough exploration in the Cape Sable region before the advance of civilization changes or exterminates its primeval conditions.
>
> A highway now under construction between Miami and Cape Sable will soon offer facilities for the further exploration of localities heretofore difficult of access from a boat; but, unfortunately, it will open the region to the inevitable advance of civilization with its accompanying unnecessary destruction and vandalism.

The settlement at Flamingo is gone now, but there is a visitor center, a campground, boat launch, and lodge. The area is protected but heavily used by recreationists. It is also at the lower end of the Everglades drainage; the health of the plants and animals depends on what happens upstream. Even though the Everglades is recognized as an International Biosphere Reserve, it is still surrounded by a gnarly babel of legal, private, and public concerns.

Everglades restoration is a complicated issue, far too involved to discuss fully here, and needs the cooperation of surrounding agricultural interests to determine when and how much water is released and who is to foot the bill for cleaning up the pollution that, mostly by those same agricultural interests, has been dumped into the Glades. The Everglades-Kissimmee freshwater marsh system once dominated this part of Florida. Since 1936, more marshland has been destroyed (4 million acres) than exists today (about 2.7 million acres).

On the way to the park, I passed through flat fields being showered by huge truck-mounted sprayers in the middle of the day. Most of that water would be lost to the sun's heat before it had a chance to soak into the soil. The early morning hours would have been a better time to turn on the sprayers, but then nearby residents using their showers would have lost water pressure. Those fields had once been part of the Everglades, hardy grasses and hammock islands surrounded by a thin sheet of water moseying to the ocean. Agriculture and progress nibbled the edges and the Glades shrank.

A cool breeze blew over the campground and evening approached. When the sun went down, the breeze stilled and the skeeters came out—

nowhere near the torrent that would accompany summer. Fred Harden had showed me a picture taken when he was doing mosquito research here in the 1960s. I could barely detect his jean-clad leg under the thick congress of blood-hungry insects. Old-timers said when they wanted to talk to their neighbor, they threw a rock through the mosquito cloud and yelled through the hole.

Mosquito larvae form the basis of the food supply for aquatic animals. It is true that only the adult females bite for blood; the males drink nectar. Females can live on nectar, too, but a blood meal greatly increases the number of eggs they can produce. I do not mind donating a little blood to keep nature healthy, but have to admit that more than a few minutes of being steadily punctured by procreation-driven insects tests my patience.

A florid sunrise dominated Florida Bay in the early morning. I had plenty of time to meander some trails before meeting with Alíce Warren-Bradley, natural areas manager of the Deering Estate at Cutler. I set out on the Anhinga Trail, a boardwalk built over Taylor Slough. Large bass guarded their holes in anticipation of breeding season. A turtle pumped through the clear, tea-colored water. Warblers picked off insects in the vegetation along the waterway and sunlight glinted off the iridescent plumage of a purple gallinule.

Anhingas were nesting and alternated between watching over the downy young and drying their wings. Also known as water turkeys or snake birds, anhingas ride low in the water and from a distance only their long necks and tapered beaks, with which they spear fish, show above the surface. Anhingas do not feed in salt water. Because they dive for food and also easily lose body heat, they often orient themselves facing away from the sun and stretch out their wings to dry and to regulate their body heat.

Geologically, the Everglades formed at about the same time as the Okefenokee Swamp. In more recent memory, both had resident populations of people who preferred living off the land. Like the Okefenokee folk, Everglades residents had to find new homes when the land became a National Park in 1947. But federal protection did not bring salvation to the land.

Residents and farmers require dry land; little by little more of the natural Everglades has been removed, reducing the habitat of the Florida panther, the region's top predator, a solitary animal, requiring a range of several hundred square miles. Biologists estimate that panthers number less than thirty individuals within Everglades National Park, with a few more in the Big Cypress Swamp. Recently a healthy female panther was struck and killed by an automobile. She carried three unborn kittens.

But why worry about the plants and animals and insects? Because if they thrive, then it is healthy for people, too. If the water is dirty, the fish are rotting, the vegetation is dying, it is not safe for humans. It seems simple enough to understand.

I love the Everglades for what the ecosystem represents, but, to be honest, the place scares me. Perhaps it is the size. I feel a pull from those watery acres and feel that if I entered them, I might never return. This is a beautiful place, even if it does not inspire the same awe that comes from Yosemite or Yellowstone. Even if the Everglades is not visually stimulating to everyone, it is infinitely more important for Florida's overall environmental health: for all creatures, whether finned, fured, feathered, leaved, or those of the human species. It saddens me to ponder on what humans have inflicted upon that soggy land in the past and what we continue to do, but give me higher, drier land beneath my feet. I prefer to love the Everglades from a distance.

It was time to leave the Glades and return to my hometown, Miami. On the trip down I toyed with the idea of driving through the neighborhoods where I had lived and where my grandparents used to live. But no one can really go home again, and I decided against it.

I arrived just in time for my appointment with Alíce at the Charles Deering Estate. The estate closed after Hurricane Andrew and only reopened in March of 1999. Alíce brought out an aerial photograph of the estate that showed hardly a twig standing after the blow, except for some royal palms attending Deering's distinctive keyhole-shaped yacht basin. Skies had begun to cloud up on my way to the park and rain began falling as Alíce and I talked.

The town of Cutler was founded near here in the 1880s, two stores, a school, and about thirty homesteads, including one owned by a family named Richmond. Mail was delivered to Fuzzard's dock; he was also the postmaster. A road hammered across the exposed limerock led to Coconut Grove. In 1900, the Richmonds enlarged their home and opened the first inn between Coconut Grove and Key West. Between 1914 and 1920, Charles Deering acquired the Richmond Cottage and other land. He remodeled the inn to use as his residence while the Stone House was being built in 1922, and razed all the other buildings that had formed Cutler.

It was often easier to deliver supplies and materials to the Stone House by sea rather than overland. From the yacht basin Charles had a one-mile-long channel dredged across shallow Biscayne Bay to facilitate larger boats—and probably those stealthy boats that delivered all that expensive illegal wine as well. At night, the channel entrance was found by lining up lights left blazing across the front of the house. There was almost no wood used in the structure. Having come through the great Chicago fire, Deering had an extreme fear of fire and even had water pipes laid through the pine rockland. If a fire came, he planned to flood the pineland to protect his home. After the main residence was completed, Deering left the Richmond Cottage standing a stone's throw away. All cooking was done there—there are no kitchen facilities in the Stone House.

The Richmond Cottage, park staff found, was only resting on its foundation. Hurricane Andrew lifted the entire structure up and slammed it back down, smashing it to smithereens. The Stone House was severely damaged by the storm surge. That hidden wine cellar was flooded. Bottles shattered and those that remained whole were infiltrated by salt water. All the labels washed off.

During the estate's closure, overseen by a multitude of state, local, and federal agencies, the structures were rebuilt, this time to withstand a hurricane. The Richmond Cottage looks like the original wooden structure (and a lot of the original material was grubbed out of the storm debris), but it is constructed of concrete block and sheathed in wood. Only the ground floors in either structure are open because the upper levels are not yet up to code. The ceiling of the large art room had to be restored. It boasts patterned plaster squares reflecting Charles's love of nature; similar shapes—pelicans, dolphins, flowers, shells, pine cones—are carved into the tops of pillars supporting covered walkways.

Because of time lost rebuilding after Andrew, the park is just getting on its feet again. Aside from protecting a historical and natural area, the estate offers guided tours; a prime goal is increased environmental education for middle school students. Meetings, weddings, and other social events are held at the estate. Alíce has dreams for what the Deering Estate can provide for Dade County residents and visitors.

Alíce had to attend another planning meeting, but first she arranged a tour for me with guide Ernie Lent. Ernie moved to South Florida in the 1960s. Before coming to the Deering Estate, he worked in the Everglades. All of the tour guides are well trained and Ernie's experience in the Glades gives him a wide view of the region's natural areas. It is obvious he enjoys sharing the land's natural and cultural history.

The rain had ceased for the moment but we opted to ride in the covered tram through the hammock down the original Cutler roadway, which, before Postmaster Fuzzard improved it, had been a narrow Indian trail. We stopped at a Tequesta Indian burial mound and Ernie mentioned that when the Seminoles came after the Tequestas were gone, they also respected the sacred mound. A solution hole near the road was barely damp after the rain. A feral cat dashed through the undergrowth. Foxes, raccoons, and opossums live on the protected land along with exotic snakes—stowaways on ships or released by owners. Staff catch them when possible and find new homes. The snakes keep the raccoon population manageable, but seem to make no dent in the number of feral cats. Most of the hammock areas had been cleared of hurricane damage, but we encountered a cleanup crew resting from the never-ending chore. It was springtime and conditions were not so bad, but as summer heated up, it would be even tougher work.

We emerged from the hammock tunnel to the pine rockland with only a thin scattering of tall slash pines. Not only were many mature pines snapped in the winds, salt water had weakened the survivors and beetles moved in for the kill. Seedlings planted after the hurricane were now four and five feet tall. A southern section of pine rockland fared better. Land managers hope to conduct prescribed burns someday, but the park is next to expensive homes and owners are not always supportive of flames so close to their property.

Showers had washed the skies blue again as I left the park and came to Red Road—a familiar name, but I could not remember where it went. It was after 3:00 P.M. Schools were letting out. Traffic picked up. I felt like a possum in the middle of Interstate 95 and ended up in South Miami, a strange mix of businesses that have not changed a lick since 1980 plus a grand new Barnes and Noble. I turned west on Sunset Drive, and drove and drove through lands, now encased in asphalt and concrete, that grew pines when I was a kid, until I finally reached what I knew must be the turnpike, but there was no entrance. I continued on for a few more blocks. The houses never slackened and it seemed as if they might just march on to the Gulf of Mexico—but somewhere out there, the Everglades were allowed to flow and development had had to stop.

Finally, I turned north and drove until I reached the Tamiami Trail, another familiar name, and turned east again. There had to be an entrance to the turnpike from the Trail—and there was. During this unscheduled tour, I'd passed through neighborhoods impressive with spacious green yards bordered by tropical flowering plants—deep crimson, bright pink, and fluorescent orange—and neighborhoods crammed together with hardly enough room between houses for grass to grow, much less anything else. Spanking new stucco homes mingled with elders built of limestone and surrounded by rock walls silvered with age.

Miami bore a Spanish influence in my childhood, but it has since become a full-fledged international city and lives life in the fast lane. Parts of it are still beautiful and I do understand why so many people want to live there. There is just too much of it for me. An excess of excess, and too much of a good thing is not always best. I had allowed another day to explore but the turnpike offered escape and I took it. I could not wait to flee.

By the time I was born, John K. Small had been gone for more than a decade. His heart had been failing, but he had not let others know of his declining health. Complaining was not his way. Because he had kept silent, most of his colleagues were taken by surprise at his death. His passing was truly mourned because of his skills and because he was a fine person. He met almost every hardship with a smile and made light of it.

He was knocked down by a car in downtown Miami and, even while trussed up in a hospital bed with a broken left ankle and a cracked right knee, wrote to Harper on April 11, 1935: "Miami auto drivers are no more affected by red lights than are those of New York, so someone has to be hit occasionally."[8]

Many of Dr. Small's travelogues were published in the *Journal of the New York Botanical Garden*, but the garden did not fund its employees' private publications. Small bore the expense of printing his *Flora of the Southeastern United States* in 1903. It was not meant to be a field book for it contained nearly fourteen hundred pages. The book did assure a place for its author as one of the era's foremost botanical taxonomists. His greatly revised 1933 *Flora* appeared smaller than the other volumes because it was printed on thinner paper. Actually it contained 1,554 pages and described more than 5,500 species.

More than two dozen travelogues published in the *Journal* were aimed at amateur botanists and others he hoped to win over to his side. Among his 419 publications, ranging from a few pages to his monumental *Flora*, are a *Flora of the Florida Keys* and *Flora of Miami* in 1913, *From Eden to Sahara: Florida's Tragedy* in 1929, and many other works on shrubs, ferns, and irises. One of his last published articles was written in favor of the proposed Everglades National Park. The tone was subdued, quite different from his passionate accounts. Perhaps Small had unconsciously slowed down. He was working on *Ferns of the Southeastern States* when he died; it was published posthumously in 1938.

In Jacksonville's *Times-Union* of February 6, 1938, Mary W. Diddell, another of Small's fern scouts, wrote that in late November 1936, Small went to Central and West Florida with the St. John brothers and had intended to continue to Miami, but was taken sick and returned to Jacksonville, where he rested two days before going back to New York. As she waited at the station with Dr. Small, Mary asked when he would be coming back and he replied with his whimsical smile, "When I can get another $52.65." He had rallied in the spring of 1937 and wrote his friends that he would be returning soon, but became ill that summer. He was better by fall and began working again, but Dr. Small would not see Florida again.

John Kunkel Small died at his home on January 20, 1938, no doubt dreaming of another trip to the paradise he knew as Florida. Not quite seventy, he was no longer a young man, but he had had many more things to accomplish. What he wanted to save most of all was Florida and that was an impossible task.

H. Harold Hume wrote in an appreciation of Dr. Small, "He brought to the work to which he has sent himself thorough training, a retentive memory, keen discernment of form and color, unswerving devotion to his undertaking, and physical stamina such as few possess. No journey was too difficult, no road too hard, no morass too deep to stop him."[9]

After Small's death, Roland wrote an admonishing letter to the *Miami Herald* in February 1938, because he felt they had not devoted enough attention to the botanist's death and his contributions to the knowledge of Florida's flora. Harper stated that Small "'put Miami on the map' in botanical circles . . . He had a very genial disposition, and will be greatly missed by all who knew him." I am sure Roland missed John K., who had the sense and graciousness to overlook Harper's irascible ways and concentrate on his strengths.

Each of the men in this book seem bound by slender threads. Nearly every one eventually tramped over the same ground, seeking what the others had found and what the predecessors might have missed. They all pursued an understanding of nature until their deaths. John Kunkel Small was no exception. Even when his heart warned him to take it easy, he was not one to sit back and surrender. Perhaps if he had curtailed his fieldwork, he might have added a year or two to his life, but he would not.

Before making the trek to Miami, I called Everglades National Park hoping to speak with someone about Dr. Small's association with the area. I was handed off to four departments before encountering someone who even remotely recognized the name and even he deflected my inquiry. Park staff, I realize, have more immediate concerns—the Everglades' overall health and keeping up with thousands of visitors—but it is a shame they have lost sight of John Kunkel Small. Maybe this abbreviated portrait will revive his memory.

CHAPTER 12

Saving a Swamp

Roland Harper
(August 11, 1878–April 30, 1966)

Francis Harper
(November 17, 1886–November 17, 1972)

As the rising sun dispels the mist, the birds are more vociferous than later in the day: the bobwhite pipes, the joree calls and sings, the redbird give a cheery *o-leet, o-leet,* an unseen woodpecker drums, and the pine warbler trills dreamily. Soon the earth warms beneath a brightening sky, and the pine lizards come forth from their nocturnal retreats in crevices of the bark, to bask and run on the fallen trunks or to bob up and down in displaying their brilliant throats to their ladyloves. As morning wears on, a breeze stirs the myriads of pine needles into murmuring music that brings peace and delight to one's soul.

—Francis Harper, "A Voice From the Pines," 1932

In the foregoing pages the aesthetic reasons for preserving natural scenery have been put foremost, but another and still higher motive has been touched upon. An artificial park or flower garden might be just as pleasing to the eye, to most persons at least, as any natural landscape; but from a scientific standpoint there is no comparison between them. Any sort of place can be beautified to the owner's (or the public's) taste by the expenditure of time and money, but when natural scenery is destroyed all the money in the world cannot restore it.

—Roland Harper, "Some Vanishing Scenic Features
of the Southeastern United States," 1919

THERE'S A BIG SWAMP in the Southeast. Only a smudge crosses into Florida; most of the wetland rests in Georgia. There are no roads breaching the great swamp's length or breadth. Highways and bridges have been boldly thrown over the Atchafalaya Swamp and across the Everglades, but not the Okefenokee. Creek Indians called it *O-ke-fin-o-cau,* land of trembling earth. It is a liquid world of mysterious beauty.

In 1902, a bright young botanist from Columbia University named Roland Harper began exploring the swamp. He, and later his younger brother, Francis, wrote reams of paper about the area. Both Roland and Francis were active into their eighties. Roland's career carried him mainly through Alabama, Georgia, Florida, and other southern states. Though Francis ranged far afield during his career, as far north as the frozen reaches of Canada, he managed to return to the Okefenokee several times until 1959, when other commitments, advancing years, and changing conditions in the swamp prevented his visits.

Roland was an eccentric person. Francis was also, but others will agree that Roland took the cake, so to speak. Both brothers were brilliant and excelled at their chosen profession. Both were perfectionists, idealists, and absolute sticklers for accuracy and detail. Both were ill at ease in social situations outside of their professional pursuits. Roland spent literally all of his time working. Francis sought posts far from city life whenever possible. Consider that their father had refused to accept his own diploma from a certain man because that man had made mistakes in his lectures. High ideals, indeed.

The brothers were reared in a family of academic achievers. Their father, William Harper, born in Ontario, Canada, completed his graduate studies in the physical sciences in Munich and, while there, married Bertha Tauber. The Harpers returned to America and settled in Farmington, Maine, where Roland was born August 11, 1878. A few years later, the family moved to Southbridge, Massachusetts, where Francis was born November 17, 1886. The paternal Harper was a teacher and a school administrator. The family moved to Dalton, Georgia, in 1887, and lived there until 1892, when Harper became superintendent of schools in Americus, Georgia.

Francis was just a lad when his older brother enrolled in the University of Georgia in 1894 as an engineering student. Clarence Knowlton, a boyhood friend of Roland's, had become curious about plants and wrote to Harper urging him to get interested so the two could exchange specimens, but Roland liked photography and railroads. While matriculating at Georgia, Roland took botany only because it was required; he could see no value in plants for an engineer.

During the first months of class students learned the parts of a plant, which Roland found pretty dry. Using Gray's *School and Field Botany,* Chapman's *Flora,* and Wood's *Class-book* students learned to identify plants using descriptions and taxonomic keys. That appealed to his strong organizational tendencies and lit a fire under Roland, "it gave me something of a thrill." Soon, he had identified one hundred and forty plant species, said to be a record at the time.

In Americus for the summers, Roland cruised the surrounding countryside for plants and found many species unfamiliar to him. Following roads and railroads, and making his own paths, he walked miles and miles, sometimes taking the train in one direction and returning on foot. His first new species, *Scirpus atrovirons,* a sedge, was discovered a few miles from his Athens abode.

After graduating, Roland took a civil service exam for a position in the

U.S. Coast and Geodetic Survey. Though he passed, he did not rate high enough for an immediate appointment. If he had, he might have stuck with engineering. Instead, he moved with his family when they returned to Southbridge in 1897. Roland took a job in an optical factory, but botany's scientific classification system lured him and he spent free time studying local flora. A scholarship to New York's Columbia University opened a whole new world.

The New York Botanical Garden was not formally opened until 1900, but Columbia's herbarium had been incorporated into the garden and students used it freely. There, Roland met John K. Small, Nathaniel L. Britton, and other learned botanists. Small assured Harper that *Scirpus* was a new species. Every summer botanists from around the country visited the garden for a few weeks. "It was certainly a stimulating environment for a young botanist, which can hardly be matched anywhere today," Roland remarked.[1]

Students looked at chromosomes under a microscope, Harper recalled, but no one knew their function. Few were interested in the infant field of ecology, but being the kind of man he was, Harper read everything about the new science. Classifying plants by their habitat appealed to him and Harper became one of ecology's early proponents.

Roland earned his Ph.D. in 1905 for his study of Georgia's Altamaha Grit region. His *Phytogeographical Sketch of the Altamaha Grit Region of Georgia,* published in 1906, was a milestone in defining the relationship between plants and geology. He joined the Geological Survey of Alabama at Tuscaloosa in 1905, served with the Florida Geological Survey from 1908–31, and then returned to Alabama and remained with the geological survey until his death in 1966. During those Georgia explorations, he became acquainted with the Okefenokee Swamp and published the first modern introduction to the region in 1909.

Around 1900, Roland began filling notebooks, though he had not kept field notes up to that point. Nearly every evening, he sat down with his field book and wrote in his diary, translating each abbreviation, keeping an accurate record of where he had been and what he had seen. Transferring information from field notes to diary helped him remember events and his organizational fetish insured a reliable record. Then he proceeded to write an avalanche of letters to colleagues on an old typewriter, making a carbon copy for his records, passing along news, asking for news, issuing parenthetical warnings—"(*More about that later.*)" for example—and always offering his critical comments.

Roland scavenged trash piles for information; people began saving their papers for him rather than have him pick through their rubbish. Post office waste cans were exceedingly fertile, for northern students tossed out their hometown newspapers. In this way, Roland kept up with news from far beyond his own province. He clipped and saved columns, too, often stuffing them into his letters. Roland published about five hundred articles during his life, not all on botany. His published works are invaluable to other scientists and his unpublished records afford a glimpse into the man and times not too far past. A profile of him in the April 29, 1923, issue of the *Arkansas Democrat* stated, "He collects facts like a vacuum sweeper gathers dust."

He had made three cameras while in Georgia, but got no pictures worth publishing. After acquiring his first Kodak in 1900, Roland kicked off an orgy of picture-taking that ended four thousand photographs later. This photographic record alone is a significant treasure.

Roland Harper never learned to drive. He took the train or bus, or cadged rides from friends; on at least one occasion he made a survey from the bridge of a boat steaming up the Apalachicola River because the flood plain of the lower portion of the river was too low, tangled, and isolated to be explored on foot. Roland was enamored of following train tracks. In the last few years, some of the paths Roland strolled have been converted to Rails to Trails, like the one from Tallahassee to St. Marks and another running along Highway 301 through Bushnell, Florida.

He preferred slow travel and honed his "car window notes." By scanning edges of a large tract, he formed a general image of plant communities by observing outstanding features such as topography, soils, and dominant vegetation. Of course, nothing beat going over the ground foot by foot, but the initial reconnaissance afforded a good idea of what he would later find. Roland spent hours in the field under varying conditions and others who accompanied him reported he never complained.

As mentioned, Harper never learned to drive, and he never owned a car, but he journeyed widely. Many of the years he worked in Alabama were Depression years and he went months without receiving a paycheck. He never smoked, either. Roland looked exactly as one might expect: lean, with a neatly trimmed mustache, appearing as debonair as

Cary Grant. His eyes penetrate even from a photograph and people who knew him related that he closely watched their reactions during conversations.

Most of Roland's later work was done in Alabama and west Florida. A red-letter day came on September 24, 1910, when he found a disjunct outcrop of Altamaha Grit about four and a half miles southeast of Chipley, Florida. Growing in the thin soil, Roland found a plant called *Chondrophora virgata,* renamed *Bigelowia nuttallii.* In the years since Roland walked there, the land has been partially timbered and grazed. Several years later, geologists determined that the outcrop was not Altamaha Grit, but an exposed Citronelle Formation—about fifteen million years younger than Altamaha Grit.

The exposed rocks are a familiar landmark to older Chipley residents and they were a popular picnic destination back when a horse and buggy was the preferred transportation. One woman's future husband popped the question to her on the way there one afternoon. The Nature Conservancy bought the 373-acre property in 1990 because it is a fine example of longleaf pine and wiregrass habitat and to protect the outcrop and the *Bigelowia,* a federally listed endangered species. Rock Hill Preserve is not open to the public, but the Conservancy holds field trips and volunteer workdays.

While living in Tallahassee, Roland became acquainted with Dr. Herman Kurz, botanist from the then Florida State College for Women. Luckily, Dr. Kurz owned a car. The two went to Lake Miccosukee east of town on February 18, 1924, where Harper discovered an endemic shrub *Grossularia echinella.* The scientific name has been changed to *Ribes echinellum* and it is now considered endangered. Only one other population is known, in South Carolina. In Florida, Miccosukee gooseberry, as the plant is commonly known, grows on private land and is protected by a conservation easement, a legal agreement between the landowner and The Nature Conservancy.

Harperocallis flava, Harper's beauty, grows in wet areas of Franklin and Liberty Counties. Each year, Louise Kirn, of the Apalachicola National Forest, herds groups of volunteers into areas of the forest where the endangered plant is known to exist. Its yellow flower stands out against the green backdrop. Harper's beauty is monotypic, the only plant in the genus, and appears to do well in areas recently burned, perhaps because of increased nutrients and decreased competition.

FIG. 21. Citronelle Formation on The Nature Conservancy's Rock Hill Preserve near Chipley, Florida, first described by Roland Harper as a southernmost outcrop of Altamaha Grit. Longleaf pines and wiregrass pose in the distance.
Photo by author.

It took a bit of doing before Roland saw his report on the Okefenokee published in the *Popular Science Monthly* seven years after his 1902 visit. He had to rewrite parts and edit it to a workable length. In the article, Roland described the Okefenokee, chronicled early explorations—which had the air of a novice pointer sniffing around a hidden quail covey and not quite knowing what to do about it—and reported, "the islands are known to have supported a small if not permanent population . . . a large family of white people is said to be living on one of the islands near the head of the Suwannee River."[2]

The swamp was, of course, first investigated by native people. For some it proved to be a sanctuary from opposing tribes. Spanish explorers probably struggled through parts of the wet expanses. William Bartram ventured near but did not enter the Okefenokee and could only relate what Indians had told him of the enchanted haven: it was a most blissful spot, inhabited by a peculiar Indian race with uncommonly lovely women who first offered tender ministrations to those who became lost but then quickly shooed the wanderers away, as the women's husbands were inclined to attack strangers.

David Glenn, a Georgia land lottery surveyor, mapped the southeastern corner of the swamp in 1805. Between 1812 and 1814, Dr. William Baldwin, a botanist living at St. Marys, explored the area and came within twelve miles of the "celebrated Okefanoka," probably Traders Hill, but dared go no nearer. Hunters may have probed the edges, but left no written accounts. Other Georgia land lottery surveyors mapped the northern and western areas of the swamp in 1814.

General Charles Floyd marched across the swamp several times in efforts to protect settlers and chase Indians from their hiding places between September 1838 and January 1839. Floyd and his officers penned their observations and the accounts were published in regional newspapers. General Floyd's reports were also submitted to Governor Gilmer. The state of Georgia commissioned a land survey in 1850, but the men were able to survey only portions of the edges. Two of the surveyors compiled some of the earliest detailed observations of the area's natural history.

Maurice and William Thompson splashed through the western swamp in 1866 while searching for the ivory-billed woodpecker. English traveler Paul Fountain claimed to be the first naturalist to visit the swamp in 1871 and 1876. Roland surmised that Fountain must have come near the great wetland, but his descriptions better suited the swamps of the upper Suwannee River. Charles Pendleton and George W. Haines, local newspaper editors, investigated the Okefenokee in 1875. The Georgia Geological Survey and the *Atlanta Constitution* cooperated for the first exploration of the watery wilderness in November and December 1875. Two months were not nearly long enough to decipher the Okefenokee, but as the years progressed, each venture into the vast wetland revealed more knowledge.

White people had been living inside the swamp since at least the 1850s. Like their counterparts living far back in the Appalachian Mountains, the people known as swampers were segregated from the rest of homogenized America. Swampers retained traces of their Scots, Irish, Welsh, French, and German ancestry. In their own way, they were an amalgamation who did not easily discard their dialect and adapted to the fully adequate existence that swamp living brought. The land provided what they needed and they were unconcerned with accumulating frivolous possessions.

They raised corn, sugar cane, potatoes, peanuts, a little tobacco and cotton, and other vegetables on a few acres near their sturdy, squarely designed homes. Mature cypress and longleaf pines furnished prime building materials. Photographs from the early 1900s show well-constructed homes and outbuildings with neatly fenced yards. They raised cattle, hogs, and chickens, fished, trapped animals for fur, and hunted deer, squirrels, turkeys, and ducks for food, and gators for hides; whether they ate the tail meat or not depended upon the distance the hunter had to carry out the carcass. Hides, furs, cane syrup, and fresh ducks heaped their wagons on town days. Flour, needles, and other store-bought items they could not fashion from the swamp's bounty made the return trip. Plain clothing suited their way of life and though shoes were very much in evidence, going barefoot was more convenient. Living in the swamp, off the swamp, did not require much money. There may have been shiftless families living in rotting shacks among the swampers, but they were the exception, not the norm.

People living in the Okefenokee were, in essence, squatters. As far as Georgia was concerned, the swamp was public land owned by the state. In 1890, the legislature put a price tag on it—26½ cents an acre—and sold 380 square miles to a syndicate in 1891. The Suwanee Canal Company was formed and began buying adjacent land. Captain Henry Jackson headed the company and fancied relieving the swamp of its timber and its water. Dredges working day and night by electric lights began eating a canal into the swamp and a ditch away from it to the St. Marys River in 1891. Logs could be floated out and eventually the swamp would be drained through the ditch to the St. Marys and "reclaimed." By 1894 the ditch was abandoned; more than twelve miles of canal had been dug when the company decided it would be more cost effective to build a sawmill and send out sawn logs over a railroad. When Captain Jackson died suddenly in 1895, his father, General Henry R. Jackson, became president. In 1897, the dredges stopped working and rotted or were burned. Vegetation began springing up in the ditch and climbed the steam engines like trellises; the rails were ripped up.

After the Suwanee Canal Company shut down in 1897, the land was sold to Jackson family members in 1899. They, in turn, sold the land to the Hebard Cypress Company of Philadelphia. Hebard jammed pilings thirty-five miles across the swamp and mounted rails over the long platform in 1909. Hebard meant business. A town to support the lumbermen sprung up on Billys Island. On June 16, 1916, Georgia's governor, Hugh Dorsey, wrote to Dr. Lucien Knight, director of the Georgia Department of Archives and History, that the Hebard Company was operating the largest cypress mill in the world near Waycross and that there was enough timber to last a hundred years even if they cut day and night. Eventually, 250 miles of trestles spidered into the interior and virgin cypress fell and fell and fell until the largest concentrated stands were gone by 1925. More than 431 million board feet had been pulled out when Hebard ceased operations in 1927, about eighty-nine years short of the hundred predicted.

The Okefenokee, of course, was not completely shorn of trees. Hebard took only the marketable timber and left behind any that would not fetch a decent price. The swamp was described as being full of stumps, and that was true in some areas. Clearing pathways for trestles, cutting undesirable trees in the way of valuable timber, using trees for building and firewood—all left a landscape ruined despite the smaller cypress, pine, and worthless trees that were spared.

Before 1930 the boomtown on Billys Island was gone and the Okefenokee had begun to regenerate. It has come back differently, in ways that no one can explain because no one living now saw it then. Subtle changes in the hydrology and vegetation patterns are difficult to reconstruct. What is true once again is that graceful ringlets of moss sway elegantly from tall cypress and zephyrs in the treetops tickle the pliant needles of rangy pines defining part of the Okefenokee's ethereal beauty.

Roland Harper made his last swamp tour in 1919. His initial plant inventory in 1902, plus another in 1919, stand as the most complete listings available. His 1909 article attracted national attention to the swamp just as Hebard was gearing up to strip as much timber as could be reached.

When he first entered the Okefenokee, Roland had envisioned a dank, gloomy place and was delighted to find it anything but. There seems to be an energy about the place that exerts a pull on some people. If they dare enter, the swamp may hold fast so that the visitor never wants to leave. For others, the draw is a force to be resisted and they can only skirt the edges and boastfully say that they have penetrated the great waters when in actuality they have not. Apparently, Roland could enter the swamp, explore it, and write about it from a detached point of view. The swamp held quite a different captivation for Francis Harper.

Unlike his brother, young Francis professed an early bent toward natural history, and received encouragement from Roland and their mother. Having stemmed from a family steeped in education, it is no surprise that Francis also sought a higher degree and seemed always to be juggling several projects at any time. He was a committed scientist and published about 135 scientific and popular papers on a broad range of subjects.

Francis Harper was an undergraduate student at Cornell when a scientific team was dispatched to the Georgia wilderness in 1912 to systematically document the Okefenokee's flora and fauna. Such a reading had never been done before. Despite his brother's pioneering work there, Francis was not invited to join the expedition. Not to be outdone, he planned his own study, charged down to the swamp, hired David Lee as his guide, and completed his first examination before the Cornell team showed up. Hebard was more or less clear-cutting when both Francis and the Cornell team arrived, but they were able to speak with people who had lived in the swamp before timbering began and who could give a verbal picture of the land when the big cypress still grew there.

The designation "swamp" is misleading, for the Okefenokee is more than a swamp. Water, while abundant, is not the only feature. Islands covered with pines, bays, oaks, and thick shrubbery hump slightly above the surface and range in size from a few acres to several hundred. Extensive grassy prairies spread between the islands of trees, but their looks are deceiving; these are wet prairies where water levels vary from a few inches to several feet. Open waterways and lakes are limited and usually result from deep pockets of peat being burned away. Narrow openings cross the prairies and bogs, but these are gator paths, much like well-used game trails found on land. Prairies and bogs, or strands—shallow places thick with vegetation—are often difficult to traverse by paddling. People living in the swamp designed a flat-bottomed boat and used a forked pole to push through.

The upper reaches of the Suwannee River slice through dense cypress swamps. Linear lakes, such as Dinner Pond, Big Water, Minnies, and Billys lakes form magnificent reflective pools that change with light and wind. Charles Wharton, in *The Natural Environments of Georgia,* calls the Okefenokee a "huge, acid, peat-filled bay-lake." Albert Wright, leader of the group from Cornell University who explored the swamp in 1912, described it as one large sphagnum bog. Francis Harper called it a primeval wilderness of exceptional beauty offering unsurpassed opportunities for faunal and ecological studies.

Whether the Okefenokee originated as a series of lakes or a low stream system has not yet been determined. The Okefenokee has been evolving for millions of years, alternating between dry land and inundation by seawater. When the climate began to warm some eighteen thousand years ago, the great ice sheets melted, and sea level rose to cover the Okefenokee Basin again. The basin's groundwater table began to rise about eight thousand years ago. Rainfall increased and a clay bottom as much as four hundred feet thick in places, laid down by those overflowing and retreating seas, cradled the water in shallow ponds. Ferns, mosses, grasses, sedges, lilies, bladderworts, and other vegetation colonized the pools and their shorelines. As plants and animals died, their remains drifted to the bottom of the ponds and gradually converted to peat; the oldest peat is about seven thousand years old. Cypress trees have been around the Okefenokee for about forty-five hundred years.

The Okefenokee receives 70 to 90 percent of its water from rainfall; the rest comes from intermittent creeks and seeping springs. More than three-fourths of that water leaves the swamp via evapotranspiration—evaporation from surface soil and water plus moisture lost from the surface cells of plants. In addition, a great deal flows out of the swamp through two rivers. Hydrological studies have provided differing figures—and it is as difficult to pin down definite numbers as it is to characterize a typical year—but the Suwannee River carries about 80 percent of the outflow westward to the Gulf of Mexico and something less than 20 percent washes down the St. Marys River. The St. Marys makes a more circuitous route as it flows southward and turns east, then flows north for a time until finally, just south of Folkston, Georgia, the river turns east again toward the Atlantic. Though both rivers rise in the Okefenokee it is impossible to pinpoint just where they begin.

Of the seventy or so islands occurring in the swamp, sixty are large enough to bear names: Billys, Honey, Cowhouse (for the large numbers of cattle left to forage there), Chesser (after the family who settled it), Floyds (after the general who chased the Indians away), Blackjack, Soldiers Camp (after an 1840s army camp), and Bugaboo. Native people left mounds where they buried their dead and middens where they piled their refuse. Hardwood hammocks and pine barrens dominate the island habitats. White-tailed deer, black bears, bobcats, raccoons, and small mammals inhabit the islands. Deer feed on the succulent vegetation and bears enjoy seasonal berries and an occasional hog.

From a distance, Okefenokee's wet prairies, with sprouting maidencane, spatterdock, water lilies, golden club (called never wets in the Okefenokee), and other aquatic plants, have the look of an open grassland. The wet prairies are unique to the swamp. Simply described, they are marsh ponds lacking trees. Boat runs across the prairies used to follow gator trails, but today large blades mounted on a work boat keep the trails open.

Outboard motors stir up the peat in shallow areas and intakes can become clogged. Decomposing peat emits gases that may lift a large mat to the surface, closing a water path or at least altering its appearance. Floating peat mats are called "batteries." If a battery stays afloat, plants begin to colonize it and it becomes a "house." These houses were sometimes used as campsites being drier than the bays and often more easily reached than an island. Since they are not stably anchored they sometimes feel squishy and move when walked upon, giving the impression that the earth is trembling or quaking.

Cypress bays monopolize any place that is not a gum forest, sphagnum bog, prairie, open water, or dry island. Red bay, red maple, black gum, and dahoon holly grow around the cypress, as do tussocks of small shrubs, such as titi and huckleberry, and grasses, such as maidencane and carex. Some of these tussocks are large enough and dry enough to walk on if a traveler is so inclined. Most, however, are small.

Between the cypress bays and prairies around some of the islands—Billys, Honey, Black Jack, and Floyds—are sphagnum bogs sometimes referred to as strands. Virginia chain ferns, pitcher plants, sundews, gallberries, slash pines, bays, and black gums are widely scattered across the bog. People have tried various measures to remove peat and sphagnum moss but have not found an economical way to do it.

Walking the bogs is frequently the only way to reach some places. One waddles and wades rather than strides across a bog, sometimes sinking up to the knees or thighs. It is difficult to pinpoint where the land ends and water begins. I have canoed in the Okefenokee, but it is unlikely that I will ever attempt bog walking.

After receiving his undergraduate degree from Cornell in 1914, Francis took time out to serve in Europe during World War I, then returned to complete his Ph.D. He was a busy student, but he took time for hiking and skiing in the beautiful hills around Ithaca, New York, perhaps over some of the same territory Alexander Wilson had covered, as Ithaca is on one of the Finger Lakes not far from Ovid. His favorite partner for these excursions was a young woman who, while a student at Vassar, was one of a group of robust women working in the farm fields to replace men gone to war.

Jean Sherwood loved the outdoors as much as Francis. She was working for her masters in Agriculture at Cornell because she wanted her own farm one day. Before her Cornell days, Jean had tutored Franklin D. Roosevelt's children at Hyde Park for a time, and had been a visitor at Campobello when he was stricken with polio. Roosevelt wanted Jean to manage his orchards after graduating, but she and Francis decided to marry a few days after receiving her degree in 1923. After the wedding, the couple drove to Michigan, camping all the way.

Jean's sunny, welcoming personality was the perfect foil for Francis's sometimes aloof manner. In choosing Jean for his partner, Francis found the bridge between his occasional haughty self and other people. She may have had some idea of the life they would come to lead, for Francis would not be directed by others. A grant from the New York State Museum led them to an extended camping trip in the Adirondack Mountains, and together they wrote a handbook on the region's animals. Jean found happiness in their unusual lifestyle.

After earning his doctorate from Cornell in 1925, based on a study of the Okefenokee's mammals, Francis went to work for the Boston Society of Natural History. To say he was always a salaried employee might not be quite true. Throughout his life, Harper's income was drawn from a number of study grants obtained from various scientific societies and organizations. That first visit to the Okefenokee captivated Francis and he returned often and moved his family there for periods of time. He studied not only the ecosystem but also the people and knew the swamp better than outsiders and almost as well as the swampers who lived there. As

Harper began to study the plants and wildlife, he realized that the swampers knew more about the swamp and the habits of its denizens than his
colleagues ever could, and that their culture was adapted from earlier
societies. The swampers, however, liked to perpetuate certain "tall tales"
as a joke, like the one about the long-tailed bobcat, said to be an especially
secretive animal completely separate from the common bobcat.

One of the last known ivory-billed woodpeckers was killed on Craven
Island in 1912, though there were isolated spottings up until the 1940s.
The region's last wild Florida wolf (*Canis floridanus* now *Canis rufus*) was
killed near the swamp's edge about 1910, though an animal believed to be
a wolf was heard in 1916. Cougars, once the supreme land hunter, were
last sighted about 1916 and may yet haunt the inner reaches. Cornell's
biological assessment came not a moment too soon.

Dr. W. D. Funkhouser, a member of the Cornell group, later lectured
on swamper families at the University of Kentucky in Louisville, calling
them undernourished, diseased, inbred, and degenerate people living in
crude lean-tos and wearing next to nothing. Their English, he jeered,
"was Chaucerian, Spenserian, and Shakespearian" and barely under-
standable.[3]

Like his brother, Francis Harper was an obsessive note-taker and collector of thoughts and papers. When he began taking down their stories
verbatim, the swampers at first thought the biologist was poking fun at
them. Some became upset when he phonetically quoted their peculiar
pronunciations. Francis never meant to denigrate them, but he did observe the people through a scientist's eyes. He set out to preserve what he
could of the swamper society; a mode of living thought antiquated by
mainstream America, molded to fit an area that could be both generous
and vengeful.

But the culture Harper studied from 1912 into the 1920s was in transition. Outside the swamp, the twentieth century beckoned. The lumber
town on Billys Island had brought the outside world to the Okefenokee
folk. Old-timers were dying and radios were replacing evenings of visiting and storytelling.

A move to protect the Okefenokee, begun in 1918, was unsuccessful at
first. In 1924, Francis published an account of his 1912 initiation into the
Okefenokee ways when another push was on to preserve the great
swamp. Roland wrote letters supporting preservation and Albert Wright
lent his voice to the effort. Hebard kept cutting.

Francis was always working, but his income may have been small. His work led him to the frozen reaches of Canada and Alaska, where Jean could not follow. Four children were born to the couple over the years; when possible, the family spent as much time as they could in the Okefenokee collecting specimens for museums. Upon returning to camp, they often lived in tents, and Jean and the children helped press plants and write labels. Jean's botanical ability was of great help to her husband. All the time, Francis kept notebook and pencil at the ready to jot down his observations. The swampers came to trust him and accepted the family as their peers.

In 1929 Francis Harper left the Boston Society of Natural History and went to work for *Biological Abstracts* in Philadelphia, where he remained until 1935, when he lost his position as a result of the Depression. The Harpers had some small savings, and needed to find an inexpensive place to live, so they returned to the Okefenokee and rented a small cabin.

When rumors of a ship canal crossing the Okefenokee began circulating in 1930, Jean Harper alerted her old employer, Franklin Roosevelt. He responded that he would hate to see the Okefenokee destroyed. While conservation-minded organizations called for preservation, local businesses and newspapers lobbied for a scenic highway across the swamp. More letters passed through the mail and in February 1935, President Roosevelt wrote to Jean that he was directing Jay N. "Ding" Darling, chief of the Biological Survey, to speak to Congress on the swamp's behalf. As a result of these efforts the Okefenokee National Wildlife Refuge was created on March 30, 1937. The refuge now protects 396,000 of the swamp's 438,000 acres.

Ironically, rules and regulations governing a federally protected area forced swampers from their homes. Legally they could no longer kill the bears and bobcats that depredated their stock. Even alligators were off-limits, though an occasional one was poached until a drop in the market price of hides helped curtail that illegal practice. By 1937, though, the alligator population had dropped significantly. A far cry from the days when Allen Chesser, born in the swamp in 1859, witnessed a group feeding where gators were so thick he could have walked across their backs, an echo of William Bartram's account of alligators on the St. Johns a century earlier. The old-timers Harper knew and appreciated have passed on now, but their descendants still live near the swamp and a few work for the agencies involved in protecting the resource. They may not live the old ways, but they pass on stories to their children.

Visitors to the Okefenokee may enter from three distinct places: the Okefenokee National Wildlife Refuge, or east entrance, is at the Suwannee Canal Recreation Area off Highway 121. The north entrance is eight miles south of Waycross at the privately leased Okefenokee Swamp Park on Route 177. An interesting feature on the way to the swamp park is a stand of cat-faced pines: the bark scraped from one or more sides. The wound oozes resin that is collected and distilled into turpentine, pitch, and rosin. Stephen C. Foster State Park, the swamp's west entrance, is located seventeen miles east of Fargo, Georgia, at the end of Route 177. The most popular day use at each entrance is a canoe trip. There are seven designated campsites within the swamp and overnight canoe trips require a permit. Only seven groups may be in the park on any given night. Becoming lost or disoriented is possible, so it is imperative that someone in charge knows who is in the park, which trail they are on, and when they will be out.

Water levels fluctuate with drought and rainfall. Longer canoe trails require extensive paddling and if the water is low or if a floating peat mat has blocked the path, the only way to get through may be to get out and push or portage. If water levels fall too low, some trails may be closed. Spring is the busiest season and winter is the slack time. Winter weather varies from balmy to downright freezing; summers are always hot and humid. Even a few hours on the swamp's slow-moving waters bring a number of wondrous sights into view, but though the Okefenokee seems unspoiled and pristine, it has been subjected to human exploitation in the past and faces future threats, too.

I visited the swamp in 1997 with writer/naturalist/teacher Gil Nelson, just to explore for the afternoon. We left early on a foggy spring morning, probably later than Gil likes, for he has a penchant for being wherever he is supposed to be before sunup. The day promised to be warm.

We arrived at Stephen Foster State Park before mid-morning and plopped Gil's canoe into the water. There were a few other people out, but in a few weeks the Okefenokee would be swarming with visitors. We

FIG. 22. Early 1900s photograph of cat-faced pines oozing sap, which
was laboriously collected and distilled into turpentine.
Courtesy of Florida Archives.

paddled down the small canal to open water lined with cypress. It was
difficult to imagine a railroad passing through here. The dark water compelled me to stick my hand in a time or two. Several gators reposed on the
sunny shore, but a stray one might have lurked beneath the canoe. On
summer days when the surface water was warm, swampers used to swirl
water into a whirlpool with their hand to draw cool water to the top.
Here and there a tree or a stump rose from a tussock of grasses and small
shrubs, looking like a dish garden on steroids. The waterway narrowed
until it formed a corkscrewed passage through thick vegetation.

We tried to move the canoe without bumping into cypress knees or
grounding it—which meant we spent some time backing and turning
and going forward again. Finally we emerged into a straight wide ditch
framed by a large earthen dam. After a significant drought and several
fires during 1955–56, refuge managers decided to build a dam, or sill,
across the Suwannee River to hold water in the swamp against another
drought. The swamp was slow to refill in 1957. Construction on the sill
began in 1958 and it was dedicated in 1960. An access road and boat ramp
were added in 1969. Over the years, constant repairs to the sill and water

control structures have been required. High water breached the dam in 1979.

A four-year study of the sill was approved in 1999. Six water monitoring stations were installed in late 1999 and an additional four were set in place in early 2000. The plan calls for two years of monitoring water levels above and below the sill. During the next two years, the water control structures will be opened and the water levels monitored again. Data comparison will provide managers with a picture of the sill's effects on the swamp's hydrology.

After milling about the sill for a time we decided to return to the canoe launch for lunch. About a quarter of the way through the twisted passage we could hear the grating whine of an outboard coming toward us. It would be next to impossible for a motor boat to come barreling through this passage, yet it sounded as if someone were trying to do just that. We pulled over and waited at a wide spot. Soon a Johnboat appeared with two teenage girls in it. One handling the motor was a bit older and though she might do fine in the open (and indeed did plow past us later as we meandered back across the wide water) her method of negotiating this passage was to back off the motor as she rammed the boat into something, then let the bounce help her edge the long boat around the turns. We hoped she would not ram us; she did manage to avoid the canoe, but it was touch and go. It was rather like bumper cars on water, but it could not have been a comfortable way to proceed nor was it particularly beneficial to the waterway as the prop stirred up a lot of silt. But the girls were having a high old time.

Back at the park we ate lunch under mossy trees at the picnic area. A small museum was closed. We would have liked to see inside. Once the canoe was safely secured to the truck we headed for the privately owned Okefenokee Swamp Park, the swamp's northern entrance. Thankfully, there are still no roads across the swamp, so we drove up the west side and then around the north edge. The park was doing a brisk tourist trade and we did not stay long; the day was long in the tooth and we had a lengthy drive back to Tallahassee.

The Okefenokee was not as I had envisioned. Sunlight brightened the land and it was far from dismal. No wonder Bartram, the Harpers, and others had become infatuated with the place. My senses became absorbed in the peaceful scenery.

Water levels seemed to be a bit low at that time, and signaled the beginning of the long drought that led to 1998's fiery summer. Periodic droughts cause worries for visitors, wildlife, and refuge managers alike. With lowered rainfall, water levels drop and the Okefenokee begins to dry up. Moisture-loving plants cure in the sun, frogs and soft-shelled turtles burrow into the muck, and mud dries and breaks into slate-like plates. Fish congregate in shrinking ponds, and alligators and birds gorge on trapped animals. After a period of feasting, if the rains do not return soon, the birds and gators will begin to suffer. In extreme drought, gator holes may be the last available water. Surplus alligators must leave to find other lakes or swimming pools. Fights erupt as competition for scarce food escalates.

In spite of the calm I felt while canoeing, the reality of nature can often turn savage—or what may seem savage to some. All the animals in the swamp must eat and many of them prey on each other. The swampers' tales are full of hunting stories and observations of encounters between animals in which only one survived. I could imagine, too, a storm roiling the waters and flogging the trees while drenching rain soaked everything. All accompanied by ropes of lightning cracking like bullwhips and loosing a stampede of thunder rolling across the wet prairies. The Okefenokee is not always kind and gentle.

What worries wildlife managers is not so much the drought—though visitors are certain to remark upon it, and traveling the waterways will be more difficult if not impossible—but what comes after the drought. Sure to follow a dry season are storms, not always bearing enough rain, but certainly accompanied by lightning. There is more lightning around the Okefenokee than anyplace else in Georgia, and with lightning comes fire. The swamp depends on fire for renewal.

During the Okefenokee's development, fire has been the main force shaping the area. That may seem ludicrous in the face of so much water, but after prolonged drought the swamp is susceptible to burning. If a fire ignites and flames and smolders over the parched land long enough to burn through exposed peat layers, new ponds and waterways can form. After a fire, the cycle of renewal begins with falling rain. Seeds respond to the moisture and greedily take in nitrogen from the ashes. Water fills depressions where peat has burned away. Aquatic vegetation colonizes the spacious prairies; sphagnum bogs and island vegetation turn green.

This cycle was replayed in the 1930s, 1950s, 1970s, the early 1990s, and gave an encore performance on July 9, 1998, when lightning struck near

Honey Island. Before sudden rain extinguished it, fire burned through 5,228 acres on Honey Island Prairie, Billys Island, and a small portion of Bugaboo Island. At one time wind had pushed the fire toward Stephen Foster State Park, and refuge staff had evacuated campers and residents so they would not become trapped if fire crossed the road.

It is not a question of if, but when fire returns to the swamp. After the fires of the early 1990s, people, agencies, and companies who own land adjacent to the refuge formed the Greater Okefenokee Association of Landowners. The group has been instrumental in disseminating information among other landowners, developing the Swamps Edge Break (a 209-mile-long firebreak), and constructing thirty-two helicopter dipsites, where the aircraft can fill a huge water bucket that can then be opened over a fire. A helicopter is the only piece of equipment that can safely move on a fire in the Okefenokee. Trying to put people or heavy machinery into the swamp to extinguish a fire is just not practical or safe. Richard Bolt was killed trying to stop an escaping prescribed fire on the Pocket, in Stephen Foster State Park, in 1979. The Swamp's Edge Visitor Center at the Suwannee Canal was renamed the Richard S. Bolt Visitor Center in 1991 in his memory.

Since fire is an integral part of the ecosystem, refuge managers have spent hours planning for fires. Of primary concern is keeping the blaze within the swamp and protecting structures. If a natural fire starts inside the refuge boundaries and gives the appearance of leaving the swamp for private property, refuge staff will jump on it. Many factors determine whether such action will be successful: water levels, days since last rain, lead time, weather forecasts. If the fire is smaller than five acres, if fewer than two hours have passed since the fire began and managers learned of it, if there is a helicopter available, chances of stopping the fire rise considerably. If the fire has grown too large to stop by dropping buckets of water or fire retardant and if dry weather and wind spread it too fast, fire crews draw back to the Swamps Edge Break and wait. The break is not designed to stop a rapidly spreading fire, but it is a point from which to impede its progress. In the end, fire in the Okefenokee is not what worries the refuge staff, but how a fire will react and how to stop it if it begins to threaten private property.

By far, the most dangerous threat facing the Okefenokee is the specter of mining.

E. I. du Pont de Nemours and Co., in 1994, quietly announced plans to mine titanium from a thirty-eight-thousand-acre strip along Trail Ridge. The mine would operate twenty-four hours a day for thirty to forty years. Titanium mixed with oxygen produces titanium dioxide, a white pigment used in paint, plastics, coated paper, and the trademark "m" on those chocolate candies guaranteed to melt in your mouth, not in your hand. Department of the Interior secretary Bruce Babbitt held a press conference at the swamp in 1998 to vigorously oppose the project. Du Pont insists its mine, thirty miles along Trail Ridge and consisting of dredged holes as much as fifty feet deep, would not harm the swamp's ecology. The soils composing Trail Ridge were laid down in layers and act as a regulatory dam dictating the rate and direction of flow as well as a balance of minerals released into the waters. Mining will mix up those layers and it is impossible to even guess what that will mean for the swamp, except that it is not likely to be good.

Residents of Folkston, Georgia, are concerned. About four hundred thousand visitors per year—hunters, anglers, hikers, canoeists—leave a fair amount of money behind when they visit the swamp. Dredges clanging and banging the day and night away under the glare of bright lights are not conducive to a quality wildlife experience.

Du Pont seems willing to compromise but the federal government, so far, is unyielding in its response: "No." Of course, the government cannot prevent du Pont from mining if the company's studies indicate that no harm will come to the environment and it wants to proceed. As this is written, more studies are underway. In February 1999, du Pont signed an agreement to sell the property for $90 million. Du Pont has, by its own accounting, sunk $20 million into the project. There is staunch opposition (78 percent) to the mine from a disparate group of people: nuns, environmentalists, Harley-Davidson riders, and dentists. Swamp protectors must stay vigilant. Even though the project is on hold, the threat is still there.

The southern reaches of the Okefenokee fade into Florida's Pinhook Swamp, which segues into the Osceola National Forest. Since 1989, The Nature Conservancy has been working with the U.S. Forest Service to purchase acreage in the Pinhook to join the forest and the swamp into a corridor for black bears and other wildlife. If state and federal funding are granted and willing sellers can be found, the project will eventually total about 106,000 acres—the largest contiguous block of forested wetlands in the lower forty-eight states. Without large tracts of protected lands, wildlife adapted to certain habitat requirements could not survive. Red-cockaded woodpeckers, bobcats, bears, and people will all benefit from uniting the area. The Pinhook is the main aquifer recharge locale for Jacksonville's drinking water supply.

When Francis Harper entered the swamp in May of 1912, alligators were still mating and females were building nests. Newborn fawns were beginning to appear, but their spotted coats made them hard to find in the undergrowth. Young turkeys followed their mother as she taught them to search for food and how to negotiate a log in case a hungry snake waited on the other side. Soft-shelled turtles scooped their nests under the watchful eyes of raccoons, who hungrily waited for a treat of fresh eggs. The ivory-bill's call, a wolf's howl, and a cougar's scream could be heard if one was patient.

Spring was full-blown by that month and heading toward summer. Francis felt the hum of life in the swamp as David Lee piloted the boat to Billys Island, accompanied by familiar bird calls. Each turn of the twelve-hour trip brought a different view of forest and prairie. At Billys Island, David Lee's family rose from their beds to welcome their son home and set out food and drink for the weary travelers.

They went exploring on Honey Island the next day and Francis rested on a half-burned log in partial shade cooled by a light breeze. Pines and palmettos grew in the distance and ferns and wildflowers nearby. Cottony clouds floated through an azure sky and a dozen different birds called. He wrote this line in his journal, summing up his feelings about the swamp: "A perfect scene of perfect peace lies about me."[4]

If success or intelligence is measured by wealth or fine possessions, then the swampers would have been considered bereft indeed. But what they claimed in abundance, and what others may have viewed with veiled jealousy, was self-sufficient freedom. The people of the Okefenokee drew their living from the land. They could build a house, a wagon, or furniture from the woods, and repair almost anything that needed it. When a boat sprang a leak there was a pine nearby where chink-stopping pitch could be obtained with a little patience. There were home remedies for illness. Malaria and yellow fever had been virtual strangers to the fresh-water Okefenokee as the diseases spread along coastal towns from ships from tropical countries via mosquitoes that bred in the salt marshes.

Francis Harper was a man who adapted to the technological advances of his time. The wealth of photographs he and his brother left behind are testament to that. Judging from Francis's love affair with the Okefenokee and the swampers, he longed to stay, but he could not quite give up the modern world. He did compile the swampers' folklore and he recorded some of their singing and especially their "hollerin'," a cross between yelling and yodeling. Men hollered when returning from hunting or just when they felt like it. Each man's call sounded different and carried miles across the prairies. It was a way of letting their family know they were returning safely. More dependable than a cell phone.

Later photographs of Francis Harper in the swamp show a happy, relaxed man. Perhaps there he felt comfortable in a retreat from the demands of the outside world, but he could only stay for short periods of time. His work and commitments to family called him away. It was the life to which he had been raised and the course he followed. Harper kept scrupulous notes of his visits to the swamp and vowed to write a book about the swampers and their land, but he put it off, attending to other matters until one day in 1972 there was no longer any time left.

Because he has an interest in Georgia Cracker history, Dr. Delma Presley came to meet Jean Harper, Francis's widow, in 1975. He borrowed boxes of the naturalist's papers and began cataloging the pages, photos, and tapes. The resulting *Okefinokee Album* is a delightful compendium of a time past in the swamp and the people who called it home for awhile. Perhaps it is not the book that Francis had once envisioned; he had planned a larger work that might have been overwhelming to most readers. Presley's work covers just enough and, as a good book should, leaves the reader longing to know more.

When Francis was an undergraduate at Cornell, his freshman English professor, Lane Cooper, wondered whether "some patriotic Philadelphian [could] be induced to revive the *Travels* of the Quaker natural scientist, William Bartram?" Clemson professor William H. Mills took Francis out to the Seneca River in 1939, where Bartram had dallied on his southern sojourn. Harper and other scientists had long felt the *Travels* lacking in modern detail with regard to current species nomenclature and precise geographic locations. Harper could not let the opportunity pass.[5]

The Bartrams' writings had been of special interest to Francis for years, and this interest deepened as he became involved with the Okefenokee. He undertook an enormous project of bringing William Bartram's work into modern times; the resulting *The Travels of William Bar-*

tram, Francis Harper's Naturalist Edition, is a must for anyone seeking to follow Bartram's path.

The lives of other early naturalists attracted Francis. Natural history was his chosen profession and knowing the lives of the first describers of America's natural world, where they explored, and what they had seen, helped guide his own work. Francis was a fine field collector in his own right; his knowledge and experience ran deep in the fields of mammalogy, botany, and ornithology. *The Mammals of the Okefinokee Swamp Region of Georgia,* published by the Boston Society of Natural History in 1927, contains not only detailed studies of animal behavior, but also recollections from various swampers and descriptions of the swamp itself.

When I first saw the western and northern portions of the Okefenokee in 1997, I had known little of the Harpers and their work there. I wanted to see the eastern side of the swamp, but first a friend and writer, Janisse Ray, arranged a visit to Milton Hopkins' home in Osierfield, Georgia. Milton lives in a converted railroad depot he had moved to his farm a few years back. There, I passed an afternoon with Milton and Chris Trowell. Milton developed an interest in natural history as a young man and began sending specimens to Francis. A small rainbow darter he sent was found to be a new species and kindly named for him. When Milton entered the service during World War II, Francis wrote with fatherly advice on how to conduct himself so far from home. Milton cherished his communications with Francis and they finally met a few years before Francis's death. It was a treat for them both.

Chris, a jocular, retired professor keenly interested in the swamp's history, particularly its social history, has plowed through parts of Roland's collections. He has published a number of research papers on the Okefenokee and if he cannot answer a question about the swamp off the top of his head, he can lay his fingers on a reference in a matter of minutes.

I tore myself away, reluctantly, and headed for Waycross. All the motels were full so I drove on to Folkston. My mind processed the afternoon's conversations as I headed east and I hardly noticed driving past pinelands and fields. I spent the evening reading stacks of information generously provided by Milton and Chris.

The next morning I meandered around Folkston—not too busy in the midst of summer—and along a back road paralleling Trail Ridge. If I'd been smart I would have been out at daybreak, but I wasn't. It was a hot July day. A very hot day. By the time I entered the wildlife refuge the evapotranspiration process was going strong. Sweat dripped from my nose as I walked the boardwalk to the observation tower. There were no mosquitoes, but I encountered a few yellow flies. I did not notice any alligators floating on the surface; it might have been too hot for them. A few egrets shopped for a noontime snack as the sun headed for its zenith. I heard small plops, probably frogs or small turtles, in the water hidden by vegetation as I strolled the boardwalk back to the parking lot. Not much else was stirring in the day's heat.

My next stop was the restored Chesser homestead. I was eager to visit the Cracker dwelling that the park purchased in 1973 and began restoring in 1976. Unfortunately, it was cleaning day. As I walked the path to the house I could see clothes hung on fences, furniture lined up along the brick walk to the house, and mattresses draped over folding chairs to air. People were inside scrubbing the floors and walls, washing the soap away with a hose. Water ran out between the walls and the floor. I peeked in the doors, mindful of being sprayed. The house has five bedrooms, a large kitchen, plus other rooms. Perching on a foundation of hand-hewn fat pine blocks, it appears a solid, comfortable, roomy home.

The white swept-sand yard is fenced; daily sweeping of the yard keeps weeds at bay, lessens the chance of fire starting near the house, and makes it easy to spot snakes if they come too close. I remember seeing swept, sandy yards many years ago—they are not so common now—and I always thought they looked tidy and clean. There are a number of outbuildings, including a small barn, syrup shed, smokehouse. Francis certainly spent many hours there, and Jean, too, for if the swampers liked Francis, they must have loved Jean: a woman who shared her husband's work, learned to expertly pole a swamp boat, raised her children well while her husband was away on research trips, and always had time and concern for the Okefenokee families as if they were part of her own.

After a pause at the visitor's center and the bookstore, I stopped at the administrative office to speak with Jim Burkhart, who runs the public use program for the refuge. Originally from Pennsylvania, Burkhart came to the swamp in 1978, and if he has his way, he'll never leave. For Jim, the swamp is the closest thing to heaven on earth. I asked him how he thought the swamp looked in 1890, before timbering, and he could not hazard a guess, but there was little doubt in his mind that removing the big trees had transfigured the swamp.

FIG. 23. An alligator soaks up the sun in a marsh.
Photo by Joe Reinman. Courtesy of St. Marks National Wildlife Refuge.

The red-cockaded woodpeckers are in trouble and the ivory-bills are gone. Rumors persist that a few ivory-bills live deep in the Okefenokee. Hope lives a long time before the fact of extinction sinks in. I didn't ask Jim if he thought the birds were still there. Even if he did, he would not have said so. Such a speculation would start an all-out stampede of bird watchers and ornithologists.

Unfortunately, it was time to leave the Okefenokee. I wanted a slow drive to Tallahassee; I had lots of information to ponder.

As brothers, Francis and Roland shared a number of similar traits. They could be stubborn and opinionated and both had a list of dislikes. Once a conclusion had been reached, neither man was easily budged from it. Francis went to great lengths to form those conclusions, devoting hours to checking original sources and verifying information. For example, he once traveled to a cove in the Catskills and threw a rock into the water, counting until it hit the bottom, just as Bartram had done. They were somewhat deficient in social graces and seemed insensitive in their remarks, but such lapses were unintentional. Their friends—and both had many, many friends—overlooked their faults and valued them for their expertise.

When I began researching the Harpers I was dismayed at the lack of current information about them. Their published articles revealed little of their personalities. Aside from obituaries, there was not much of a personal note to be found. I was grateful to have the opportunity to speak with Milton, Chris, and Del, who eagerly shared their knowledge and impressions about these interesting brothers who added so much to our natural history lore.

Roland finally married in 1943, when he was sixty-five years old. The couple had no children. Roland Harper died in Tuscaloosa in 1966. The bulk of his papers are housed at the University of Alabama; in addition to correspondence, photographs, botanical lists, and scientific publications there are railroad, bus, airline, steamship, and trolley timetables that Roland had collected since childhood, cemetery records mostly from Alabama but also from Arizona, Tennessee, Florida, Connecticut, Georgia, Maine, New Jersey, New York, North Carolina, Pennsylvania, Texas, and Maryland, and booster materials promoting towns and attractions, mostly in Florida. The collection fills about two rooms. The librarian once remarked to Chris Trowell that Dr. Harper was the strangest person she had ever met.

Francis's papers reside at the University of Kansas. Like Roland, Francis left a large compilation of photographs and many field notebooks and pieces of correspondence. For Francis, the Okefenokee was always reshaping itself and it was a place for personal renewal. I do not know if he felt as if he had learned everything the swamp and the people could teach him, but until the swampers pulled up stakes and left, it was a place to which Francis and Jean returned time after time. It was home.

Del Presley related a story about Jean Harper as she neared the end of her life. She imagined Francis approaching on a white horse. Soon he would reach her and she would mount behind him and they would ride together into the swamp that they both loved and where they had spent so many happy years. I believe their spirits are there.

Appendix

Note: All Websites were accessible as of June 2000.

Apalachicola National Estuarine
Research Reserve
Visitor and Education Center
261 7th St.
Apalachicola, FL 32320
(850) 653-8063
http://inlet.geol.sc.edu/APA/
gen_info.html

Apalachicola National Forest
P.O. 579
Bristol, FL 32321
(850) 643-2282
http://www.fs.fed.us

Bartram's Garden
54 Street and Lindbergh Boulevard
Philadelphia, PA 19143
(215) 729-5281

Cape Romain National Wildlife Refuge
5801 Highway 17 North
Awendaw, SC 29429
(843) 928-3264
http://www.fws.gov

Daniel Stowe Botanical Garden
6500 South New Hope Road
Belmont, NC 28012
(704) 825-4490
http://www.stowegarden.org/
MichauxMain.html

The Deering Estate at Cutler
16701 SW 72 Avenue
Miami, FL 33157
(305) 235-1668
http://www.co.miami-dade.fl.us/
parks/deering.htm

Drayton Hall
3380 Ashley River Road
Charleston, SC 29414
(803) 766-0188
http://www.draytonhall.org

Florida Department of State
500 S. Bronough
R. A. Gray Building
Tallahassee, FL 32399
http://www.dos.state.fl.us
http://fpc.dos.state.fl.us/ (online
photographic collection)

Fort Clinch State Park
2601 Atlantic Ave.
Fernandina Beach, FL 32034
(904) 277-7274
http://www.dep.state.fl.us/parks/
District_2/FortClinch/index.html

Florida Native Plant Society
P.O. Box 690278
Vero Beach, FL 32969-0278
http://www.fnps.org/

Fort McAllister State Park
3894 Fort McAllister Road
Richmond Hill, GA 31324
(912) 727-2339
http://www.gastateparks.org

Francis Marion National Forest
Wambaw Ranger District
P.O. Box 788
McClellanville, SC 29458
(803) 887-3257

Grandfather Mountain
P.O. Box 129
Linville, NC 28646
(828) 733-2013
http://www.grandfather.com

Gulf Islands National Seashore
Superintendent
1801 Gulf Breeze Parkway
Gulf Breeze, FL 32561-5000
(850) 934-2600
http://www.nps.gov/guis/
GuisHome.htm

Hontoon Island State Park
2309 River Ridge Road
Deland, FL 32720
(904) 736-5309
http://www.dep.state.fl.us/parks/
District_3/HontoonIsland/index.html

James Island County Park
871 Riverland Drive
Charleston, SC 29412
(843) 795-7275

John Gorrie State Museum
P.O. Box 267
46 Sixth Street
Apalachicola, FL 32329-0267
(850) 653-9347
http://www.dep.state.fl.us/parks/
District_1/JohnGorrie/index.html

Magnolia Gardens
Ashley River Road
Charleston, SC 29414
(800) 367-3517
http://www.magnoliaplantation.com

Middleton Place Foundation
Ashley River Road
Charleston, SC 29414-7206
(800) 782-3608
http://www.middletonplace.org

The Montezuma Wetlands Complex
Project Office
3395 Routes 5 & 20 East
Seneca Falls, NY 13148
(315) 365-2371
http://www.fws.gov

Natchez Trace Parkway
Superintendent
RR 1, NT-143
Tupelo, MS 38801
(601) 680-4025
http://www.nps.gov/natr/

National Audubon Society
700 Broadway
New York, NY 10003
(212) 979-3000
http://www.audubon.org

National Forests in North Carolina
160A Zillicoa St.
Asheville, NC 28802
(828) 257-4200
http://www.fs.fed.us

The Nature Conservancy
Apalachicola Bluffs and Ravines
Preserve
P.O. Box 393
Bristol, FL 32321
(850) 643-2756
http://www.tnc.org

Okefenokee National Wildlife Refuge
Rt. 2, Box 3330
Folkston, GA 31537
(912) 496-7836
http://www.fws.gov

Okefenokee Swamp Park
Waycross, GA 31501
(912) 283-0583

Osceola National Forest
P.O. Box 70
Olustee, FL 32072
(904) 752-2577
http://www.fs.fed.us

St. George Island State Park
1900 E. Gulf Beach Dr.
St. George Island, FL 32328
(850) 927-2111
http://www.dep.state.fl.us/parks/
District_1/StGeorgeIsland/index.html

St. Joseph Peninsula State Park
8899 Cape San Blas Road
Port St. Joe, FL 32456
(850) 227-1327
http://www.dep.state.fl.us/parks/
District_1/StJoseph/index.html

St. Vincent National Wildlife Refuge
P.O. Box 447
Apalachicola, FL 32329
(850) 653-8808
http://www.fws.gov

Savannah National Wildlife Refuge
1000 Business Center Drive, Suite 10
Savannah, GA 31405
(912) 652-4415
http://www.fws.gov

Sierra Club
85 Second Street, Second Floor
San Francisco, CA 94105-3441
(415) 977-5500
http://www.sierraclub.org

Skidaway Island State Park
52 Diamond Causeway
Savannah, GA 31411
(912) 598-2300
http://www.gastateparks.org

Stephen C. Foster State Park
Rt. 1, Box 131
Fargo, GA 31631
(912) 637-5274
http://www.gastateparks.org

Thurmond Lake
Rt. 1, Box 12
Clarks Hill, SC 29821-9703
(800) 533-3478

Torreya State Park
Rt. 2, Box 70
Bristol, FL 32321
(850) 643-2674
http://www.dep.state.fl.us/parks/
District_1/Torreya/index.html

The Wilson Ornithological Society
Museum of Zoology
University of Michigan
Ann Arbor, MI 48109-1079

Notes

1. First Contact

1. According to several volumes of the *Florida Handbook*, published yearly since 1947 in Tallahassee by the Peninsula Publishing Company and compiled by the late Allen Morris, Florida has become the largest beef-producing state east of the Mississippi.
2. Duncan, *Hernando de Soto*, 417–24. While the thought progression is sometimes difficult to follow in de Biedma and A Gentleman of Elvas, *Narratives of De Soto*, 23, the translation contains interesting descriptions of the southeastern landscape, wildlife, and native people, including dispassionate accounts of their customs, murders, and enslavement.
3. Wright, *Thirteen Colonies*, 179.
4. Ewan, *John Banister*, 92–93. Another account of his death on page 22 of Gilbert's *John Abbot* relates that "Banister slipped, fell, and was killed while collecting plants."
5. Lawson, *New Voyage*, 267.
6. Ibid., 243.

2. Illuminating Natural History

1. Catesby, *Catesby's Birds*, 137.
2. Frick and Stearns, *Colonial Audubon*, 45–46.
3. Catesby, *Catesby's Birds*, 150–51.
4. Bartram, W., *Travels*, 200.
5. Catesby, *Catesby's Birds*, 144.
6. Savage, *Lost Heritage*, 85.
7. Catesby, *Catesby's Birds*, 139.
8. Ibid., 140–41.
9. Ibid., 138.
10. Ibid.

3. The Bartram Legacy

1. Mohan, "St. Johns," 46.
2. Bartram, W., *Travels*, 120.
3. Ibid., 114–15.
4. Ibid., 102.
5. Ibid., 105.

4. The Intriguing Naturalist

1. Drayton Papers, property of Drayton Hall, a National Trust Historic Site in Charleston, South Carolina.
2. Savage and Savage, *André and François Michaux*, 75.
3. Ibid., 89.
4. Ibid., 98.
5. Ibid., 149–50.
6. On page 135 of *Wildflowers of the Carolina Lowcountry and Lower Pee Dee*, Richard Porcher states that native people used extracts from the mayapple as purgatives, for skin disorders, and for tumorous growths. Today's researchers form the basis of a drug to treat lymphocytic leukemia and testicular cancer from alkaloids found in the plant's rhizomes.

5. A Peculiar Liking for Insects

1. Remington, "John Abbot," 29.
2. Ibid., 30.
3. Dow, "John Abbot," 70.
4. Hunter, *Letters of Alexander Wilson*, 308–9.
5. Gilbert, *John Abbot*, 66.
6. Ibid., 80.

6. *The Lovely Face of Nature*

1. Wilson, *Life and Letters*, 405.
2. Ibid., 207.
3. Ibid., 274.
4. Hopkins, *Our Country*, 76–80.

7. *The Man Who Painted Birds*

1. Proby, *Audubon in Florida*, 9.
2. Ibid., 15.
3. Ibid., 30–31.
4. Ibid., 313. This same passage appears almost verbatim in Audubon's own account of his birth in the New World, quoted on page 33 of John Chancellor's 1978 biography of Audubon: "my Parents say, under the dark foliage of an Orange Tree, with a load of Golden Fruit and blossoms upon which fed that airy Silph the Hum Bird, whilst I received the tender cares of a Mother ever since kind to me."
5. Audubon, *Himself*, 197–98.
6. Audubon, *Audubon's America*, 3–14.

8. *The Garden of Eden*

1. Ken Wurdack relates that, like torreya, *Croomia* has a relative in China and another in Japan. The northernmost American population is found in Dekalb County, Alabama, almost in Tennessee.
2. Latrobe, *Rambler in North America*, Vol. 2, 33–45. The Bellamy Road between Pensacola and St. Augustine was completed in 1826. Crews left high stumps in the sixteen-foot-wide clearing and built inadequate bridges and causeways. Today U.S. 27 follows part of the Bellamy Road east of Tallahassee and U.S. 90 follows its path west of the capital city.

9. *Medicine Man*

1. Kimball, "Reminiscences of Chapman," 5.
2. Chapman, "Torreya taxifolia, Arnott," 251.
3. John Kunkel Small Collection, Chapman-Torrey unpublished letters, Florida Archives, Tallahassee, Florida.

10. *Walking in Heaven's Light*

1. Wolfe, *Son of the Wilderness*, 107.
2. Muir, *Walk to the Gulf*, xx.
3. Ibid., 87.
4. Ibid., 89–90.
5. Ibid., 107.
6. Ibid., 91.
7. Ibid., 101.
8. Ibid., 133.
9. Muir, *Boyhood*, 243.

11. *A Voice for Florida Conservation*

1. Small Collection, Florida Archives.
2. Harwood, *Vizcaya*, 21.
3. Call, *Invasive Exotic*, 2.
4. Small, "Lost Cacti," 165–172.
5. Small, "Of Grottoes," 30–37. Roland Harper wrote a fine article on those fern grottoes in a 1916 issue of *American Fern Journal.*
6. Small, "Spring Meets Autumn," 60–74.
7. Small, "Historic Trails." 212.
8. Small Collection, Florida Archives.
9. Ibid.
10. Ibid.

12. *Saving a Swamp*

1. Harper, R., "Autobiographical Notes."
2. Harper, R., "Okefinokee Swamp," 610.
3. Russell, *Okefenokee Swamp*, 82.
4. McQueen and Mizell, *History of Okefenokee*, 182.
5. Bartram, W., *Travels: Naturalists Edition*, v.

Selected Bibliography

A number of people shared their knowledge of these men and are mentioned in the acknowledgments. The following writings have been most useful in compiling this book. Some of them contain conflicting images, but they are meant to be a starting point for those who wish to learn more about natural history. Read carefully.

Adams, Alexander B. *John James Audubon: A Biography.* New York: G. P. Putnam's Sons, 1966.

Allen, Elsa Guerdrum. *The History of American Ornithology Before Audubon.* New York: Russell & Russell, 1969.

———. "A Third Set of John Abbot Bird Drawings." *The Auk* 59 (1942): 563–71.

Ambrose, Stephen. *Undaunted Courage: Meriwether Lewis, Thomas Jefferson, and the Opening of the American West.* New York: Simon and Schuster, 1997.

Audubon, John James. *Audubon, by Himself.* Edited by Alice Ford. Garden City, N.Y.: The Natural History Press, 1969.

———. *Audubon's America.* Edited by Donald Culross Peattie. Boston: Houghton Mifflin, 1940.

Austin, Daniel F., with Anita F. Cholewa, Rita B. Lassiter, and Bruce F. Hansen. *The Florida of John Kunkel Small: His Species and Types, Collecting Localities, Bibliography, and Selected Reprinted Works.* Contributions from the New York Botanical Garden, vol. 18. New York: New York Botanical Garden, 1987.

Barnhart, John Hendley. "The Passing of Doctor Small." *Journal of the New York Botanical Garden* 39, no. 460 (1938): 73–79.

Bartram, John. *The Correspondence of John Bartram, 1734–1777.* Edited by Edmund Berkeley and Dorothy Smith Berkeley. Gainesville: University Press of Florida, 1992.

Bartram, William. *Travels and Other Writings.* New York: Literary Classics of the United States, Penguin Books, 1996.

———. *William Bartram in Florida 1774.* Edited by Helen G. Cruickshank. Cocoa: Florida Federation of Garden Clubs, 1986.

———. *William Bartram's Travels: Francis Harper's Naturalist Edition.* Edited by Francis Harper. Athens: University of Georgia Press, 1998.

Bassett, Anna Stowell. "Some Georgia Records of John Abbot, Naturalist." *The Auk* 55 (1938): 244–54.

Bell, C. Ritchie, and Bryan J. Taylor. *Florida Wild Flowers and Roadside Plants.* Chapel Hill: Laurel Hill Press, 1982.

Belleville, Bill. *River of Lakes: A Journey on Florida's St. Johns River.* Athens: University of Georgia Press, 2000.

Bennett, Charles E. *Twelve on the River St. Johns.* Jacksonville: University of North Florida Press, 1989.

Berkeley, Edmund, and Dorothy Smith Berkeley. *The Life and Travels of John Bartram: From Lake Ontario to the River St. John.* Tallahassee: University Presses of Florida, 1990.

Brewer, T. M. *Wilson's American Ornithology.* Boston: Otis, Broaders, and Company, 1840.

Burt, Al. *The Tropic of Cracker.* Gainesville: University Press of Florida, 1999.

Byrd, William. *The Secret Diary of William Byrd of Westover, 1709–1712.* Edited by Louis B. Wright and Marion Tinling. New York: G. P. Putnam's Sons, 1963.

Call, James. "Invasive Exotic Plants: Visitors That Never Leave." *Florida Wildlife* 53, no. 3 (May–June 1999): 2–7.

Callaway, E. E. *In the Beginning: Creation—Evolution—Garden of Eden and Noah's Ark.* New York: Carlton Press, 1966.

Cantwell, Robert. *Alexander Wilson: Naturalist and Pioneer.* Philadelphia and New York: J. B. Lippincott, 1961.

Catesby, Mark. *Catesby's Birds of Colonial America.* Edited by Alan Feduccia. Chapel Hill: University of North Carolina Press, 1985.

———. *The Natural History of Carolina, Florida and the Bahama Islands.* Savannah: Beehive Press, 1974.

Chancellor, John. *Audubon.* New York: Viking Press, 1978.

Chapman, A. W. *Flora of the Southern United States: Containing an Abridged Description of the Flowering Plants and Ferns of Tennessee, North and South Carolina, Georgia, Alabama, Mississippi, and Florida: Arranged According to the Natural System.* New York: Ivison, Phinney, and Co., 1860.

———. "A List of the Plants Growing Spontaneously in the Vicinity of Quincy, Florida." *The Western Journal of Medicine and Surgery* (June 1845): 461–483.

———. "Torreya taxifolia, Arnott: A Reminiscence." *Botanical Gazette* 10, no. 4 (1885): 250–54.

Coker, W. C. "The Garden of André Michaux." *Journal of the Elisha Mitchell Scientific Society* 27, no. 2 (1911): 65–72.

Coker, William Chambers, and Henry Roland Totten. *Trees of the Southeastern States.* Chapel Hill: University of North Carolina Press, 1937.

Craighead, Frank C., Sr. *The Trees of South Florida: The Natural Environments and Their Succession.* Vol. I. Coral Gables: University of Miami Press, 1971.

Croom, Hardy Bryan. "Floral Calendar of Middle Florida." *American Journal of Science* 24 (1834): 69–78.

De Biedma, Luys Hernandez, and A Gentleman of Elvas. *Narratives of De Soto in the Conquest of Florida.* Translated by Buckingham Smith. Gainesville, Fla.: Kallman Publishing, 1968.

Delatte, Carolyn. *Lucy Audubon, A Biography.* Baton Rouge: Louisiana State University Press, 1982.

Delcourt, Hazel R. "Roland McMillan Harper: Recorder of Early Twentieth-Century Landscapes in the South." *Pioneer America* (December 1978): 30–50.

Dow, Robert Percy. "John Abbot, of Georgia." *Journal of the New York Entomological Society* 22 (1914): 65–72.

Dugger, Shepherd M. *The Balsam Groves of Grandfather Mountain.* Banner Elk, N.C.: Puddingstone Press of Lees-Mcrae College, 1974.

Duncan, David Ewing. *Hernando de Soto: A Savage Quest in the Americas.* Norman: University of Oklahoma Press, 1996.

Duncan, Wilbur H., and Leonard E. Foote. *Wildflowers of the Southeastern United States.* Athens: University of Georgia Press, 1975.

Durant, Mary, and Michael Harwood. *On the Road with John James Audubon.* New York: Dodd, Mead and Company, 1980.

Ehrlich, Paul R., David S. Dobkin, and Darryl Wheye. *The Birder's Handbook.* New York: Simon and Schuster, 1988.

Ewan, Joseph, and Nesta Ewan. *John Banister and His Natural History of Virginia 1678–1692.* Urbana: University of Illinois Press, 1970.

Faxon, Walter. "John Abbot's Drawings of the Birds of Georgia." *The Auk* 13 (1896): 204–15.

Fox, Stephen. *John Muir and His Legacy: The American Conservation Movement.* Boston: Little, Brown and Company, 1981.

Frick, George Frederick, and Raymond Phineas Stearns. *Mark Catesby: The Colonial Audubon.* Urbana: University of Illinois Press, 1961.

Gannon, Michael. *Florida: A Short History.* Gainesville: University Press of Florida, 1992.

———, ed. *The New History of Florida.* Gainesville: University Press of Florida, 1996.

Gilbert, Pamela. *John Abbot: Birds, Butterflies and Other Wonders.* London: Merrell Holberton Publishers, 1998.

Harper, Francis. "The Mammals of the Okefinokee Swamp Region of Georgia." *Proceedings of the Boston Society of Natural History* 38, no. 7 (1927): 191–396.

———. "Okefinokee Swamp as a Reservation." *Natural History* 20, no. 1 (1920): 28–41.

———. "The Okefinokee Wilderness." *National Geographic Magazine* 65, no. 5 (1934): 597–624.

———. "A Voice from the Pines." *Natural History* 32, no. 3 (1932): 280–88.

Harper, Francis, and Delma E. Presley. *Okefinokee Album.* Athens: University of Georgia Press, 1981.

Harper, Roland M. "Autobiographical Notes." 1954, Milton Hopkins private collection.

———. "Historical Notes on the Relation of Fires to Forests." *Proceedings, First Annual Tall Timbers Fire Ecology Conference, March 1–2, 1962.* Tall Timbers Research Station, Tallahassee (1962): 11–29.

———. "Okefinokee Swamp." *Popular Science Monthly* (June 1909): 596–614.

———. "Some Vanishing Scenic Features of the Southeastern United States." *Natural History* 19, no. 2 (1919): 192–204.

————. "Studying the Georgia Flora and Some Red-Letter Days in the Life of a Botanist." *Castanea: the Journal of the Southern Appalachian Botanical Club* 32, no. 1 (1967): 1–17.

Harwood, Kathryn Chapman. *The Lives of Vizcaya: Annals of a Great House.* Miami: Banyan Books, 1985.

Herbst, Josephine. *New Green World.* New York: Hastings House Publishers, 1954.

Hindle, Brooke. *The Pursuit of Science in Revolutionary America, 1735–1789.* Chapel Hill: University of North Carolina Press, 1956.

Hodges, Margaret. *Making a Difference: The Story of an American Family.* New York: Charles Scribner's Sons, 1989.

Holbrook, Stewart H. *The Old Post Road.* New York: McGraw-Hill, 1962.

Hopkins, Albert A. *Our Country and Its Resources.* New York: Munn and Co., 1917.

Hopkins, John M. "Forty-five Years with the Okefenokee Swamp, 1900–1945." *Georgia Society of Naturalists,* Bulletin No. 4: 1–69.

Hudson, Charles. *Knights of Spain: Warrior of the Sun.* Athens: University of Georgia Press, 1997.

Jefferson, Thomas. *Thomas Jefferson's Garden Book, 1766–1824, with relevant extracts from his other writings.* Annotated by Edwin Morris Betts. Philadelphia: American Philosophical Society, 1944.

Kalm, Peter. *Travels in North America.* Volumes 1 and 2. New York: Dover, 1966.

Kimball, Winifred. "Reminiscences of Alvan Wentworth Chapman." *Journal of the New York Botanical Garden* 22, no. 253 (1921): 1–11.

Langeland, K. A., and K. Craddock Burks, eds. *Identification & Biology of Non-Native Plants in Florida's Natural Areas.* Gainesville: University of Florida, 1998.

Larson, Lewis H. *Aboriginal Subsistence Technology on the Southeastern Coastal Plain During the Late Prehistoric Period.* Gainesville: University Presses of Florida, 1980.

Latrobe, Charles Joseph. *The Rambler in North America.* Vol. 2. New York: Harper and Brothers, 1835.

Lawson, John. *A New Voyage to Carolina.* Edited by Hugh Talmage Lefler. Chapel Hill: University of North Carolina Press, 1967.

Littlefield, Doris Bayley. *Vizcaya.* Miami: Matori Enterprises II, 1983.

McIlhenny, E. A. *The Alligator's Life History.* Berkeley: Ten Speed Press, 1987.

McPhee, John. *Oranges.* New York: Noonday Press, 1991.

McQueen, A. S., and Hamp Mizell. *History of the Okefenokee Swamp.* Clinton, S.C.: Press of Jacobs and Company, 1926.

Melham, Tom. *John Muir's Wild America.* Washington, D.C.: The National Geographic Society, 1976.

Mohan, Geoffrey. "St. Johns." In *The Rivers of Florida,* edited by Del Marth and Marty Marth, 45–49. Sarasota, Fla.: Pineapple Press, 1990.

Morris, Allen. *Florida Place Names: Alachua to Zolfo Springs.* Sarasota, Fla.: Pineapple Press, 1995.

Muir, John. *The Story of My Boyhood and Youth.* Boston: Houghton Mifflin, 1947.

————. *A Thousand-Mile Walk to the Gulf.* Boston: Houghton Mifflin, 1916.

————. *The Wilderness World of John Muir.* Edited by Edwin Way Teale. Boston: Houghton Mifflin, 1954.

Myer, William E. *Indian Trails of the Southeast.* Nashville: Blue and Gray Press, 1971.

Myers, Ronald L., and John J. Ewel, eds. *Ecosystems of Florida.* Orlando: University of Central Florida Press, 1990.

Nicholson, Rob. "Chasing Ghosts." *Natural History* (1990): 8–13.

O'Toole, Patricia. "Dawn in the Garden of Good and Evil." *Smithsonian* 26, no. 7 (1998): 138–54.

Plate, Robert. *Alexander Wilson, Wanderer in the Wilderness.* New York: David McKay, 1966.

Porcher, Richard D. *Wildflowers of the Carolina Lowcountry and Lower Pee Dee.* Columbia: University of South Carolina Press, 1995.

Proby, Kathryn Hall. *Audubon in Florida.* Coral Gables: University of Miami Press, 1974.

Randazzo, Anthony F., and Douglas S. Jones, eds. *The Geology of Florida.* Gainesville: University Press of Florida, 1997.

Redfearn, D. H. "The Steamboat Home: Presumption as to Order of Death in a Common Calamity." *Florida Law Journal* 9, no. 5 (May 1935): 405–24.

Remington, C. L. "John Abbot; Notes on My Life." *Lepidopterists' News* 2, no. 3 (1948): 28–30.

Rhoads, Samuel N. "Georgia's Rarities Further Discovered in a Second American Portfolio of John Abbot's Bird Plates." *The Auk* 35, no. 3 (1918): 271–86.

Riley, Laura, and William Riley. *Guide to the National Wildlife Refuges.* New York: Macmillan, 1992.

Rogers, William Warren, and Erica R. Clark. *The Croom Family and Goodwood Plantation: Land, Litigation, and Southern Lives.* Athens: University of Georgia Press, 1999.

Rogers, William Warren, and Lee Willis III. *At the Water's Edge: A Pictorial and Narrative History of Apalachicola and Franklin County.* Virginia Beach: Donning Company, 1997.

Rogers-Price, Vivian, and William W. Griffin. "John Abbot: Pioneer Artist-naturalist of Georgia." *Antiques* (October 1983): 768–75.

Rourke, Constance. *Audubon.* New York: Harcourt, Brace and Company, 1936.

Russell, Franklin. *The Okefenokee Swamp.* New York: Time-Life Books, 1973.

Savage, Henry, Jr. *Lost Heritage: Wilderness America Through the Eyes of Seven Pre-Audubon Naturalists.* New York: William Morrow, 1970.

Savage, Henry, Jr., and Elizabeth Savage. *André and François André Michaux.* Charlottesville: University Press of Virginia, 1986.

Schlesinger, Arthur M., Jr., ed. *The Almanac of American History.* New York: Barnes and Noble Books, 1993.

Simmons, Glen, and Laura Ogden. *Gladesmen: Gator Hunters, Moonshiners, and Skiffers.* Gainesville: University Press of Florida, 1998.

Simpson, Charles Torrey, *Out of Doors in Florida, The Adventures of a Naturalist,*

Together with Essays on the Wild Life and the Geology of the State. Miami: E. B. Douglas Co., 1923.

Slaughter, Thomas P. *The Natures of John and William Bartram.* New York: Alfred A. Knopf, 1996.

Small, John Kunkel. "Coastwise Dunes and Lagoons: A Record of Botanical Exploration in Florida in the Spring of 1918." *Journal of The New York Botanical Garden* 20 (October 1919): 191–207.

———. *From Eden to Sahara: Florida's Tragedy.* Lancaster, Penn.: Science Press Printing Company, 1929.

———. "Historic Trails, by Land and by Water: A Record of Exploration in Florida in December 1919." *Journal of The New York Botanical Garden* 22 (November–December 1921): 103–222.

———. "In Quest of Lost Cacti: Cactus Hunting in the Carolinas in Winter." *Journal of The New York Botanical Garden* 21 (September 1920): 161–78.

———. "The Land Where Spring Meets Autumn." *Journal of The New York Botanical Garden* 25 (1924): 53–94.

———. "Of Grottoes and Ancient Dunes: A Record of Exploration in Florida in December 1918." *Journal of The New York Botanical Garden* 21 (February 1920): 103–222.

———. "The Proposed Everglades National Park, U.S.A." *Nature* 140 (August 1937): 263–66.

———. "A Winter Collecting Trip in Florida." *Journal of The New York Botanical Garden* 19 (April 1918): 69–77.

———. Papers and letters. John Kunkel Small Collection, Florida Archives, Tallahassee, Florida.

Smith, Charles M. *From Andersonville to Freedom.* Providence: The Society, 1894.

Smith, Herbert F. *John Muir.* New York: Twayne Publishers, 1965.

Stewart, Doug. "Mark Catesby." *Smithsonian* 28, no. 6 (1997): 96–103.

Trelease, William. "Alvin Wentworth Chapman." *The American Naturalist* 33, no. 392 (1899): 643–46.

Trowell, C. T. *Exploring the Okefenokee, Roland M. Harper in the Okefenokee Swamp.* Research Paper No. 2, September 1988.

———. *Okefenokee, Profiles of the Past.* Okefenokee Wildlife League, Special Publication No. 1, 1998.

———. *Life on the Okefenokee Frontier.* Special Publication No. 3, 1998.

———. *Jackson's Folly.* Special Publication No. 4, 1998.

———. *Okefenokee, The Hebard Lumber Company.* Special Publication No. 5, 1998.

———. *Seeking a Sanctuary, A Chronicle of Efforts to Preserve the Okefenokee.* Special Publication No. 6, 1998.

Turner, Frederick. *Rediscovering America: John Muir in His Time and Ours.* New York: Viking, 1985.

Vitale, Alice Thoms. *Leaves in Myth, Magic & Medicine.* New York: Stewart, Tabori and Chang, 1997.

Welch, William C., and Greg Grant. *The Southern Heirloom Garden.* Dallas: Taylor Publishing, 1995.

Wharton, Charles H. *The Natural Environments of Georgia.* Atlanta: Geologic and Water Resources Division and Georgia Department of Natural Resources, Bulletin 114, 1978.

Williams, Charlie. "Carolina 1796, '. . . d'un nouveau Magnolia.'" *Magnolia* 32, no. 2 (Summer 1997): 15–31.

Wilson, Alexander. *The Life and Letters of Alexander Wilson.* Edited by Clark Hunter. Philadelphia: American Philosophical Society, 1983.

Wolfe, Linnie Marsh. *Son of the Wilderness: The Life of John Muir.* New York: Alfred A. Knopf, 1945.

Wright, Albert Hazen. *Our Georgia-Florida Frontier: The Okefinokee Swamp, its History and Cartography.* Vol. 1. Ithaca: A. H. Wright, 1945.

Wright, Louis B. *The American Heritage History of the Thirteen Colonies.* New York: American Heritage Publishing, 1967.

———. *South Carolina: A History.* New York: W. W. Norton and Company; Nashville: American Association for State and Local History, 1976.

Index

GAIL FISHMAN, a native Floridian, has twelve years of experience in the conservation field. She lives in Tallahassee and travels to faraway places whenever possible.

Related titles from University Press of Florida

The Life and Travels of John Bartram: From Lake Ontario to the River St. John, edited by Edmund Berkeley and Dorothy Smith Berkeley

Some Kind of Paradise: A Chronicle of Man and the Land in Florida, by Mark Derr

Swamp Song: A Natural History of Florida's Swamps, by Ron Larson

Southwest Florida's Wetland Wilderness: Big Cypress Swamp and the Ten Thousand Islands, by Jeff Ripple, photographs by Clyde Butcher

The Wild Heart of Florida: Florida Writers on Florida's Wildlands, edited by Jeff Ripple and Susan Cerulean

Read more about these and other books on our Website at http://www.upf.com